THE MAN THEY COULD NOT HANG

THE TRUE STORY OF JOHN LEE

MIKE HOLGATE
& IAN DAVID WAUGH

SUTTON PUBLISHING

First published in the United Kingdom in 2005 by
Sutton Publishing Limited · Phoenix Mill
Thrupp · Stroud · Gloucestershire · GL5 2BU

British Library Cataloguing in Publication Data
A catalogue record for this book is available from the British Library.

ISBN 0-7509-3652-5

Typeset in 11.5/14 Photina.
Typesetting and origination by
Sutton Publishing Limited.
Printed and bound in England by
J.H. Haynes & Co. Ltd, Sparkford.

To the memory of Torbay's 'Mr History',
John Pike (1921–2004)

Contents

Preface and Acknowledgements

Mike Holgate's interest in the case of John Lee was stimulated by the BBC2 television documentary *The Man They Could Not Hang*, presented by Melvyn Bragg and broadcast on 1 February 1975. Mike was then living in Torquay near the scene of the Babbacombe Murder. The programme featured music performed by Fairport Convention from their folk-rock album '*Babbacombe' Lee*. A year later, singer-guitarist Mike supported the band in concert on a tour of the West Country. At this time his father was carrying out some family history research after hearing from a relative that a branch of the Holgate family named Lee might be descended from the infamous criminal. This myth was quickly dispelled after receiving assistance from Torquay Borough Librarian John Pike, who had acted as a researcher and appeared in the BBC programme.

In 1990, Mike joined the staff of Torquay Library as a part-time reference library assistant; the aim was to supplement his income as a musician and further his knowledge in order to fulfil a vague ambition to become a local history writer. In this new post he regularly carried out searches on behalf of would-be authors planning to write a book about John Lee, none of which was ever written. When he realised that no one had devoted a full volume to the subject since John Lee's autobiography was first published in 1908, he decided to write one himself. This was made possible by the encouragement and cooperation of John Pike, by this time retired from the Library Service and established as an eminent author on local history. He generously handed over the results of his research started in 1959, which Mike bolstered with evidence from recently declassified archives obtained from the Public Record Office. The result was *The Secret of the Babbacombe Murder*, published in South Devon by Peninsula Press in 1995, which later that year formed the basis for an episode of Granada Television's crime series *In Suspicious Circumstances* presented by the actor Edward Woodward.

Reading the book rekindled the interest of broadcast producer and presenter Ian Waugh, who had been told tales of John Lee by his grandfather. In 1999, he visited Torquay Library and obtained advice from Mike Holgate. His first objective was to transcribe the witness statements of the magistrate's hearing from the Torquay Court Records held at the Public Record Office. When this was achieved he produced a booklet entitled *Who Killed Emma Keyse?* Ian then turned his attention to the daunting task of transcribing hundreds of handwritten Home Office and Prison Commission documents relating to the case and launched a comprehensive website about John Lee. This was visited by a recently retired policeman, Don Hanson, who contacted Ian and passed on an invaluable file of John Lee's correspondence with his supporter Stephen

Bryan, which had been deposited at the Exeter Prison Museum. Together with a tantalisingly plausible tale of Lee's last resting place, obtained by following up a story told to Exeter publisher Chips Barber, which ironically led back to the town of Tavistock where Ian had been raised, there was now enough material to team up with Mike and produce a book.

Mike and Ian have collaborated and researched, with varying degrees of success, three intriguing aspects of the life of John Lee: How did he escape the death penalty? What became of him after serving life imprisonment? Was he guilty of the Babbacombe Murder? They do not claim to have found all the answers, although their research belies much of the folklore and press coverage surrounding this fascinating subject. They have strived to produce a comprehensive overview of the case, extensively quoting official documents, contemporary newspaper reports, expert opinion, titbits of local gossip and the letters and personal accounts of the principal characters involved.

Before approaching a publisher, Ian and Mike sought advice from a mutual acquaintance, Stewart Evans, renowned author of *Jack the Ripper*, then finalising *The Chronicles of James Berry* – a biography of the executioner who failed in his duty to hang John Lee. Stewart kindly recommended the authors to Sutton Publishing Ltd, whose editor, Christopher Feeney, immediately commissioned the work.

The authors gratefully acknowledge the assistance of those people already mentioned and are indebted to the following individuals and organisations for providing various segments of a story whose telling can be likened to piecing together a giant jigsaw puzzle. If anyone reading this book can provide any of the missing pieces of information, then Ian and Mike would certainly be glad to hear from them. Look us up at www.murderresearch.com.

LIBRARY SERVICES

This project would not have started without access to the local history archive at Torquay Central Library. Many past and present members of the reference staff have contributed invaluable help and assistance, and grateful thanks are due to Mike Dowdell, Ann Howard, Lorna Smith, Lesley Byers and Mark Pool for their ongoing advice and encouragement. Many thanks also to library users Ray Strevett, Don Collinson, Terry Leaman and Mike Wells for interrupting their own research to turn up vital snippets of information.

Many other libraries have been contacted at home and abroad in our quest, and the authors would like to express their appreciation to staff members of the following institutions:

England: London: Guildhall, Marylebone, Southwark, City of Westminster Archives; Bradford; Exeter (West Country Studies Library); Gloucester; Leigh; Manchester; Newcastle-upon-Tyne; Newton Abbot; Plymouth; Redruth;
USA: Brooklyn; Buffalo; Chicago; Milwaukee; New York; University of Wisconsin; Illinois State Library;
Canada: Toronto;
Australia: State Library of New South Wales; State Library of Victoria.

RECORDS AND DOCUMENTS

Grateful thanks to Dr Stephen Smith for conducting the time-consuming search for the Torquay Court Records at The National Archive, Kew. A special mention is also due to the staff of that establishment for locating and supplying copies of Admiralty, Assize, Home Office and Prison Commission records relating to John Lee. Appreciation to Ian Mulholland, Governor of Exeter Prison, for permission to quote the correspondence of John Lee, Stephen Bryan, Mrs Caunter, Fred Farmer and George Bond. With thanks to the Galleries of Justice, Nottingham, an educational organisation educating the wider community about crime, punishment and the law – and its librarian/archivist Bev Baker for permission to quote from documents in the Epton Collection. Special thanks to K.M.J. Caine of the Devon Record Office, for information relating to the workhouse records of the Tavistock Institution; Pamela Clarke, Deputy Registrar, for information from the Royal Archives, Windsor Castle: Douglas Parkhouse, Cemetery Superintendent, Tavistock, for undertaking the search of burial records, Derek Reed, solicitor, Woollcoombe, Beer & Watts, Newton Abbot, for providing a copy of the will of Mary Lee; Steve Daily, Curator of Research Collections, Milwaukee Historical Society, for a search of naturalisation records; the State of Wisconsin Department of Health and Family Services for locating vital records relating to the Lee family; Bob Gartz for information regarding the records and graves of the Lee family in Milwaukee; Alan Elliott for locating the family records of Elizabeth Harris in Australia.

MISCELLANEOUS

Appreciation to the following organisations, which provided assistance in a variety of ways: BBC South West, British Film Institute, Devon Family History Society, Lincoln County Council, London Metropolitan Archives, National Film and Television Archive, Plymouth District Land Registry, Probate Registry, Salvation Army, Surrey County Council, Tavistock Town Council, Teignbridge District Council, Torbay Council, Torquay Museum, Television South West (TSW) Film and Television Archive, Wellcome Trust. Also, special thanks to the following individuals for their contributions to the project: the late Leslie Lownds Pateman CBE, Gordon Honeycombe, Susan Arn, Edna White, Wendy Harvey and Sandra and Shirley Harris. Kind assistance was also received from the late Frank Keyse (a descendant of the murder victim's family) and his widow, Margaret.

NEWSPAPERS, JOURNALS AND BOOKS

For dealing with our frequent and persistent enquiries for copies of contemporary newspaper reports we thankfully acknowledge the diligent cooperation of staff members at the British Newspaper Library, Colindale. For permission to quote extracts from newspapers, journals and books, grateful thanks are extended to the representatives of the following copyright holders: Duncan Currall, MD of Westcountry Publications (*Herald Express*, *Express and Echo*, *Western Morning News*); Mike Roberts, MD of Torquay News Ltd (*Torquay Times and South Devon Advertiser*); Colin Brent, editor of the *Tavistock Times and Gazette*; Paul Robertson, editor of the *Newcastle Evening Chronicle*; Jenny Potter, managing editor of the *Radio Times*; Kate White of Guinness Publishing Ltd. Last, but not least, we would like to thank our 'partner in crime', barrister Barry Phillips, contributor to the law journal *Counsel*, and its editor, Stephanie Hawthorne.

ILLUSTRATIONS

Supplementing photographs and illustrations from the authors' own collection is *The View from my Bedroom Window*, painted by Emma Keyse in 1876, photographed by Shane Edgar and reproduced courtesy of Torre Abbey Historic House and Gallery, Torquay. Special thanks to David Mason of Torbay Postcard Club for providing postcards of St Marychurch Parish Church and 'John Lee's Mother'. A portrait of P.S. Abraham Nott, photographs of The Glen and South Devon business advertisements have been provided courtesy of Torbay Library Services. Thanks also to John Draisay, County Archivist, Devon Record Office, for providing a Crown Copyright copy of the cheque obtained for stolen goods by John Lee (QS4/Midsummer 1883). The majority of the line drawings illustrating the text were originally published in contemporary editions of the *Devon County Standard, Illustrated London News, Torquay Directory and South Devon Journal, Harper's New Monthly Magazine*, provided by Torbay Library Services, and the *Illustrated Police News, Sunday Chronicle, The Builder*, obtained from the British Newspaper Library. Further sketches from an extra supplement to the *Devon County Standard* and a souvenir *Record of the Dates of the Visits to Babbacombe by Members of the Royal Family* have been copied from originals held at Torquay Museum. Paul Williams provided illustrations from the Edwardian magazine *Famous Crimes*. Ian Waugh re-created plans of The Glen and the map of the 'Babbacombe Murder Trail'. Timothy Lau adapted technical drawings of the scaffold from an original held at The National Archives (HO 144/148//A38492).

Prologue

On a damp overcast morning in February 1885, an expectant hush fell over the large crowd gathered outside Exeter Prison. At 8 a.m. the prison bell tolled the death knell for John Lee, a twenty-year-old servant sentenced to death for a crime rightfully described by the trial judge as 'one of the most cruel and barbarous murders ever committed'.

The apparently motiveless murder of elderly Emma Keyse at her seaside villa The Glen at Babbacombe, Torquay, had shocked the sensibilities of everybody in the locality. The elderly victim had been callously bludgeoned to death with blows to the head before her throat was slashed and her lifeless body set on fire. Any moment now the black flag would be hoisted above the prison to signal that the evil perpetrator had paid the full penalty of the law for killing a lady he himself described as 'my best friend'. She had taken him into her service and shown a kindly interest in his welfare, despite the fact that he had served six months' hard labour in this very prison for stealing from his previous employer.

The View from my Bedroom Window – painted by Emma Keyse.

The crowd grew uneasy as the minutes passed by without the expected pronouncement. Perhaps the miserable wretch had finally abandoned his stubborn protestations of innocence and admitted his guilt, delaying the proceedings with a protracted confession? Half an hour later there was still no news. Surely the condemned man had been granted a last-minute reprieve? Perhaps there was some truth in the written statement made earlier by the prisoner in his death cell, implicating the lover of his half-sister, Elizabeth Harris, who was expecting an illegitimate child conceived while she was the cook at The Glen.

Speculation continued for a further twenty minutes, until members of the press suddenly emerged from the prison gate and rushed towards the telegraph office. They were immediately engulfed by people clamouring for information. A besieged reporter breathlessly revealed:

'It's a bungle!'

'What?'

'Can't hang the man!'

'What do you mean?'

'They've tried three times and he's still not dead!'

Inside the prison, shocked officials, whose onerous responsibility it was to carry out the death sentence, were reliving the full horror of what had occurred. It was their painful duty to witness the execution – and more than one had fortified himself with a drop of Dutch courage, although nothing could have prepared them for the harrowing scenes that were to follow. They had assembled anxiously at the appointed hour as the prisoner mounted the scaffold, stood calm and erect, then glanced skywards for a moment before the executioner, James Berry, made the necessary preparations for his grim task. He quickly pinioned the condemned man's legs, drew a white cap over his head, then tightened the noose around his neck: 'Have you anything to say?' he whispered.

'No,' came the firm reply. 'Drop away!'

The hangman hesitated while the prison chaplain read a somewhat prophetic passage from the service from the Burial of the Dead: 'Now is the Christ risen from the dead . . .'.

At the appropriate moment, Berry pulled a lever to activate the 'drop', then gasped in amazement as the trapdoors merely sagged slightly, leaving the prisoner precariously suspended between life and death! 'Quick, stamp on it!' he shouted to the warders.

Distressing scenes followed as desperate efforts were made to force the 'trap' open. Warders jumped on the doors, risking falling into the pit with the prisoner had they been successful, but after several minutes the bewildered prisoner was led to one side while the apparatus was repeatedly tested and found to be working perfectly. Visibly shaken, Berry made a second attempt. Heaving with all his might, he succeeded only in bending the lever, then abandoned his post to add his weight to that of the prisoner standing helplessly on the trap – all to no avail!

'This is terrible,' cried the anguished Governor. 'Take the prisoner away!'

Carpenters were summoned to diagnose the problem and a saw was passed around the frame of the trapdoors to relieve possible pressure, in case they were swollen from the overnight rain. As a final test, a warder balanced on the 'trap' while clinging onto the hangman's rope and the doors fell away easily. Satisfied that the fault had now been remedied, the Governor recalled the prisoner to face his ordeal for a third time. The

The Man They Could Not Hang.

witnesses were in a great state of shock, and the Chaplain trembled as he read more in hope than expectation: 'Man that is born of woman hath but a short time to live . . .'.

Perspiring freely, Berry grasped the lever with both hands, determined that this time John Lee would keep his appointment in Hell. The bolt was drawn and the scaffold shuddered.

'Is it all over?' pleaded the Chaplain, who was too afraid to look.

'In God's name, put a stop to this!' demanded Mr Caird, the surgeon. 'You may experiment as much as you like on a sack of flour, but you shall not experiment on this man any longer.'

The Reverend Pitkin opened his eyes and almost collapsed when he realised that Lee had survived a third attempt on his life. He immediately informed the Under-Sheriff, Henry James, 'I cannot carry on!'

Following a huddled conference, it was agreed to postpone the proceedings pending instructions from the Home Secretary. John Lee was returned to his cell, seemingly unaffected by his torment, but he reacted angrily when Berry came in to remove his bonds. 'Don't do that,' he protested. 'I want to be hung!'

'Have no fear,' reassured the Chaplain, with tears in his eyes. 'By the laws of England they cannot put you on the scaffold again!'

Lee recovered his composure, then suddenly remembered an extraordinary occurrence which he recounted to the incredulous chaplain: 'I saw it all in a dream! I was led down to the scaffold and it would not work – after three attempts, they brought me back to my cell!'

The Reverend Pitkin's assurance to Lee that he was legally protected from having to face the death penalty again was misinformed. However, the Home Secretary, Sir William Harcourt, was empowered to commute the sentence on humanitarian grounds, if he felt it appropriate. Lee's agonising experience brought about a wave of public sympathy and indignation that was typified by Queen Victoria, who reacted strongly in favour of Lee, even though she had been personally acquainted with the murder victim. She made her feelings known in a telegram to the Home Secretary: 'I am horrified at the disgraceful scenes at Exeter at Lee's execution. Surely Lee cannot now be executed. It would be too cruel. Imprisonment for life seems the only alternative.' Sir William concurred and told a packed House of Commons: 'It would shock the feelings of everyone if a man had twice to pay the pangs of imminent death.'

Circuit barrister Mr Molesworth St Aubyn, who had conducted the inept defence of Lee, could not disguise his relief in a letter to the Reverend Pitkin: 'I am one of those who was never satisfied of his guilt. What a marvellous thing if he turns out to be innocent. At any rate he must have a nerve of iron. What will become of him now, I wonder?'

Meanwhile, a thrill of astonishment and disbelief swept through the country as the story caught the public imagination. The sensational morning's events certainly brought about a remarkable change of opinion. A reviled murderer suddenly became the object of heartfelt sympathy after enduring a terrible ordeal on the scaffold. Reinforced by the startling revelation that the prisoner had prophesied he would not die, a legend was created as John Lee became the only condemned person in the history of capital punishment to survive the 'long drop', gaining instant immortality as 'The Man They Could Not Hang'.

Adapted from eyewitness accounts.

JOHN LEE RETURNS TO THE WORLD

At eight o'clock on the morning of the 18th of December, 1907, the iron gates of a prison opened, and out into the light of day stepped two middle-aged men.

One man was an official in civilian clothes. He bore the hallmarks of drill and discipline. The other man . . .

The other man! He looked hunted and cowed like a creature crushed and broken. He seemed to hang back as if he were afraid of the light of day. He appeared to draw no happy inspiration from God's sunshine. He fumbled at his overcoat pockets as if the very possession of a pocket was a new sensation. He trod gingerly, as if the earth concealed a pitfall.

Away they went by cab and rail to Newton Abbot. There the two men walked to the police-station, where the official announced that he was a warder from Portland Convict Prison in charge of John Lee, convict, on ticket-of-leave.

John Lee handed his ticket to the police officer, who read it.

What was it that made the policeman start as he read? What was it that made him look so curiously at the tall, thin, clean-shaven elderly man before him?

It was this: Certain particulars on the ticket showed that on February 4th, 1885, *the bearer was sentenced to death* at Exeter Assizes for murder at Babbacombe. The man was 'Babbacombe' Lee.

'Babbacombe' Lee was on his way to spend Christmas with his aged mother – *John Lee, the man they could not hang*, the man under whose feet the grim mechanism of the scaffold had mysteriously failed in its appointed work.

The story of his life's ordeal John Lee himself will tell in the following pages. It is the story of one, who, rightly or wrongly, was doomed in the first flush of manhood to a torture more fiendish than the human mind, unaided by the Demon of Circumstances, could have devised. It is the story of a man dangled in the jaws of death, and hurried thence to a living tomb whose terrors make even death seem merciful.

From his terrible ordeal, John Lee emerges with the cry, 'I am innocent' still on his lips. And who that has not suffered will not listen?

Introduction to *The Man They Could Not Hang*, John Lee, 1908

Babbacombe
Murder Trail

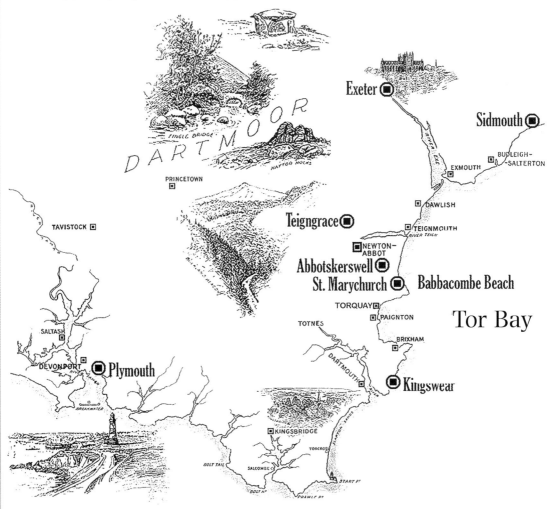

Key

Abbotskerswell – birthplace of John Lee
Babbacombe Beach – home of Emma Keyse at The Glen
Exeter – where the infamous execution took place
Kingswear – where Lee worked in a hotel and as a railway porter
Plymouth – where Lee served in the navy and was later arrested for theft
St Marychurch – last resting place of Emma Keyse
Sidmouth – where Emma Keyse's mother was reputed to have cared for Princess Victoria
Teigngrace – where Emma Keyse was baptised

CHAPTER 1

The lure of the sea

We came to Babbacombe, a small bay . . . It is a beautiful spot . . . Red cliffs and rocks with wooded hills like Italy and reminding one of a ballet or play where nymphs appear – such rocks and grottos, with the deepest sea on which there was no ripple.

– Queen Victoria's Journal, 1846

When wealthy spinster Emma Keyse employed a rough country lad called John Lee to work on her South Devon coastal estate in 1878, she little realised that a relationship had been forged which would end in personal tragedy for her and criminal infamy for him. Many years later, he recalled their first meeting, when she assessed his suitability for a position in her household: 'I went to Babbacombe. Just by the sea-shore was an old house called "The Glen," and in that house lived the lady who was to be my mistress – Miss Keyse. I saw her with my mother. She seemed to be pleased with me, so pleased that she engaged me at once. I was to receive three shillings a week. What a happy day that was for me. If I had only known what was to happen afterwards!' (Lee, 1908).

'What was to happen afterwards' resulted in John Lee being accused of launching a murderous attack on Emma Keyse. Police were called to her home in the early hours of the morning on Saturday 15 November 1884, and their suspicions were quickly aroused by the presence of the only male servant. Despite his plea of innocence, John Lee was found culpable and condemned in time-honoured fashion 'to be taken to a place of execution and thereby hanged by the neck until dead'. Incredibly, the hangman was thwarted when the trapdoors of the scaffold resolutely refused to swing open beneath the feet of the condemned man. The attempt had to be abandoned and as a consequence, the death penalty was commuted to life imprisonment following the personal intervention of Queen Victoria.

The Queen was one of three British monarchs who had favoured The Glen with a visit. She was enraptured by the delights of Babbacombe, which was part of fashionable Torquay and renowned as 'The Queen of the Watering Places'. The holiday resort first rose to prominence shortly

John Lee.

Princess Victoria in 1834.

after the Battle of Waterloo. In July 1815, Napoleon Bonaparte became an invaluable tourist attraction when he was held offshore by the Royal Navy en route to exile on the isle of St Helena. The town received the royal seal of approval in August 1833, when the Duchess of Kent and her fourteen-year-old daughter, Princess Victoria, attended a regatta and were greeted by a cheering crowd as the royal yacht landed unexpectedly at Torquay Harbour. Their Royal Highnesses were accommodated at a nearby hostelry, soon to be renamed the Royal Hotel by the proud proprietor, before continuing with the main purpose of their visit, making the short journey to Babbacombe. Their destination was the home of Emma Keyse and her twice-widowed mother, Elizabeth Whitehead, who had briefly served the royal family at a crucial moment in British history.

At Christmas 1819, while residing in Sidmouth, Elizabeth helped to care for Princess Victoria when the infant's debt-ridden parents fled from their London creditors and arrived in the East Devon resort where they were offered accommodation at Woolbrook Glen. During the royal family's seven-week stay, there was consternation in the nursery when a boy fired his rifle at some birds in the garden. A coloured pane of glass now indicates the spot where a pellet crashed through a window and narrowly missed the head of the royal baby. Worse was to follow in January 1820, when Edward, the Duke of Kent, returned from a long walk in the rain. He delayed changing out of his wet clothes, preferring to spend some time playing with his baby daughter. As a result, he caught a feverish chill and developed pneumonia, from which he quickly died. Within a week, Victoria's grandfather, 'Mad' King George III, was also dead, and with a lack of male heirs, the seven-month-old princess took an unwitting step towards eventually claiming the throne in 1837.

As Elizabeth Whitehead and the Duchess of Kent renewed their acquaintance over tea in the music room of The Glen, Princess Victoria, who was destined to become the nation's longest-serving monarch, was kept company by her hostess's seventeen-year-old daughter from her first marriage, Emma Keyse – the future victim of the infamous Babbacombe Murder.

She was born in 1816 at Edmonton, London, the youngest child of wealthy socialites Thomas and Elizabeth Keyse. Emma's father died when she was aged only five, and her mother soon remarried another gentleman of independent means, George Whitehead. The family settled for some years on a country estate at Teigngrace, near the South Devon market town of Newton Abbot, but by 1830 they were living in Babbacombe, which was then a small fishing hamlet, thriving on plentiful catches of sprat and

The room where Emma Keyse entertained Princess Victoria.

pilchard. The community grew around Babbacombe Beach, which had its own tavern, the Cary Arms, and a coastguard station with revenue officers monitoring the activities of local smugglers.

George Whitehead passed away in 1831 and was buried in the graveyard of the parish church in the neighbouring district of St Marychurch. Isambard Kingdom Brunel would later make a generous donation towards the rebuilding of the church. The Great Western Railway engineer bought land in the area while supervising the stretch of line between Exeter and Torquay. In 1854, he performed a tremendous service for Elizabeth Whitehead when he involved himself in a campaign to foil a plan to build a gas-works near her home on Babbacombe Beach. Following protests, the case went before a parliamentary committee where Brunel spoke eloquently against the proposal and won the day in the House of Lords. The local press triumphantly announced the victory: 'Mr Brunel . . . succeeded, by the expression of his opinion and great influence, in driving the nuisance from Babbacombe' (Pateman, 1991).

Emma Keyse's two brothers and four sisters from her mother's two marriages gradually left home to make their way in the world. Her sisters all married men of

A portrait of Emma Keyse on her
twenty-first birthday.

substance, while Emma remained a lifelong spinster. It is often said that she became a lady-in-waiting or matron of honour to Queen Victoria. This claim is totally unfounded, although she and her mother entertained royalty on a further occasion, when, in 1852, the royal yacht anchored in Babbacombe Bay. Queen Victoria stayed on board while her husband, Prince Albert, and their sons Prince Alfred and Albert the Prince of Wales were rowed to Babbacombe Beach. The young princes were entertained by Elizabeth Whitehead, while Emma Keyse had the honour of conducting the Prince Consort around the grounds of The Glen. As the royal party left Babbacombe, the landlord of the Cary Arms, William Gasking, presented the visitors with a copy of a lithograph depicting the royal yacht *Victoria and Albert* with a naval escort passing through Babbacombe Bay in 1846. On that occasion, bad weather had prevented the royal couple from landing. The Prince of Wales (later Edward VII) returned twice more to Babbacombe, in 1878 and 1880, and during the latter visit handed a half-sovereign to each of the household servants of Miss Keyse. The youngest of these was the cook Amelia Lee whose troublesome brother John would be accused of the seemingly senseless killing of Emma Keyse four years later.

Born on 15 August 1864 at Abbotskerswell, an agricultural village situated midway between Torquay and Newton Abbot, John Henry George Lee was the second child of John and Mary. He attended the village school with his sister Amelia, who was two years older. The children also had an elder half-sister, Elizabeth Harris, the illegitimate daughter of their mother, who was raised by her grandparents in the nearby village of Kingsteignton. All three children, known to the family as Jack, Millie and Lizzie, would at some point find employment in the service of Emma Keyse some years after she inherited the Glen estate upon the death of her mother in 1871.

The 13-acre estate extended from the rolling grassy cliff top of Babbacombe Downs to the shingle beach some 300 feet below. Access to and from the seashore was only possible on foot via an extremely steep winding track, and as she grew older, this may have been a factor in Emma Keyse's decision to dispose of the property at auction shortly before her death. A later advertisement gives a graphic description of the splendour of the location. The principal residence mentioned is 'The Vine', while the cottage situated 'immediately above the beach' is where Emma Keyse chose to reside.

The Glen on Babbacombe Beach (centre) with The Vine in the trees above.

Formerly known as 'Beach House', then 'Babbicombe' (an earlier derivation of the place name Babbacombe), it became forever remembered as simply 'The Glen':

> Occupying one of the loveliest stations on the coast of Devon, and unequalled in its attractions as a yachting station. . . . This property has been several times visited and admired by the Queen and other members of the Royal family. The grounds comprise the whole of one side of a most picturesque Glen, and extend to the seashore. They are of singular beauty, and are well planted and tastefully laid out in shrubberies, woodland and wilderness walks, with winding paths leading to secluded nooks, commanding magnificent views of the coast scenery extending to Portland Bill, as well as of the far-famed Babbacombe Bay. There are also lawns, suitable for croquet or tennis, kitchen and other gardens.
>
> The principal residence stands on a level plateau at a good elevation in a sheltered and charming situation. It contains lofty hall, drawing and dining rooms, each 27 feet in length; breakfast room, Nine Bedrooms and man servant's room, good kitchen and offices; 3-stalled stable, loft, and coach house. Hard and soft waters are laid on. There is also a cottage situated on small level lawn immediately above the beach, approached by colonnade, and containing entrance hall, dining room pretty ante-room, conservatory,

leading to a drawing room; handsome music or billiard room, 34 feet x 19ft. 6in.
(detached), but connected with a main building by a covered passage; ten bedrooms and
dressing rooms, and extensive cellarage. (*Torquay Times*, 23 August 1889)

The 1881 census shows that the property was occupied by Emma Keyse accompanied
by two long-serving elderly maids, sisters Eliza and Jane Neck, a young gardener, Simon
Bartlett, and the cook, Amelia Lee, who was soon to leave and be replaced by her half-
sister Elizabeth Harris. At the age of fourteen, John Lee joined The Glen household
shortly after the Prince of Wales had made a brief visit to Babbacombe in September
1878 (the date is incorrectly given as August 1879 in our illustration of the souvenir
produced by the proprietor of the Cary Arms). The Prince was rowed to Babbacombe
Beach and invited to tea by Miss Keyse, but arrangements had been made for him to
dine alfresco at the Cary Arms. By the time the Prince of Wales returned with his wife,
Princess Alexandra, and their two sons, Prince Albert Victor and Prince George (the
future King George V), in May 1880, John Lee had left the household, albeit temporarily.

With royal visitors in the habit of turning up unannounced, a spare bedroom at The
Glen called the 'Honeysuckle Room', and dubbed the 'Queen's Room' by the household
servants, was kept in constant readiness in case a member of the royal family required

An alfresco picnic at the Cary Arms.

A. LORIMER,

Proprietor.

CARY ARMS HOTEL,

BABBACOMBE.

In kind Remembrance of the Jubilee Year of ..
Her most Gracious Majesty the Queen.

The Landlord of the "Cary Arms Inn," will supply to his Customers this Summer, a Copy of this Record of the Dates of the Visits to Babbicombe by Members of the Royal Family. .

1ST AUGUST, 1833—The Duchess of Kent, with her daughter the Princess Victoria, landed at Torquay, and after a brief stay at the Royal Hotel, paid a visit to Mrs. Whitehead at Babbicombe.

AUGUST, 1846—The Royal Squadron, with Her most Gracious Majesty the Queen and Prince Albert and others on board, anchored in the Bay.

ON MONDAY, JULY 19TH, 1852—At three o'clock p.m., the Royal Squadron was observed by the preventive men on the heights at Babbicombe steering for Torquay; bearing 20 to 25 miles S.E. The active Coastguards at Babbicombe were immediately numbered in their uniforms, and were soon afloat in a fine boat to do honor to the Royal Standard of England. As soon as the boat was seen by the Squadron, the Royal Yacht altered its course, and soon came within hail. His Royal Highness Prince Albert and his Private Secretary, stepped into the boat and were immediately pulled on shore. The excitement among the inhabitants of the beautiful hamlet of Babbicombe was immense, and they crowded the shore and every part of the hills to give expression to their feelings of loyalty. Mrs. Whitehead received the Royal party as they landed, and Mr. Gasking, the proprietor of the beautiful hotel, the "Cary Arms" which is so picturesquely situated at the foot of the cliff, caused mahogany planks to be laid down to facilitate the passage of the Royal party over the beach.

His Royal Highness walked to the top of the hill, where he engaged a carriage belonging to Henry Manning, coach proprietor of St. Mary Church, requesting to be driven to the principal parts of Torquay. His Royal Highness went through the New Terrace Drive from Torquay by Meadfoot to Babbicombe Hill, where an immense number of persons had assembled to show respect to the Consort of our beloved Queen. Miss Keyse had the honor of conducting the Prince through the celebrated grounds of Mrs. Whitehead, with which his Royal Highness expressed himself highly gratified.

During the time Prince Albert was thus employed, the Prince of Wales and his brother landed with Captain Crispin, and were engaged in examining and enjoying the beauties of Mrs. Whitehead's house and grounds.

At the request of Her Majesty, Lieutenant Shairp, of the Coastguard Service, went on board the Royal Yacht, and was graciously requested to steer the Barge along the coast, the scenery of which was much admired, and sketches were taken of some of the point most interesting. The urbanity of the Royal party was the delight of all who had the pleasure of enjoying an intercourse so unexpected and so novel.

On the Royal party leaving Babbicombe, Mr. Gasking, of the "Cary Arms" had the honor of presenting the Princes with a lithograph view of Babbicombe, taken in 1846, when Her Majesty graciously anchored in the Bay, and the Royal Squadron is seen at anchor.

AUGUST 5TH, 1879—Another visit of His Royal Highness the Prince of Wales, who took tea at the "Cary Arms," accompanied by Lord Charles Beresford and party.

MAY 18TH, 1880—Another visit by their Royal Highnesses, the Prince and Princess of Wales, and two sons, Prince Albert Victor of Wales and Prince George Frederick of Wales, and the Duchess of Sutherland.

Cary Arms souvenir of royal visits to Babbacombe.

overnight accommodation. There was no such luxury, however, for the lowly servant John Lee, who slept downstairs on a fold-down bed in the pantry. He had been offered employment by Miss Keyse when she required someone to work in the stables: 'So there I was in my first situation. I had nothing much to do. The pony was about thirty years old, I believe. They told me that it once belonged to my mistress's mother, and that it had been more or less pensioned off for its old age. I had to look after it just as one would nurse some infirm creature. I put it in its stable at night or took it out for exercise. When I was not looking after the pony I was generally going about with Miss Keyse. When she went visiting I used to bring her home at night. I was the boy' (Lee, 1908).

The grandeur of The Glen was quite a change of surroundings for the son of a clay miner raised in a small rented cottage in a relatively poverty-stricken village. *The Great Western Illustrated Railway Guide* from this period carries this description of Babbacombe, which then had a population of around 1,000 people:

> From Babbacombe Downs, where the best houses are to be found, one of the most delightful of the delightful views in South Devon is to be found. The eyes wander along the eastern coast to Teignmouth, Starcross, over the Exe to Exmouth, and past this point to those of Budleigh Salterton and Sidmouth. The rich dark red of the rocks, the deep tone of the sea, and the brilliant green of the meadows topping the undulating cliffs form, with the vast expanse of the sky, a most lovely panorama. Below, lies the well-sheltered beach, whence our view, looking eastward, is taken. Here the waters are clear

A GWR sketch showing The Glen on Babbacome Beach.

as crystal, and splash over an expanse of such well-rounded pebbles, that the bather is guaranteed from injury. To the eastward rises a mass of roseate rock, while to the right lies the undercliffe, where the closely-sheltered houses promise a pleasant refuge for the invalid. . . . Above, on the breezy downs, quite a town may now be seen, and here, visitors seeking invigorating sea-side air, may readily find it, while sojourning in houses well guaranteed from extreme heat, even in the hottest weather.

Babbacombe possesses the advantage of being rural and retired, while it is only a drive of two or three miles over a road (which is a perfect avenue of fine trees), and by the sea-wall, into charming Torquay. The walks east and west over the downs are unparalleled. Indeed, Babbacombe, with its lofty rocks, its beetling cliffs, and its masses of deep shadowy foliage, is a place to be remembered.

Living and working in this wonderful setting, John Lee was inspired to see more of the world as he became captivated by the lure of the sea:

I ought to explain that Babbacombe was a prosperous fishing village. The place was full of old sailors, who used to tell me queer yarns. All kinds of strange craft used to come in and anchor in the bay. They were mainly small trading vessels, but every now and then a big man-of-war, one of the old-fashioned kind – would come in, and then I used to spend the whole afternoons on the beach, watching the ships and jack tars.

Time went on, and every day I became more and more fascinated with a new idea that had taken possession of me. I would be a sailor. (Lee, 1908)

Following heated arguments, John overcame considerable opposition from his father and got his wish, joining the Royal Navy on 1 October 1879. Initially, all went well in his new career as he was stationed on a succession of training ships at Plymouth. At Christmas 1880, he was awarded a book, *The Bear Hunters of the Rocky Mountains* by Anne Bowman, in recognition of his success, receiving the 'Admiralty Prize for general progress. First prize, first instruction'. However, in January 1882, his dream of going to sea and travelling to exotic countries was dashed. At the age of eighteen, Lee's life in the Royal Navy came to a sudden end when he was taken seriously ill:

I was stricken down with pneumonia, and sent to the Royal Naval Hospital. For some days I lay between life and death till they pulled me through – but at what a price!

The doctors told me that I was of no more use to the Navy. I was invalided out. My career was closed. I still possess my discharge papers, setting forth the reason of my discharge and describing my character as 'Very good.'

My heart was broken. There seemed to be nothing left for me to do. (Lee, 1908)

This setback was the crucial event in what Lee described as 'a clutch of circumstances' that were to lead the would-be sailor back to The Glen and criminal notoriety two years later. That fateful year 'A Visitor's Opinion of Torquay', which was first published in the *Cheltenham Examiner*, was proudly reproduced in the *Torquay Directory*, 27 August 1884:

Invalids resting outside the Cary Arms.

'Anywhere, anywhere out of the *town*,' was the scattering cry this month among the remnant left in London of the nomadic band known as Society. As chronicler of that favoured corporation, our vocation was at an end, and we 'did' Torquay. . . . It does not boast the bracing qualities of the more favoured northern resorts, but for those who do not require to be strung up to a muscular pitch, who are in a normal state of good health, and who merely wish for quiet, cool sea breeze, beautiful drives, objects of romantic and historic interest within a day's outing, every luxury and refinement that the 19th century can give, moderate charges for housing of every degree, and good boating, Torquay holds its own against any other sea-coast place in England. For those too delicate or fragile to brave sharper air, it stands alone.

The season of Torquay, as everybody knows, is winter – then it is crowded with rich invalids, and also with pleasure seekers, young and old – and prices rise in proportion. Then the great hotels are crowded, and the sheltered villas, peering out on the sea from quiet leafy nooks, find ready tenants. Now the same accommodation can be had for probably one half the winter charge. The appliances for warding off the cold winds of winter and spring also ward off the too ardent regards of the sun – and for summer residences the houses are charming. . . . The drive to Babbacombe, a suburb, and now almost part and parcel of Torquay proper, gives some lovely sea views. . . . The sojourner there could make a separate excursion each day for a month to some place of interest, and still leave the field un-exhausted. . . . Torquay has one more recommendation; it enjoys an immunity from severe thunder-storms.

This flattering testimonial of the delights of the area provided excellent publicity for the fast-growing holiday resort, although bad news was soon to follow. That winter Torquay hogged the headlines with lurid details of a dastardly crime. Furthermore, the assertion of the *Cheltenham Examiner* that the town enjoyed an 'immunity from severe thunder-storms' proved to be a fallacy when All Saints Church, Babbacombe, and St Marychurch Parish Church were struck by lightning on 30 January 1885. Perhaps this was an omen of things to come, for the date coincided with the opening of the Devon County Assizes at Exeter Castle and the eagerly awaited trial of the man accused of committing the vile and despicable 'Babbacombe Murder'.

CHAPTER 2

Troubles and misfortunes

The tragedy, by whomsoever enacted, has put an end to the philanthropic exertions of Miss Keyse on behalf of the prisoner Lee.

– Torquay Directory, 26 November 1884

John Lee described his youth as a 'long series of troubles' and 'misfortunes'. These began at the age of eighteen, when he was forced to relinquish his naval career on health grounds and return to South Devon to seek alternative employment. In the first nine months of 1882, he moved between three jobs. The first, and longest, period was spent in a position as 'boots', cleaning the footwear of guests at the Yacht Club Hotel, Kingswear. Dissatisfied with this lowly occupation, he gained employment as a porter at Kingswear Railway Station; then, a month later, early in October, was transferred to the goods department at Torre Station, Torquay. He had only been there one week when fate intervened in the shape of his former employer Emma Keyse who presented him with a golden opportunity to further his prospects: 'Miss Keyse had been keeping an eye on me. She used to write to me and give me good advice. You can understand, therefore, how one morning my heart positively leapt for joy when I received a letter from her in which she told me that she had arranged for me to go as footman to Colonel Brownlow at Torquay. I gratefully accepted the offer, entered the colonel's service – and happened on my second great misfortune' (Lee, 1908).

Lee's 'second great misfortune' was a self-inflicted act of crass stupidity committed only six months later, when he stole valuables from his new employer, the Brownlows, while they were holidaying abroad. The young servant was apprehended in Plymouth attempting to pawn the family silver. Victorian moral values were harsh, and his crime virtually ensured that Lee would never again be employed in a position of trust. The case came before the magistrates at Torquay Police Court on Wednesday 9 May, lasted two days and warranted prominent coverage in the *Torquay Times and South Devon Advertiser (Torquay Times)*, Saturday 12 May 1883:

John Lee, footman, was charged with stealing a quantity of silver plate belonging to his employer, Colonel Brownlow, of Ridgehill, Middle Warberry Road. Mr. Creed, solicitor, defended.

Michael Kisler, butler at Ridgehill, said the prisoner was footman at the establishment. On Wednesday, April 25th witness cleaned the plate, which was kept in a little room,

The prisoner's career.

locked up in some boxes. The keys of the plate chest were placed on a shelf whereupon was kept the glass. He identified two small silver candlesticks produced as a portion of the plate he cleaned; also a tray and pair of snuffers and a pair of larger candlesticks. All these articles he placed carefully away in the boxes. While cleaning the plate he had occasion to go to the door. Lee assisted him in the work, and when witness went to the door he left him with the goods. He was not absent longer than four or five minutes. After finishing cleaning, he locked the plate in its chest and the chest in the room. On the 1st May Detective Slee came to witness and in consequence of what he said, a search was made of the plate boxes. There were missing two plated candlesticks, two silver candlesticks, snuffers and tray. Lee went away on the previous Saturday and returned at night: he said he had been away because his father was ill. On Monday morning witness found that Lee had gone away again, and was told that that he had set off to see his father. Prisoner did not come back again, and witness had not been seen until he was placed in the dock. Witness and Slee, on May 3rd, went to prisoner's bedroom door, which they found locked. Having got a key to fit the lock they opened the door and searched the room. They found two keys . . . One of the keys found in the room opened the door of the room in which the plate was kept.

Cross-examined: There were not two keys to the plate-room. Prisoner had been in Colonel Brownlow's employ for six months, three months of which time the Colonel had been away.

Mark Emdon, pawnbroker and jeweller, 48 Fore Street, Devonport, said that on April 28th, at half-past two in the afternoon, prisoner had rang his side-door bell. He said he was recommended to witness to sell a pair of silver candlesticks. Witness was suspicious of him and asked him inside, when he produced a small pair of candlesticks. Being asked if he had anything else, he took a pair of snuffers out of his pocket. Witness inquired for the tray, and prisoner told him he had forgotten it, but would bring it down the next time he came. He had a paper parcel in his hand, and witness asked him what it contained. He said he had there two candlesticks, which he produced. Being told they were odd candlesticks, he said he would make up the pair when he brought the tray. Witness went

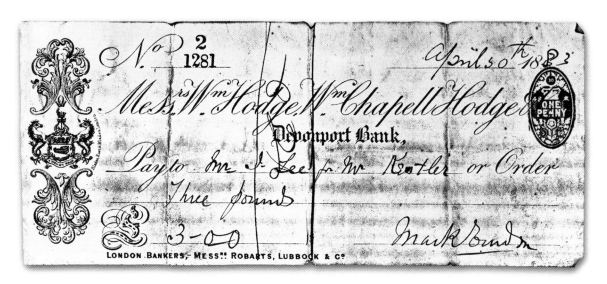

The cheque received by John Lee for stolen goods.

to get some scales to weigh the silver, and took the opportunity of looking for a policeman. Not seeing one, he returned and proceeded to ascertain the weight of the silver. Then he offered prisoner £3 for it, and he agreed to accept it. Witness said he had no money, and must give a cheque for the amount. This he did, post-dating it. Prisoner told him that he came from a Mr. Kisler, of Union Street, Torquay, who was the owner of the property. Witness's cheque was made payable to 'J. Lee for Mr. Kisler.' He agreed to give him 30s. for the large plated candlesticks when he brought the other two to make up the pair. When prisoner left the shop witness followed him to the corner of the street and saw him standing outside an outfitting establishment. Anticipating that he may attempt to cash the cheque there, witness took steps to prevent it, and immediately went to the police-station. There was only an inspector on duty, however, and, he had to go to the residence of a detective. In the meantime the prisoner had returned to his house, and complained that he could not get his cheque cashed, because it was not properly dated. Witness afterwards ascertained that prisoner had presented the cheque at the outfitting establishment. On Monday morning, about 11 o'clock, the prisoner came into the witness's shop and took a snuffers' tray from his breast pocket. He was asked for the other candlesticks, and he replied that he could not bring them. He also said the cheque was wrongly dated, and produced it in order that he might alter it. Witness went to get his scales, intending again to communicate with a policeman. Having obtained an officer he sent him to the side-door in order to wait until he should be called in. Witness went back and told the prisoner he must give a better account of the articles than he already had, because he had discovered that there was no Mr. Kisler residing in Union Street, Torquay. He was unable to do so, and witness eventually gave him into custody. The value of the property produced was at least £20.

John Slee, police constable, said that in consequence of a communication from Devonport police, he on May 1st went to Colonel Brownlow's house and saw the butler, Mr. Kisler, with whom he searched the plate chests. The articles produced were missing. On Wednesday May 2nd, he again went to Ridgehill and entered Lee's bedroom, with results stated by the witness Kisler. He went to Devonport on May 8th, where he received prisoner into custody from the police. When charged with stealing the articles, he said, 'It's no use to deny it; I took the candlesticks and snuffers on Saturday morning and the tray on Monday morning. I don't know what could make me do it.' Witness brought him to the Torquay police-station and locked him up.

This was the case for the prosecution.

Mr. Creed, on behalf of the prisoner, did not attempt to deny the charge. He said the prisoner had hitherto borne a good character. It was a first offence, and he would submit that it was one of those cases which it was intended might be dealt with summarily. . . . The vicar of Abbotskerswell (the home of the prisoner) testified to his good character, and he had served two years in the navy, being discharged in January 1882, invalided, and his character was marked 'Very good.' Lee had also been employed as a porter at Kingswear railway station. His action in this matter, respectably and honestly connected as he was, to him (Mr. Creed) was inexplicable. It was evident that if a man had intended to be detected he could not have acted more foolishly than the prisoner had. . . .

[Next day] The Bench said they had considered all that Mr. Creed had said. They were very sorry that a young man who appeared to have hitherto borne a good character should have committed an offence of such a grave character, namely, of a servant in a position of trust taking a considerable number of articles belonging to his master – and proceeding with them to another town – Plymouth – to pledge them. A fact which weighed with the Bench was that having taken a certain amount of the goods and pawned them on Saturday, he went back after the tray had been asked for, and brought it on the Monday. Therefore it looked as though the prisoner had a determination to continue the offence he had commenced on Saturday. When a servant acted in this way the Bench deemed that they could not do otherwise than send him for trial. Therefore they committed him to take his trial at the Exeter Quarter Sessions to be held in July. Mr. Fortescue added that the Bench considered it their duty to say a word of commendation of Mr. Emdon, the pawnbroker, for the manner he had acted. They wished that all pawnbrokers would pursue a similar course in matters of this kind.

DETECTIVE SLEE

Victorian courts took a dim view of servants transgressing against their masters, and once Lee's solicitor had failed in his argument for the case to be dealt with by a fine imposed by the magistrates, a custodial sentence was the predictable outcome of Lee's trial at Exeter Assizes, which was reported briefly in the *Torquay Times*, Saturday 16 July 1883:

John Lee, 18, footman pleaded guilty to having, on the 28th April, at Tormohon, stolen a pair of silver candle sticks, two plated ditto, silver snuffers and tray, and other articles, the property of the Hon. Colonel E. Brownlow. Mr. Molesworth St. Aubyn, M.P., who appeared for the prosecution, asked the Court to be lenient in consideration of prisoner's previous good character. Lee was a servant in the employ of Colonel Brownlow, and in the absence of his master yielded to a sudden temptation and made away with these goods, which, however, had all been recovered. Prisoner was sentenced to six months' imprisonment with hard labour.

While he was serving his 'lenient' sentence at Exeter Prison, having already spent three months remanded in custody awaiting trial, Lee's future prospects as a convicted felon looked decidedly grim, but he was offered yet another lifeline by Emma Keyse, whom he had let down badly after she had recommended him to Colonel Brownlow. Despite this breach of trust, she evidently still thought well of Lee, believing he had simply been 'led astray'. On New Year's Day 1884, shortly before Lee's imminent release, her letter to the governor was passed to the prison chaplain, the Reverend John Pitkin, with an offer which would enable the prisoner to rebuild his life and gain a 'character' reference:

Emma Keyse.

Sir, I hope you will excuse my troubling you, but I feel anxious to know what report you can give me of John Lee? Whether he has conducted himself satisfactorily, and whether those who have had much to do with him can give a good report, and whether you consider that he truly and really feels the great sin he has been led into, and whether he is really penitent. I shall be grateful, if you will make careful enquiries, in addition to your own personal opinion. He lived with me as a lad, and I liked him very much, and found him very honest and truthful and obedient. I had no particular fault to find with him, but considered his was a simple-minded, easy disposition that would be easily led astray, and hoped, by being on a training-ship, he would gain stability of character and purpose, and was very sorry that his health would not admit of his remaining. I feel much interested in his family and himself; and have told his mother that I will take him back into my service, and to work in the garden with my gardener for a while, to be able to give him a character, until something desirable may turn up.

He will live in the house, and sleep as before, in my pantry. But it depends upon what character you may give, and if you consider I may really trust him. We trusted him so implicitly when he was here, that I do not feel disposed to be mistrustful now. Still, it is a serious matter, and I should like to hear from you about him, and what you think of the matter. I cannot give him much in the way of wages; and he must promise to be content to keep in of an evening, and to be very steady. I could not have anxiety to be looking after him constantly; being a lady it would not be pleasant. Two of my servants have lived nearly forty years here (my late mother's servants), and the other is half-sister of John Lee. So they would all be interested in him. I was in hopes that I should have an opportunity of his going with some people I know to the Colonies, but that has fallen through; they are supplied. I think it would be desirable when he is older, and his principles are more firm. But I fear he would even now be too easily lead astray, though I hope this severe lesson will have taught him more strength of purpose for good.

I hope you will excuse my thus troubling you, but feel anxious to hear what report you can give. And if you can kindly talk to him about being steady, quiet and not seeking companions, I should be grateful.

Awaiting your reply,

I remain, Dear Sir,
Emma Whitehead Keyse.

(Pitkin, 1918)

John Lee gratefully accepted the opportunity to work temporarily for a token wage while Miss Keyse attempted to find him gainful employment elsewhere and give him a fresh start in life:

'I feel much interested in his family and himself; and have told his mother that I will take him back into my service . . .'

'MISS KEYSE IS A FRIEND TO THE PRISONER

Once again a hand was near to help me. My kind old friend, Miss Keyse, had written to the governor of the prison, asking for my character. As soon as she received it she wrote to me at Abbotskerswell, and asked me to go and see her. Accompanied by my sister Millie, I went over to Babbacombe one afternoon and had a long talk with Miss Keyse. I have often thought of that day since. She was so kind to me: she seemed to be more gracious than ever. After she had spoken to me she sent me to the vicar. In the end I was taken back into the household at 'The Glen'. (Lee, 1908)

Lee's gratitude was short-lived, however, for prospective employers, mindful of the unpleasant experience of Colonel Brownlow, were not easily persuaded by Miss Keyse's pleas to 'give the poor boy another chance'. As the months went by and she failed to find him a suitable position, Lee became argumentative and disrespectful. He began to refer to her in derogatory terms as 'the old woman'. It was as if he began to blame the elderly lady for the hopelessness of the position his crime had placed him in. The situation was exacerbated when he became engaged to a local dressmaker, as he was not earning enough to support a wife. Early in October 1884, his fiancée, Katie Farmer, was dealing with the grief of the sudden loss of her widowed mother when she received an unexpected shock from Lee. Frustrated by his lack of prospects, Lee chose this sensitive moment to write a letter suggesting that they break off their relationship:

October 10th, 1884

My dearest Katie,

I am very unsettled in what I am going to do in my future life. I am tired of service and am going to look out for something else and to do something which may not be to your liking. And my dear, don't let me keep you from going anywhere where it will be for your good. You may get a better chance by going away, and we might not always be the same as we are now, in love. My dear, I implore you, if you think we shall not come together, let us break off our engagement before it is too late. I am beginning to love you so much it will break my heart if we should leave in time to come. Do let us break off at once. My dearest, let what you have gone by die out of our thoughts, but our love never can. My dearest, you have been the kindest I ever met with, in love and all things. I shall ever love you the same; and I shall leave the town as soon as possible. I shall feel it very much my darling. If I had kept your company when first I seen you. I would have married you and made you happy. I am unsettled now, and don't know what my fate may be, my darling own love. Good-bye my sweetest love, from one who will ever love you the same.

John Lee

Miss Kate Farmer

Lee evidently changed his mind and the couple were reunited when Katie immediately responded with the following loving reply (subsequent events would lead to both letters appearing in the press):

My dearest love,

    Your letter to hand, which has caused me the greatest pain and grief. What can you possibly mean by telling me one time you will [never] leave me and then writing to know if I wish to break off our engagement. It is no use to tell. I can't make it out. As you are so undecided about what you intend to do for the future, are you also undecided about me? Do you think seriously of what you are doing before you give me up. I tell you now the same as I told you before, our engagement shall be not broken off with my consent. As regards what you intend in the future, if it was your lot to break stones in the street, I will not say no. Have a little pity for me and think how dearly I love you. Perhaps if I had loved you less you might have valued me a little more. As to my getting another chance away, do you think I want anyone better than the one I love? If you knew how you were deceived, you would never mention it. Why not have you told me last night when I mentioned about going away? What you write then would not come so hard for me. There is one thing I wish particularly to know. That is, do you think I wish you to marry me before you see your way clear? No my darling I am prepared to battle my way until you see fit to make me your wife. I will never be the one to grumble at waiting for you. Jack, think if we part you will be the cause of grieving me to death and breaking my heart. After what you said to me on Sunday, I never dreamt of your writing to me in the same strain as your last letter was written. But never mind, I freely forgive you, but at the same time will not give you up. My Mother will naturally come into your mind. Would to God it had been my funeral you went to instead of hers. Then I should have never have got your letter and you would never have written it. She was my only friend, but I have always depended upon you to be something more than a friend to me. You have been my chief support in all my troubles and helped me to bear them better than I could else. Before concluding I should very much like to see you once more as I have something to say which can't be written. You ask me if I should be annoyed if you sent me a present. You must fancy me annoyed with you which you know could never be. Nothing will give me more pleasure than to receive anything from the hands of one whom I love devotedly. Whatever it is it will die with me and my love. Grant my last request by coming down tomorrow evening (Wednesday).

    Accept my fondest and truest love, and believe me ever your true love.

Katie Farmer

Friction within The Glen continued to mount when Miss Keyse, who had been trying to sell her estate for some considerable time, succeeded in finding a buyer for the property at an auction conducted in London on 28 October. Later that day, she paid the servants their quarterly salaries, owed in arrears, and Lee was bitterly upset to learn that she had reduced his wages from half a crown to the miserly sum of two shillings a week. What she planned to do after disposing of what had been her home for over half a century never emerged, but it was patently clear that she had no further use for a manservant. Tragically, a little over two weeks after reassuring Lee that she would try and persuade the new owners to keep him on, she was dead and suspicion for her brutal murder quickly fell upon 'the only man in the house'.

During the subsequent inquest, magistrate's hearing and murder trial, Lee was not required to venture any information about what happened that fateful night. It wasn't until many years later when he sold his 'life story' to a newspaper (also published in paperback) that the public eventually got the opportunity to hear his version of events:

And so I come to November 14, 1884. The first thing I distinctly remember is seeing my step-sister, Elizabeth Harris, going to her bedroom. It was teatime. As she looked queer I asked her what was the matter. She said she didn't feel well. 'Shall I fetch Dr. Chilcote?' I said. She replied, rather shortly I thought, 'Oh, no, no!' I was afterwards told that she was in bed. At all events, I did not see her for the rest of that day.

At seven o'clock I went to the post, as was my duty every day. Then I went round to see Miss Farmer, and at ten o'clock I returned to 'The Glen.' After supper I went in to prayers with Eliza and Jane Neck. Miss Keyse said the prayers. It was always a touching little service. I shall never forget the picture – old Miss Keyse reading the prayers and a chapter from the bible.

In a quarter of an hour the prayers were said, and at eleven o'clock I went to bed in the pantry. The other two servants didn't go just then. Jane was in the pantry putting away some things. She used to go about her work, although I was asleep, or, perhaps, getting into bed. She never worried about me. Miss Keyse never used to go to bed till one or two o'clock in the morning. I think Jane Neck stayed up for about half-an-hour. The last thing she did was to put a nib of cocoa on the kitchen hob for our mistress. This was done every night. Miss Keyse used to go into the kitchen herself and carry the cocoa up to her bedroom. On this particular night I think I was asleep before Jane had finished. But I do know that Miss Keyse had told Jane to tell me that there was a note in the pantry for me to take to Colonel McLean's [Miss Keyse's brother-in-law] in the morning, with a brace of pheasants. Miss Keyse often left notes like that, and I attended to them in the morning.

The next thing I remember is being roused up before daybreak by my step-sister shouting 'Fire! Fire!' I jumped out of bed and put on my shirt, socks, and trousers. At the top of the stairs I saw the three women. The house was full of smoke. Eliza Neck was shouting: 'Where's Miss Keyse? Where's Miss Keyse?'

We rushed into Miss Keyse's bedroom. The old lady was not there. Terror-stricken, Eliza Neck went running about the rooms upstairs, but there was no sign of Miss Keyse. I could see flames coming out of my mistress's room, and also out of another room. Eliza was the first to go into the dining-room. Jane and I waited outside. The smoke was so thick that I could hardly see her. I heard Jane call out, 'We shall all be stifled!'

Realising the danger I rushed headlong into the dining-room in order to open the windows. I tried to open the French window on the right, but I couldn't. So I pushed my arm through the glass. I cut my arm and left a bit of flesh on the pane. I could feel the blood pouring down my sleeve and soaking it. But what did it matter?

I little thought that afterwards my fate would practically turn on that trivial circumstance. The smoke was now pouring out of the room, and we looked about us.

'We rushed into Miss Keyse's bedroom. The old lady was not there.'

'Oh! Where is Miss Keyse?' I heard one of the women say. As she spoke I looked round. My mind recoils with horror as I think of it. There spread before me, was the answer to my cry. My poor dear mistress was lying on the carpet – a ghastly sight. I can see her eyes staring out from the hair which had fallen about her face. I can still see her hands. They were blue and 'clawlike' – drawn up in convulsions of death. I just took one glance at the body and went out.

Jane and I at once called a man named Stiggins [Stigings], who was living in one of Miss Keyse's cottages on the beach. He was a fisherman. Then I went back to the house. I remember that we also called Mr. Gaskin [Gasking], the landlord of the Cary Arms. Several other people came as well. I went back to the dining-room. The smoke had now gone. Miss Keyse was lying by the sofa. There was blood on her throat. The body looked as if an attempt had been made to burn it, but I did not notice any paper about or oil.

FINDING THE BODY of MISS KEYSE

'My poor dear mistress was lying on the carpet – a ghastly sight.'

With the assistance of Mr. Gaskin I carried the body outside. Nearly all the clothes had been burnt off it, Mr. Gaskin lifted her by the head, and I took her by the feet.

Next I remember that I went back into the dining-room, and helped to put out the fire. The people in the house wanted someone to go and break the news to Colonel McLean. I was sent. I ran all the way to the house in Torquay, and threw some gravel up at the servant's window. After the gravel had been rattling against the panes for several moments the window was thrown up and a servant put out her head. 'There's been a fire at Miss Keyse's,' I said. 'Tell Mrs. McLean [the victim's sister] I want her.'

I was admitted into the hall, and presently I saw Mrs. McLean standing on top of the landing. 'Miss Keyse's place has been on fire,' I told her, 'and the poor old lady is badly burnt.' On my way back to 'The Glen' I met the chimney sweep. I think I also called a policeman.

At the trial something was said about an axe. It is quite true that I was asked for one when they were putting out the fire. They wanted to chop down a beam. I went out to the woodhouse and got the axe I knew would be there.

How quickly that terrible morning passed! Still less did I pause to recollect that on the night before the tragedy, I was the only man in the house!

As soon as things got a bit quiet I wanted to go to the doctor to get my arm dressed. By that time my shirt was soaked with blood. At the door of 'The Glen' there was a policeman, I told him where I was going. Holding up a hand he said: 'You can't go there alone. I must go with you.' I protested strongly against such absurd treatment. The real meaning of it did not dawn on me. However, the policeman went to the superintendent, and asked him if he was to go with me to the surgery. 'No,' said the superintendent. 'Let him go himself.'

After my arm had been dressed I went back to the house, and sat down with the firemen in the kitchen. Suddenly the superintendent called me to him. 'Lee,' he said, 'you will be

Sergeant Abraham Nott accompanied Lee to the police station.

apprehended on suspicion.' I said, 'On suspicion? – Oh!' I was too astonished to say anything else. He answered, 'You are the only man in the house!' Almost dazed, I was handed over to the sergeant. I could hardly speak. I could not think. My tongue was tied. As I was going through my step-sister, Elizabeth Harris, said to me: 'Where are you going to?' I said, 'I am taken on suspicion.' She answered, 'I know you didn't do it!'

As I left the house for Torquay police-station I heard Mr. Gaskin say that 'something foul' had been done. That is all I know about the murder of Miss Keyse. I take Almighty God as my judge – I have spoken the truth. Miss Keyse was my best friend. . . .

Immediately after I had been arrested I was marched all the way to Torquay police-station in front of a policeman. No crowd accompanied me. I was not handcuffed. I simply trudged along as if I was bent on some errand. Behind me was the sergeant. I made no attempt to escape. I wanted to see the whole business through from beginning to end. I had nothing to be afraid of. In a sense I was quite happy. When we got to Torquay I was formally charged, and put into a cell. As I heard the door clang upon me my heart sank. For a second time I was within prison walls. I sat down, my head in my hands, and strove to realise what had befallen me. Theft I had already suffered for. I was now charged with murder! (Lee, 1908)

CHAPTER 3

News of the Babbacombe tragedy

DEATHS: On the 15th Nov., at The Glen, Babbacombe. EMMA ANN WHITEHEAD KEYSE, youngest daughter of the late Thomas Keyse Esq., of New Hall, Middlesex, and of the late Mrs Whitehead, widow of George Whithead Esq., of Weston House, Somerset, and of The Glen, Babbacombe.

– The Times, 21 November 1884

The genteel inhabitants and visitors of Torquay society were horrified to hear that one of their number had allegedly been murdered by one of her own servants. The gruesome particulars were revealed in the *Torquay Times* of Friday 21 November 1884:

The small village of Babbacombe, about one-and-a-half miles from Torquay, was thrown into a state of the wildest excitement on Saturday morning by a report that an aged and well-known lady of the place had been cruelly and brutally murdered. At first the rumours were believed to be exaggerated, but as the morning wore on, and more details came to light, the conviction gained ground that a terrible deed had been committed – mysteriously, silently, and with a fiendish disregard of other lives in the house, and of the premises, and their handsome contents – for all appearances point to the conclusion that the hand which did the murder, if murder it be, set fire to the house, with the intention, undoubtedly, of hiding all traces of the ghastly act.

'Babbacombe' [The Glen] is a charming residence at the foot of the steep decline to the Beach, surrounded with pretty gardens, and having all the attributes which go to the making up of a pleasant marine villa. It is we understand, reckoned a valuable property, with a marketable value of £13,000. Gasking's Cary Arms stands close by, and there are a few fishermen's houses in the same vicinity. But the spot is a weird and lonely one in the winter, and especially unsuitable for the living-place of an aged and solitary female. The approach to it is such that no vehicles can be got near it, and the occupant has to mount a very rough and steep hill in order to reach the high-road. The house has been in the occupation of Miss Keyse, a lady between 60 and 70 years, for a very long period. . . .

The establishment consisted of the mistress, three maid-servants, and a man-servant, and it appears that although Miss Keyse has shown herself to be of a slightly eccentric turn of mind, her household has always been well conducted. The shocking occurrence seems to have taken place about half-past three on Saturday morning. At that time Mr. Gasking, of the Cary Arms, was awakened from his sleep by some shouting outside,

Residence of the late Miss Keyse: 'the spot is a weird and lonely one . . . and especially unsuitable
for the living-place of an aged and solitary female'.

and, hurriedly dressing himself, he went downstairs. The same shouts also called up Richard Harris, a fisherman, living close by, in a small house opposite 'Babbacombe.' However, Mr. Gasking was before him and, at the direction of the servants of the deceased woman, who are said to have raised cries for help, he rushed to Miss Keyse's residence, passing through the garden gate, and entered the house. He could see smoke and other indications of fire, which drew his attentions to the dining-room. Before entering this apartment, there was observed in the passage, a pool of blood, and a moment later a terrible sight presented itself. On the floor near a table, was the body of Miss Keyse, with a terrible gash in her throat, injuries to the head, the flesh charred, and almost every shred of the night-clothes which she had been wearing, burnt off her. Mr. Gasking raised her, and with other assistance, carried the poor old lady to an outhouse near the gates of the villa, where she was placed with as much decency as the circumstances would permit. Meanwhile the coastguard and the police had been summoned, and the fire brigade at Torquay informed of the fire. The engines proceeded to the brow of the hill, but the fishermen and other helpers had worked with willing hands, and had subdued the flames, which had been confined to the dining-room and two bedrooms. Under any circumstances the engine could not have assisted in extinguishing the fire without incurring serious risk, so deep in the glen are the premises situated.

The persons who went into the house agree that there was no fire in the grate and that no lamp or anything of the kind was burning. The cook is understood to have been the first to awake. The fire was finally got under about five o'clock. Sergeant Nott, of St. Marychurch, and P.C. Meech were soon on the premises.

About half-past nine o'clock Doctor Steele and Doctor Chilcote, two medical practitioners in the district, went down to the Beach and there examined the body of Miss Keyse. They found the skull to be fractured and the throat cut, all the deep vessels being divided and the windpipe severed.

If it were not for the fractured skull the supposition of suicide might have some foundation, although Miss Keyse only on the previous day was in the best health and spirits, did some shopping, talked with several people in St. Marychurch, and seemed as far removed as possible from the condition of an intending suicide. . . .

The manservant John Lee was arrested on Saturday on suspicion of being concerned in the tragic occurrence.

The Glen suddenly became a ghoulish attraction, drawing large numbers of people to view the scene of the crime. The tragedy also stimulated a flourishing trade in souvenirs, with local photographers clamouring to sell their wares.

An argument broke out when Charles Collis, who had taken a studio portrait of John Lee, did not take kindly to a competitor, Benjamin Pearce, offering the same photograph to his customers. In his next advertisement, he issued this warning to would-be customers: 'Mr Collis, of Fleet Street, Torquay, having the only original Negative Plate, the public are cautioned against purchasing *Vile and Spurious Copies.*'

Although the local papers were content to run these advertisements in the columns alongside their copious reports of the murder, they expressed dismay that the story was reaching a wider audience: 'The daily newspapers, both metropolitan and provincial,

Charles Collis, the photographer who had taken this studio portrait of John Lee, warned would-be customers: 'the public are cautioned against purchasing *Vile and Spurious Copies*.'

have devoted considerable space to the Babbacombe tragedy, in the absence of more stirring news' (*Torquay Directory*, 3 December 1884). It was particularly galling that upper-class patrons were exposed to bad publicity about the resort when the unsavoury incident was featured in a leading society journal. The article elevated general dogsbody John Lee to the status of 'butler':

The Murder at Babbicombe

The village of Babbicombe, situated on the shore of a small bay on the South Devon coast, between Teignmouth and Torquay, was the scene of a cruel murder perpetrated on Saturday, the 15th inst. An elderly maiden lady, Miss Emma Keyse, sixty-eight years of age, resided in a pretty marine villa at the foot of the cliff, surrounded by wooded pleasure-grounds, which is called 'The Glen'. She is said to have dwelt there more than forty years. The house, which is shown in our illustration [overleaf], was a low thatched building, but sufficiently commodious; and Miss Keyse, living there with none of her family or friends, often entertained visitors and private yachting parties. She kept three female servants, one of whom had a half-brother, John Lee, twenty-years old, and he was

Scene of the murder at Babbacombe.

the butler in Miss Keyse's household. In the night, or between three and four in the morning, the cook smelt burning, and gave the alarm. It was discovered that the house had been set on fire in three places, in the drawing-room, in the dining-room, and in Miss Keyse's bed-room. The dead body of the unfortunate lady was found in the dining-room, with a deep gash across the throat, and with the side of the head smashed, as by a blow with some heavy instrument. No one had broken into the house. John Lee, whose behaviour and appearance at the time seemed very suspicious, is charged with the murder. His previous character was bad, as he underwent six months' imprisonment for stealing plate from a former master; and he was under notice to quit the service of Miss Keyse. (*Illustrated London News*, 29 November 1884)

For the international market, the story was sensationalised beyond all recognition, which brought this indignant reaction from the editor of the *Torquay Times*, 12 December 1884:

Two days after the murder of Miss Keyse at Babbacombe, there was published in the New York Herald an article, which has been brought under our notice, purporting to be an account of the shocking occurrence, in which nothing but the barest outline was in accordance with the facts. Evidently these few facts had been telegraphed across the Atlantic, and had there been expanded by an imaginative writer into a tissue of romantic lies, utterly falsifying the account as to the relations of time, persons and places, and introducing as the motive of the horrible deed a romantic attachment instead of the vulgar spite which is the only motive really apparent. Such journalism may be smart, and it may pay for a time, or if only occasionally indulged in, but it certainly behoves all honest journalists to condemn and expose such abominable impositions on the credulity of the public. Better stale news if true than such fictitious fancies published in order to gratify the morbid craving of the multitude for sensation. We refrain from reprinting the account in consideration for the feelings of the relatives of the deceased lady, but are not willing to pass over quite without notice such a shameful and yet shameless instance of dishonest journalism.

Within twenty-four hours of the murder, the offending article, suggesting that John Lee was in love with 'Miss Key' (*sic*), appeared in the *New York Herald* and Canada's *Toronto Globe*:

Torquay, the fashionable winter watering place on the south coast, is at present stirred by a sensation of a most ghastly character. Nearly adjoining Torquay is the smart fishing village of Babbacombe. Conspicuous for many years among the residents of Babbacombe has been Miss Key an aristocratic, wealthy and unmarried woman of middle age. The lady resided in a palatial villa and was regarded by the families as an angel because of charities, and her accomplishments and entertainments were the envy of most of the fashionable visitors to Torquay. Some time ago Miss Key took into her personal service, as a valet, a young and good-looking man, named John Lee. He had come down from London, and bore such testimonials as to worth and character from personal friends of the Key family that he found little difficulty in entering the service of the lady. His duties finally resolved themselves into those of an escort, and he waited upon his patron wherever she went. This started much gossip on the part of the envious, and this gossip became much exaggerated. Last night the people of Babbacombe were startled by the discovery of flames issuing from the mansion in which Miss Key resided. The fire had evidently been burning for some time, as the flames broke simultaneously through windows in the different walls. The villagers went to the scene in a body and the coast guard and local police soon got control of the fire from without. They found that the mansion had been securely closed and that the windows and doors had all been fastened. An entrance was forced and the fire extinguished. Miss Key was found lying upon the parlour floor – dead. Her person was nude, and the body partly charred. An investigation revealed the fact that her throat had been cut and her skull fractured.

There were evidences that the lady had been dragged down stair before she was killed, and that preceding all this and after a terrible struggle in her private apartments she had been assaulted. All the jewellery and portable valuables belonging to the lady were missing, and not a shilling of money was left in the house. The murder was at once set

'He confessed his guilt and fully told the story.'

down to jealousy, and the robbery was set down as a ruse to misdirect suspicion. No trace of John Lee could be found, and it was feared that he too had been murdered. The country was at once scoured by the police and the enraged fishermen who eagerly joined in the chase for the criminals. After an all-night search John Lee was found concealed in a stable not far from the scene of the murder. A large sum of money and much of the missing jewellery were found upon his person. He was at once arrested and charged with the crime.

He confessed his guilt and fully told the story. He admitted he was an ex-convict and had obtained employment in the service of Miss Key, by means of forged letters. He said he had fallen in love with the lady, and having no means to secure an acquaintance with her, resorted to his deceit for that purpose. After he had been in her employ for a time and had secured kindly recognition in his capacity as valet, his ardour getting the better of his judgement; he mistook the lady's favours for more than it meant, and made an avowal of love.

Miss Key was horrified, and attempted to correct his folly by showing him that his suit was both hopeless and absurd. He persisted, and Miss Key finally ordered him out of her service and accused him of being a mercenary adventurer. On the evening of the murder he forced another interview upon his mistress, and when she again treated his overtures with contempt he became enraged and attacked her.

His passions once aroused he lost all control of his moral senses he said, and after the assault he struck her senseless so that she could not interfere with his escape. When he saw that the blow was apparently fatal, he resolved to rob the house and flee. After he had gathered up his plunder he noticed signs of consciousness in his victim, and then being desperate broke her skull and cut her throat. It then occurred to him, to drag her remains down stairs, close the doors and windows and fire the house in the hope of burying the crime in mystery. He believed that if he could have got out of the country, the crime would never have been attributed to him. The prisoner is under special guard, threats of mob violence having been made against him.

Emma Keyse had worshipped at St Marychurch Parish Church, and on Sunday 23 November, the Reverend Arthur Bouchier Wrey delivered an emotional sermon which he later published and put on sale. It was recorded at length in the *Torquay Directory*, 26 November 1884:

The death of Miss Keyse was the theme of the vicar's discourse on Sunday morning at the parish church of St. Marychurch, where she was a regular attendant. The Rev. A.B. Wrey commenting upon the murder said it all seemed conflictingly strange that one who served God so well and so consistently, with so much sacrifice of self, time, and effort,

St Marychurch Parish Church.

CONVEYING BODY TO THE OUTHOUSE

'The coffin had to be conveyed to the summit by relays of bearers under the direction of Mr. Gasking.'

should have fallen an innocent victim to a heartless, cold-blooded stealthy murderer. God's ways and thoughts were not as theirs. Often times man could not explain nor discern the reason why such things were, but, although this might silence them, yet it did not really satisfy, and the question was still thought, if not expressed, 'Why did God let that poor, good old lady be murdered?' Looking to their Bibles for guidance to an answer, they found that the Evil One had an immense power given to him to do evil in the last times between the first advent and the second advent of the Son of God, and, though the victory of evil over good might be often apparent, when they looked at any single events, these events, when joined together and worked out by God or by His permission, did not shew the evil victorious, but the reverse. The preacher proceeded to point out another lesson which he thought capable of being drawn from the awful event which had horrified them all. We all know – he said – the exceeding beauty of this Babbacombe Glen, and the ever changing and fresh views which have delighted all who have passed through those grounds by their winding paths. The good kind lady owner took more delight than anyone else possibly could have in those well-known and beautiful views of her lovely seaside home. She thought it a Paradise. Royalty, too, had ennobled it. The Queen and her Prince Consort had in their early years paid a visit to it, and had felt and expressed its charms. The Prince of Wales more than once visited it, bringing the Princess of Wales on one occasion, telling her she must see this most lovely glen of lovely Devon. No wonder, then, that our dear old friend should have prided herself in owning such a place, even though she may have valued it and spoken of it at times in somewhat extravagant terms. A slight fault this in one of such simplicity of character. But now see how all is changed. All is vanity. 'Vanity of vanities,' sayeth the

Preacher, 'all is vanity.' This unique spot on earth, favoured so lavishly by Nature, favoured by Royalty, and every other visitor, will henceforth be marked and known – oh, horrors! – thus, 'See that yonder glen and that thatched house by the seaside? That is the scene of that atrocious and vile murder of 1884.'

Three days earlier, the Reverend Wrey had officiated at the funeral of Emma Keyse. The tragic circumstances surrounding her death produced intense sympathy and vast crowds lined the route from Babbacombe Downs to St Marychurch Parish Church. The impressive arrangements had been matched on only two other occasions in the district: for the funerals of the solicitor and chairman of the Torquay Local Board of Health, William Kitson, known as 'The Maker of Torquay', and the Bishop of Exeter, Henry Phillpotts, who had resided for many years in Babbacombe at his villa Bishopstowe. In addition to the numerous local worthies who attended the funeral of Miss Keyse, the mourners also included an Admiral of the Fleet, two retired army generals, the Chief Constable of Devon, a former deputy chief constable of the county and at least ten churchmen. The event was keenly observed by the press and every minute detail was recorded in the *Torquay Directory*, 26 November 1884:

> The remains of the late Miss Keyse were buried on Thursday in the churchyard of St. Marychurch where the family have a vault. On all sides there were signs of general mourning; the shops and places of business in St. Marychurch and Babbacombe were closed, and nearly everyone to be met with were attired more or less in black.
>
> Owing to the difficulty of access down the steep road to the house it was arranged that the cortege should form at the top of the hill. The coffin had to be conveyed to the summit by relays of bearers under the direction of Mr. Gasking, who had entire superintendence of the arrangements, and soon after twelve o'clock the carriages began

'After the service in the church the procession . . . proceeded to the grave at the eastern end of the yard . . . and here the melancholy rites were completed.'

to arrive; several hundred persons were already there, but a very large number, including many from Torquay, proceeded to the church.

The coffin was placed in a hearse having open panels, and was covered with a number of beautiful and costly wreaths and other floral tributes of affection and esteem from relatives and friends. The remains of the deceased lady were enclosed in three coffins, consisting of a shell, a leaden coffin, and a coffin of polished oak, the latter being fitted with brass furniture. The inscription on the breast-plate was as follows:– 'Emma Ann Whitehead Keyse, aged 68 years; died 15th November 1884.'

Precisely at half-past twelve the procession was set in motion; first came about sixty tradesmen and other inhabitants walking two and two; then followed the coastguard and fishermen, the undertaker, and bearers. After these came the hearse, succeeded by members of the family in mourning coaches, and a long line of private carriages, numbering about thirty in all. The party passed across the Downs, and along by the Hampton Road, to the Town Hall, where a temporary halt took place in consequence of the crowded conditions of the somewhat contracted thoroughfare. The churchyard itself was crowded with spectators, amongst whom there seemed to be but one feeling – that of sorrow for the fate of the unfortunate deceased.

Arriving at the lynch-gate the coffin was removed from the hearse and placed on trestles until the rest of the cortege had arrived. The Rev. A.B. Wrey, many of the local clergy, and the choir, then led the mournful procession to the church, which was crowded with a congregation draped in mourning attire. Immediately following the coffin were Mr G. Whitehead, of Edinburgh, half brother of the deceased, and the two servants, Jane and Elizabeth Neck. Elizabeth Harris, the cook, who is half sister to the prisoner, was not present. . . . As the coffin was borne up the aisle to the temporary resting place the organist (Mr. T. Hoylands-Smith) played Mendelssohn's 'O rest in the Lord.' The remainder of the service, chiefly choral, was most solemn and impressive.

After the service in the church the procession was reformed, and proceeded to the grave at the eastern end of the yard, not far distant from the last resting place of Bishop Phillpotts, and here the melancholy rites were completed.

With Miss Keyse laid to rest, attention now focused on bringing the culprit to justice. The outcome of the ongoing legal proceedings was eagerly anticipated by the editor of the *Torquay Times*, 21 November 1884:

Horror at the tragic fate of a highly respected lady whose long life has been spent in this neighbourhood has been the prevailing sensation during the last week. Babbacombe, the name of a delightful marine village, well known to residents and visitors in Torquay but very little known to others, has suddenly attained an unenviable notoriety and become a household word all over the country. . . . One of the most remarkable features in the case is the apparent absence of any sufficient motive to account for the crime. That the lady was highly respected by all her neighbours was made abundantly clear at the funeral yesterday, at which there was an attendance larger than has been known at a funeral at St. Marychurch except on two occasions. She was quiet, benevolent, and in particular very kind to her servants, two of whom had been with her for nearly half a century, and the young man who has been accused of the murder had been taken into her service from motives of benevolence. The mystery which therefore still enshrouds the fearful crime stimulates the public curiosity, while the shocking details are horrible enough to satisfy the most morbid craving for sensation. We hope that before many days have passed the painful enquiry may be completed and the mystery solved, so that the public mind may not be kept long in a state of such painful uncertainty as exists at present; and that the responsibility for the terrible crime may be brought clearly home to the true culprit; and then *fiat justitia!*

CHAPTER 4

Committed for trial

John Lee the Butler is now sent for trial,
Committed for murder there is no denial,
Whether he done it, it is hard to say,
It will be proved on some future day . . .

– T. Brooks, song publisher, Bristol, December 1884

The chilling drama surrounding the death of Emma Keyse would be recounted by a total of twenty-six witnesses who had been summoned to give evidence during the preliminary stages of the formal investigation. The South Devon Coroner, Sydney Hacker, came in for criticism from the Chairman of the Magistrate's Hearing, W.L. Bridges, for allowing the inquest to take on too much of a judicial character. The magistrates could only commit the defendant for trial at the Devon County Assizes if they found there was a case to answer, while, unusually, the Coroner went further than was usual, invoking his full powers to determine not only whether the deceased lady had died by natural causes or met with a violent end, but inviting the jury to name the person or persons responsible for her death. In this respect, the inquest became a needlessly protracted affair lasting five days over a period of two weeks. By the fourth day, the press noted that even the jurymen were growing weary: 'Some surprise was caused by a member of the jury clapping his hands to accelerate the arrival of the Coroner' (*Torquay Times*, 28 November 1884).

THE INQUEST
Two days after the death of Emma Keyse, the inquest opened in the music room of The Glen. The proceedings were held on 17, 18, 21 and 28 November before a verdict was finally delivered on 1 December. At the outset, Police-Sergeant Abraham Nott presented the evidence to the inquest, while John Lee was not represented. As soon as the Coroner's intentions became apparent, solicitor Isadore Carter was appointed to represent the Crown and Reginald Gwynne Templer was engaged on behalf of the defendant. The inquest was by far the most interesting aspect of the legal proceedings as witnesses were often allowed to express opinions as opposed to fact. There were also some unguarded comments from John Lee as he attempted to cross-examine witnesses who also faced a barrage of questions from the Coroner, police officers, jurors and Templer. The witness statements and comments reproduced below are adapted from

verbatim reports of the inquest in the *Torquay Times and South Devon Advertiser* with additional dialogue relating to servants Eliza Neck and Elizabeth Harris taken from the *East and South Devon Advertiser*. The evidence has been arranged in chronological order to coincide with the events that occurred on the night in question:

The Coroner's Opening Address

The Coroner, addressing the jury, said: You are summoned here this morning as you are doubtless all aware, to hold an enquiry into the circumstances under which the lady whose body you shall have view, came to her death. The circumstances under which she was found dead are circumstances which suggest grave suspicions, and it will be for you to carefully give your attention to the evidence brought before you, as suspicion is directed to a man who at present is in the hands of the police, and for whom this enquiry may turn out very serious. The circumstances have been reported in the newspapers, and it is my duty, in opening this inquest, to call your attention to this point – that it is necessary for you, in approaching this inquiry, to be perfectly unbiased by anything that has come to you from the public papers or from any private source. You will have evidence submitted to you which will, I expect, from the information I have received, only enable us to commence this enquiry. It will probably, therefore, be necessary to adjourn the enquiry to enable the police to obtain further evidence and institute further proceedings in the matter for our assistance. I propose to swear one of the constables – a police-sergeant – so that we can take his evidence here at this house, and so that he may show us round the place and indicate the various points, which will enable us to understand the evidence brought forward at the Town Hall, to which place I propose to adjourn to take the remainder of the evidence. Having viewed the body you will be taken round the house by the police-sergeant, and, with the plan of the house in our minds, we shall be in a position to understand the evidence at the Town Hall.

Sergeant Nott was then sworn and conducted the Coroner and the jury over the house. The body was lying in one of the bedrooms, where it was viewed by the jury in private.

The inquest was resumed in the Public House of the Town Hall, which was crowded long before the Coroner and jury arrived. Lee was present. He was brought up from the Torquay Police Station in a cab by P.C. Bastin, and looked pale and distressed. He was trembling violently. The jury commenced their examination of the house about a quarter-past eleven, and it was nearly half-past twelve before they reached the Town Hall. . . .

The Coroner said: In proceeding with our inquest, I propose to take what evidence we have available, and, as I said in opening the inquest, I shall then adjourn to some convenient day to enable the police to prosecute their enquiries and obtain any further evidence they may be able to. . . . At this point the prisoner Lee was brought into the room, and the whole of the spectators endeavoured to get a look at him. His face was now flushed, but his appearance was more natural than when he arrived in the cab. He stood at the bottom of the table, and the Coroner addressing him said: It is my duty to inform you that this is an enquiry into the circumstances under which Miss Keyse came to her death. And it is my duty to tell you that it is an enquiry which may turn out to be

St Marychurch Town Hall: 'Having viewed the body you will be taken round the house by the police-sergeant, and, with the plan of the house in our minds, we shall be in a position to understand the evidence at the Town Hall.'

a very serious one for you, and that you have a right to be present and to make any statement, if you think it advisable to do so. You must understand that you are not compelled to give any evidence, and that if you do give any it may afterwards be used as evidence against you. You may ask a question of any witness if you like. You may sit down if you wish to be present. Prisoner sat down in charge of a constable.

THE WITNESSES

THE GLEN

William Delf Bowden, Surveyor to the St Marychurch Local Board of Health, produced plans and, later in the proceedings, a model of The Glen. He described the salient features of the house giving details of the size and location of the various rooms, doors and windows.

George Whitehead, the stepbrother of the victim, resided in Edinburgh and admitted having little recent contact with Emma Keyse before her death. Yet, at the inquest he was allowed to speculate on possible motives of robbery and whether John Lee stood to benefit from his employer's will. Somewhat surprisingly, the Coroner did not check the amateur sleuth when he delivered the result of his own investigation into what he prejudged to be 'murder':

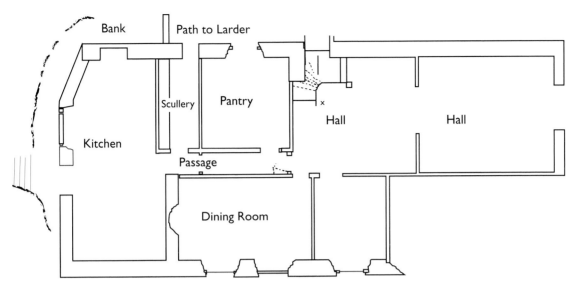

The Glen – ground-floor plan.

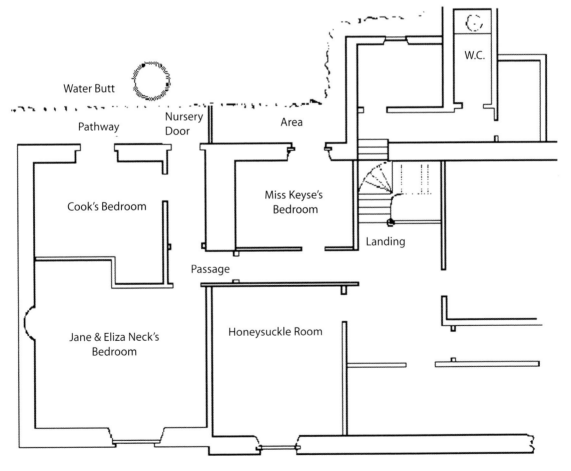

The Glen – first-floor plan.

George Whitehead: I have not looked into any of her papers yet, and I know nothing as to her will, except I have been told that she had made one. I also heard of her intention to make one a fortnight ago. I do not think she kept money about the house. She paid her bills by cheque. On Sunday morning I made a close scrutiny of the outside of the house, but I could not see the slightest sign of any forcible entry. There was no scratch or mark outside, I also made a minute inspection of the inside of the house. I went first of all upstairs to the bedroom which Miss Keyse used to occupy, which I found had been set on fire at the corner of the bed. The bed cover was burnt. The bed had not been occupied, for the water-bottle was high up as though placed there without being pushed down. Miss Keyse had undressed herself and her clothes were lying close to the bed. I went downstairs and examined the place where the murder had been committed, and found traces of blood. I inspected the dining-room and I found the place in great confusion. The furniture is much damaged. I have no knowledge of the circumstances. . . .

In reply to a juror: If anything had occurred outside, the man Lee must have heard it. The head of the bed was within six feet of where the unfortunate lady fell in the hall.

This witness did not appear before the magistrates or at the trial.

THE HOUSEHOLD SERVANTS

In evidence the three female servants gave a quaint insight into the strict regime at The Glen. Elizabeth Harris told the court that she did not know the Christian name of her employer and rarely saw her between morning and evening prayers. The long-serving Neck sisters had strictly defined roles. Parlour maid Jane's duties included cleaning, locking up at night and acting as go-between for her mistress and the lowly cook and manservant. Lady's maid Eliza's domain was the bedroom, where she helped to dress her mistress, prepared her boudoir and locked away personal valuables each night.

Elizabeth Harris was the first witness called at the inquest. Her initial testimony gave no indication of the more serious disclosures she would make when recalled at a later date:

Elizabeth Harris: I live at the Glen, Babbacombe, the house of Miss Keyse. I am cook. I saw her for the last time in the morning at 10.30. This was at prayers, in the dining-room. . . . I went to bed about five o'clock as I was ill. . . . I was wakened by the smell of smoke. I was not woke up by a noise . . . I called to Jane and Eliza three or four times before I could make them hear. I had not dressed myself then. . . . The passage was full of smoke. I went into the 'honeysuckle' room and threw water on the walls. Lee was wearing a shirt and a pair of trousers. We said nothing to each other. . . . It was half an hour before I went downstairs and found the dining-room on fire. John was there, and I think while I was there Mr Gasking came in. I saw Miss Keyse's body on the floor in front of the couch. . . . I saw Mr Gasking and John carry Miss Keyse out. Miss Keyse's clothes were burnt, but there were no flames about her. I did not notice any blood then. Afterwards I saw the pool of blood in the hall.

In reply to questions from members of the Jury: It was about five minutes after calling the other servants before I saw John Lee. . . . I did not go close to the body. . . . I was not aware what had happened to Miss Keyse when I went into the dining room. . . . I have not been ill long. I asked Jane not to say anything about my illness to Miss Keyse as she might think more of it than was necessary. Jane and Eliza went to Miss Keyse's room. I went to the honeysuckle room. I thought Miss Keyse was in her bedroom at first, but whilst we were carrying the water, I heard Jane say she was not there.

Continuing evidence: I slept more sound during the earlier part of the night than in the morning, but I don't remember waking up. I told the Police Sergeant that if I had not gone back to bed when I did we should have all been burnt in our beds.

The Neck sisters' recollections would prove crucial to the case against John Lee, particularly their rather confused versions of events regarding his state of dress when the fire was discovered and at what stage he was seen with blood on his person. The prosecution would claim that Lee immediately appeared outside the pantry dressed in shirt, collar and trousers when Eliza Neck descended the stairs and that he then helped Jane Neck to safety, leaving bloodstains on her nightdress – before sustaining cuts to his arm while tackling the fire on his return from the Cary Arms with Gasking:

Jane Neck: I live at Miss Keyse's 'Babbacombe,' I am parlour maid there. I have been in the employment of the deceased since 1836. . . . I last saw her alive about 12.40 on Friday night. . . . After prayers I went downstairs and made tea and toast. . . . Eliza had not gone to bed, but I saw John in bed about 11.00. He was asleep when I went into the bedroom. I went to bed about 12.40. It is my custom, after I have put away the books, and done little things, to go out, but to come back again and tell Miss Keyse the time, and wish her goodnight. This is my usual course, and I did so on Friday night. I left her cocoa on the kitchen stove. . . . When I said 'Goodnight' to Miss Keyse, she was writing in her diary. She always wrote her letters after we had gone to bed. I always take the keys and put them on a seat in her bedroom. I did this on Friday night. . . . Her watch and chains were usually left in her wardrobe but the key was left in the door. The plate box was in her bedroom. I and my sister Eliza knew where the key was kept. The plated goods were kept in the honeysuckle room. After putting the keys away, I went into my own room. . . . The door is never quite closed. . . . I was awoke by hearing Elizabeth saying there was a great deal of smoke. . . . When I came to Miss Keyse's room it was all in a blaze. I went in and pulled down the bedclothes and found that she had not been in bed at all. The hot water bottle was in the room and the bed was not disturbed. It was between three and four o'clock when this occurred. There was very dense smoke. . . . When I was coming out of the bedroom my sister called out, 'Here is Miss Keyse.' . . . When I got out of the room I saw John and he caught hold of my arm and led me to the balustrade. . . . As far as I can recollect John went to the dining-room window. The door was wide open. . . . The shutters were not open in the dining room when I went in. . . . The glass was broken when I went out on the lawn and shouted, 'Fire'. The only light in the room came from the fire burning. I am quite sure the shutters were closed when I went into the room. I cannot tell whether I opened the shutters or whether John did. The broken glass was on the floor. I did not discover the body before I went to the shutters. John Lee did not say anything to me. . . . It was about twenty minutes between the time I found the fire burning, and when I sent John to Gasking's. The first place I saw John was on the landing. I had no conversations with him until I had been out on the lawn. He did not tell me he had cut his arm until after I had been out on the lawn. . . . I noticed that his arm was bleeding when he called my attention to it. Miss Keyse occasionally came downstairs after she had been to her bedroom. On this particular night Miss Keyse intended to make up a package to be taken to Compton and she might have come downstairs again to attend to it. . . . I have known Miss Keyse occasionally come downstairs to leave a message with the occupant of the pantry. . . . I saw no blood on John's arm until after the body had been discovered. My nightdress was stained with blood, but I don't know exactly where. I touched the body of my mistress, and found it was cold. John soon returned with Mr Gasking. . . . All the servants were on good terms with Miss Keyse. She had tried to get prisoner to emigrate. . . . Miss Keyse advanced some money to John recently. He was very much put out because she did not give him what he expected, and talked about leaving.

Eliza Neck: I am ladies maid to the deceased. I have been in her employ since 1848. On Friday last at about 10.30pm, I was present at family prayers. I took up the hot water bottle and put it in the bed of the deceased about a foot from the pillow. I put her night dress ready. At 12.15, I preceded my sister to bed by a few minutes. . . . I was awoke by hearing Elizabeth Harris call out shortly before three. I made my way downstairs to the dining room at the bottom of the stairs. John Lee was there, he said, 'What is the matter?' and she replied, 'It's full of smoke.' John said, 'It's choking me.' . . . I went towards the dining room, from where smoke was coming out. I called out, 'Do bring a light,' but when I went into the dining room the wall was all a-fire. I went and got some water from the pantry and poured it on the fire. I then saw the body of the deceased for the first time. I then went out and called upstairs, 'Miss Keyse is lying on the dining room floor.' After Elizabeth Harris and Jane Neck came down I went up to the 'honeysuckle' room and helped put out the fire. I suppose John had gone for Mr Gasking. The next time I saw him was upstairs outside the nursery door, where he was bringing in water from the cask. He had only his trousers and shirt on, and his braces were hanging down. I went to the deceased's bedroom. The bed had not been slept in. The water bottle was in the same place I put it.

In reply to a juryman: Witness did not know whether John Lee was a heavy sleeper. She was the first downstairs and there found Lee. When she discovered the body Lee was not there.

PS Nott: Can you identify these matches?

Witness: They are similar to those we use. Jane always placed a box by the side of the candlestick.

Coroner: Where were the matches found?

PS Nott: In Lee's pantry.

Witness: But my sister always keeps a box in the pantry for her own use.

THE FIREFIGHTERS

An assortment of neighbours, coastguardsmen and fishermen rushed to The Glen believing that Miss Keyse had perished accidentally in the fire, but found themselves in the midst of a murder investigation. Although it was difficult to determine anything through the dense smoke which enshrouded the building, they were asked to recall at what point they had first seen blood on the prisoner. Most appear to have had their attention brought to this by Lee himself. A crucial debate concerned the axe produced as the murder weapon and whether it was near at hand when Lee was sent to fetch it to cut down burning timbers. At the subsequent trial, estimates of the time taken by him varied from one to three minutes, which, the prosecution argued, was not long enough to retrieve it from the outhouse where it was stored.

Amusingly, the ironmonger who had supplied the oil believed to have been used to start the fire had a common medical ailment which prevented him from identifying his own product:

William Salter: Miss Keyse recently had more oil in the house than usual. He last supplied a gallon of Alexandra oil to Miss Keyse on November 6th. The oil produced was apparently Alexandra oil. Could not say that the carpet produced smelt of oil, but he had a cold.

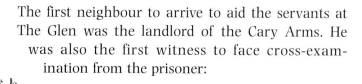

The first neighbour to arrive to aid the servants at The Glen was the landlord of the Cary Arms. He was also the first witness to face cross-examination from the prisoner:

William Gasking: My niece Mary Wilson called me up on Saturday morning about four o'clock. I got out and began to dress, and she brought me a light. When I went down I found John Lee at the nursery bedroom entrance. Volumes of smoke were coming out. I said 'Well John, what's the matter?' He replied, 'Oh! Mr. Gasking, Miss Keyse is burnt to death.' I said 'Where to?' and he said 'In the dining room.' I turned to go through the kitchen to the dining room, and I saw his sister getting water from the cask. Then I told John to knock the head of the cask in, and he got a stone and did so. I entered the kitchen door and went through the passage to the dining room door. Lee then came down the stairs and met me. I said 'Where is she?' and immediately saw Miss Keyse on the floor. The shutters of the dining room were closed. I should think I got into the dining room about quarter-past four. I went to the left hand side of the body and said 'Help to get her out of this.' He began to talk about some other matter, and I said 'Hold your tongue, John, I don't want to hear anything about that.' I also told him to 'come on' and then he helped me to move her. We took her as far as the kitchen door and then I sent John to get a carpet. John put his left hand to her arm and his right hand under her right thigh. I saw the wounds on the body. When I saw prisoner first he had on a pair of trousers, with the braces hanging behind, but no waistcoat. I can't say if his shirt sleeves were rolled up or if he was wearing boots. I folded the carpet over the body and took it, with Richard Harris, to the outhouse. When I left John, I told him to look sharp and get some water. I went back to the house and into the dining room again, where the shutters were still closed. I could not tell at the time whether the glass of the window was broken or not. I threw water on the flames, Harris, John, and my niece fetching it, until the coastguard came. I asked for a hatchet, and Harris who got it from Lee, brought it. Lee was not long in going for the hatchet. I think it was kept in the woodhouse. I don't remember seeing the prisoner in the room after the hatchet was brought. I went around afterwards to the dining room window, and saw that one of the panes of glass was broken. The outer shutters were open and fastened back. I can't say if they were shut at all that night. I am not certain how many panes of glass were broken. Had the inside shutters been open the wind would have blown in violently. I found the padding of the sofa on fire later on, and got that out. There was also a cushion on fire, and we poured water on that. Eliza had put the fire out in the bedroom above the dining room. I was told that Miss Keyse's bedroom had been set on fire. We remained in the house until daylight. After I had gone home and had my breakfast I went back to the house and saw John there. He had told me before that he wanted to go to 'Compton,' and I think he had been there by this time. I asked Lee when he broke the glass and he told me it was before he called me up. I also asked him how he did it, and he said 'With my fists,' and he showed me how he did it. . . .

In reply to a juror: When Lee helped me out with the body I saw no stain of blood on his arms. I have examined the clothes I was wearing, and can't find a trace of blood on them. If blood came off Miss Keyse's body it would have stained me as well as him. The body was as dry as bone.

In reply to the Coroner: He did not notice any blood on Lee's arms when he raised them to knock in the water butt; neither did he observe any when prisoner was bringing water to him.

John Lee: Do you remember which side of Miss Keyse you took hold of when you carried her out?

Witness: Most certainly, I carried her left side.

John Lee: You carried her right side.

Witness: I did not.

John Lee: Which side was Miss Keyse's head?

Witness: Towards the fireplace; the feet towards the door.

John Lee: It was quite the reverse when I saw it.

It is not known whether there was any family connection between fisherman Richard Harris and his wife, Elizabeth, and the household servants Elizabeth Harris and John Lee. If so, he may have helped them and their sister, Amelia, to gain positions at The Glen, for he was said to be 'much trusted' by Emma Keyse (*Devon County Standard*, 31 January 1885).

Richard Harris: I live at Beach Cottage, Babbacombe. On Saturday morning I heard John Lee singing out for Mr. Gasking. He called out several times, and mentioned my name as well. The words he used were 'Miss Keyse's house is on fire.' I went and opened the window and smelt the smoke very strong. I called my son and my sister. I went down to the steps of the kitchen door of Miss Keyse's house where I saw deceased. I got there about 3.55. Mr. Gasking was there before me. I asked whose the body was, and Mr. Gasking said it was Miss Keyse. I and Mr. Gasking carried her to the outhouse. I did not notice any blood about her. When I went back . . . I went to the well and got some buckets of water. Then I went into the house for the first time, going through the kitchen into the upstairs room, where I put the water down. I saw the prisoner several times. I did not notice blood about him. There did not seem to be any blood flowing from his arm. I might not have seen it if there had been. He told me he had cut his arm all to pieces with the glass.

Elizabeth Harris: I am the wife of Richard Harris. I followed my husband down to The Glen on Saturday morning. I saw my husband and Mr. Gasking in the outhouse, and they told me Miss Keyse was dead. I next saw my husband and Lee filling a kieve with water in the garden. I saw some blood on Lee's arm but no wound, as his shirt sleeve was down. This was about 4.30. Lee said he had cut his arm with the glass.

George Pearce: I am a coastguard stationed at Babbacombe. On Saturday morning I was in bed when I heard a noise at the door of my quarters. It was about 4.00. I came down and heard a young man named Harris say that Miss Keyse's house was on fire. I ran down there and went into the dining room. I saw Mr. Gasking and John Lee in the dining room. The former was throwing water on the fire, and the man servant was knocking away the ceiling with a pole. I went upstairs and helped put the fire out. The side of the bed in the spare room was smouldering, but I saw no flames. The walls were so hot that you could scarcely bear your hand against them. I first saw Lee in the dining room. He had a shirt and collar on, and a pair of trousers. I did not notice any blood on him at that time. The shutters were closed when I went into the dining room. I had no conversation with Lee. He said nothing to me about cutting his arm. There was no blood about the pole which prisoner had been using.

Thomas Bennett, officer of coastguard, next gave evidence. It was similar to that of Pearce. He believed prisoner had blood on his hand while in the house. Asking Lee about it, he said he had cut his hand in breaking the glass to let the smoke out. . . . A part of the prisoner's hand was swollen.

In cross-examining this witness, prisoner made the admission that he had not taken off his collar or neck-tie from the previous night. A Juror inquired of the

Coroner whether it would be right to ask prisoner what he meant, but the Coroner said it would be better to ask him nothing.

George Phillips, chief boatman of the coastguard, said: On Saturday morning about 4.00 I was called and went to the fire at Miss Keyse's. I went in, got a bucket of water, and went upstairs with it. . . . I remained there, and poured water on the fire for some time. I afterwards passed water up to others, and remained there until the fire was put out. I went in the dining-room and saw fire there, and helped put it out. I remained there until the constables came. I saw a lot of glass on the floor near the shutters, which were fastened. They were not open whilst I was there. I saw Lee when I first came in, but I had no conversation with him. I noticed he had no coat, waistcoat, or hat on, but I could see distinctly that he had a collar on. I did not see any blood on him; he was not close enough.

William Searle, coastguardsman, was not called at the inquest but gave the following evidence to the magistrates: I was called to Miss Keyse's house on Saturday morning, arriving there shortly after 4.00. I heard George Pearce ask for a hammer or hatchet, and saw prisoner, who was present, go out and bring a hatchet. He went down-stairs for it. After the fire was out witness was in the dining room. Lee came in shortly after seven o'clock, put his arm on the sideboard and said, 'Oh my poor arm!' I asked what was the matter with it, and he replied, 'I cut it by breaking the window.'

COMPTON HOUSE

John Lee volunteered to make the two-mile round trip to inform Mary McLean of Compton House that her sister had died. Along the route of his walk, the people with whom he met and discussed the tragedy were not made aware that Emma Keyse had suffered grievous injuries before being set alight:

George Russell: I live at St. Marychurch, and am a chimney sweep. At half-past five I met John Lee walking from St. Marychurch towards Wellswood. He had a lantern. He said he was going to Captain McLean's to tell Mrs McLean that her sister, Miss Keyse, was dead. I said, 'Is she really dead?' and he replied, 'Yes, she's burnt to death.' I said, 'I'm very sorry to hear it,' and he said, 'So am I.' I said, 'How did it occur?' and he said, 'We should all have been burnt to death if it hadn't been for my sister.' I said, 'How did she know it?' and he replied, 'She smelt smoke, came downstairs, and saw the sofa afire in the drawing room.' I said, 'Is that all; was there any lamp capsized?' He replied, 'No; there was no lamp there, or candle.' He also said again, 'I'm very sorry for it, but as she's dead we shall never know how 'twas done.'

Charles Henry Sutton: I am a hairdresser. I met prisoner . . . He was walking from St. Marychurch to Torquay. I asked where there had been a fire and he replied, 'It's at my house, sir. The lady is burnt to death. I should have burnt to death too in about half-an-hour if it had not been found out.' Holding his hands towards me, he said he had cut them in breaking the dining room window to let out the smoke. I asked him whether he knew the cause of the fire, but I do not remember his words. They left the impression on my mind that the fire was caused by a lamp and that nothing more could be known because Miss Keyse was the last person up in the house.

Sutton did not appear before the magistrates or at the trial.

Mary Blatchford: I am maid to Mrs. McLean. I saw John Lee on Saturday morning about half-past five. I heard a knocking and asked what was the matter. He said 'Oh, Miss Blatchford, come down!' adding 'Miss Keyse's house is burning.' I then opened the house-maid's door and went into her room and spoke to Lee through the window. I asked if it was much, and he said the dining room was burning. I asked him if the engine was there, and he said it was sent for. I said 'Where is Miss Keyse?' and he did not answer me for a moment, but then said 'Miss Keyse is hurt.' I said 'Where is she?' and at last he said 'Her's dead.' I said 'No, it isn't possible!' and he said 'Yes her is and you must tell Mrs. McLean.' I said 'I can't tell her' and he said 'You must. Jane [Neck] told me to come and tell you, and you must tell Mrs. McLean.'

Ann Bolder: I am cook at Mrs. McLean's. I saw John Lee on Saturday morning. I asked him what was the matter, and he said 'Miss Keyse's house is on fire and she is burnt to death.' I said, 'How did it happen?' and he replied 'I don't know.' I saw that his arm was bleeding. He said it was done in breaking the glass to let the smoke out.

P.C. Boughton: At 5.45 I was put in charge of the outhouse in which the body was. At 6.15, I saw John Lee coming down the hill towards the house. I asked him where he had been and he said, 'I've been to Compton; isn't this a bad job?' I said, 'Yes, it is.' Lee said, 'Isn't my arm bad?' I said, 'What's the matter?' and he replied, 'I cut it in breaking the dining room window to let out the smoke.' I told him it was a foolish thing to do, and he said, 'I was obliged to do it; the smoke was so thick I could not find my way back to the door.' At 9.00 I saw him again. He was shaking very much and I said, 'Hullo, old man, you're feeling the cold.' Prisoner replied, 'So would you if you had been running about all the morning with only your shirt and trousers on.' He added, 'Good God! That ever such a thing should happen; I've lost my best friend.' I said there was no doubt about that and asked him if he heard anything during the night. He said, 'No, I was dead asleep, and the servants had great trouble to wake me when they came down.'

THE POLICE INVESTIGATION

John Lee was not questioned by the police before setting out for Compton House. By the time he returned to The Glen the local force were out in numbers and all the criminal evidence gathered was pointing towards one suspect – 'the only man in the house':

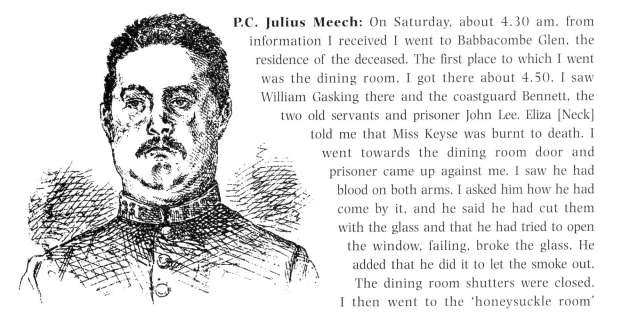

P.C. Julius Meech: On Saturday, about 4.30 am, from information I received I went to Babbacombe Glen, the residence of the deceased. The first place to which I went was the dining room, I got there about 4.50. I saw William Gasking there and the coastguard Bennett, the two old servants and prisoner John Lee. Eliza [Neck] told me that Miss Keyse was burnt to death. I went towards the dining room door and prisoner came up against me. I saw he had blood on both arms. I asked him how he had come by it, and he said he had cut them with the glass and that he had tried to open the window, failing, broke the glass. He added that he did it to let the smoke out. The dining room shutters were closed. I then went to the 'honeysuckle room'

upstairs, prisoner going with me. He tore down a curtain in that room. The fire seemed to have come up from the dining room. I looked in to Miss Keyse's room, and found it had been subdued. It appeared to me to be a separate fire. . . . A little while later I went to see the body of the deceased, and then noticed the wound on the throat. . . . After that I fetched Dr. Chilcote, and proceeded to take charge of the upstairs rooms. About 8.15 prisoner came up to me where I was standing. I noticed he was trembling and told him he was shaking and he said he was cold. He replied, 'This is a bad job for me; I've lost a good friend.'

P.C. Rounsefell: On Saturday morning last I was searching the butler's pantry at Miss Keyse's house. I examined the drawer and noticed a small stain of blood. On the side of the drawer lower down I found a further stain of blood. This led me to examine the contents of the drawer, and at the bottom I found a piece of paper containing a knife. The paper was stained with blood and there was blood and earth on the knife. I took charge of the knife and paper and handed them over to Super-intendent Barbor. I noticed a stain of blood on the right door jamb of the pantry and there were stains on the walls of the passage leading to the kitchen, on both I saw blood, on the water barrel outside the nursery door, and on the lock of the outer door leading into the road.

P.S. Abraham Nott: I am a police-sergeant stationed at St. Marychurch. On Saturday morning between five and six o'clock. I was called by a constable to go to Miss Keyse's. I immediately got up and met Meech whom I told to go for a doctor. I went to the residence of the deceased and saw an officer there. My attention was called to a pool of blood in the hall, and near it was a blood stained chair cover which was partially burnt and which smelt strongly of oil. I saw Mr. Bennett and he told me where the body was. I sent a man out to take charge of it. I then went into the kitchen and made enquiries of Jane Neck as to who had locked the doors and she told me she had done so. I next asked for John Lee and was told that he had gone to Mrs. McLean's. I went through the house and endeavoured to find any weapon. In the dining room I found a hatchet. On its head was a dark spot which I considered had the appearance of blood and also a spot or two on the side of it. I asked one of the men how it came there and was told by a fireman that it had been used to knock down the ceiling with. By that time Dr. Chilcote had arrived. I accompanied him to place where deceased lay . . . In presence of the medical gentleman and others I took four gold rings from the third finger of deceased's left hand. . . . I accompanied the superintendent of police around the house to see if we could detect any attempt at burglary. I found the dining room window had been broken – the one opposite the door. On examining the window I found blood on the outside and also on the broken glass and woodwork. In handling the glass in the window I took off a piece of skin from the inside. I saw a second piece of flesh on the inside woodwork, and allowed it to remain. Six panes of glass were broken. I came to the conclusion that no implement had been used to break the glass. There was glass outside about 3 feet away from the window. I do not think the shutters in the dining room could be opened in the dark, as you have to press in the knob. I saw slight dents on the outside of the shutters. . . . I found no signs that the house had been broken into. I found some spots of blood outside the hall door, under the veranda, and there was a spot or two on the handle of the door, both inside and out. I then went inside the house, entering by way of the hall door, which brought me to the pool of blood. . . . I afterwards discovered traces of blood by the skirting, in the space between the pool of blood and the butler's pantry. I did not observe any blood higher up than the skirting. There is some blood in one of the drawers in the pantry – a stain outside, and another inside. . . . The stained drawer is the one the knife was found in. I was with the constable when it was opened. . . . The blood was in a streak as though it had run down from the top. . . . I found two towels in the pantry, marked with blood. . . . I saw blood marks outside the pantry door, and leading into the kitchen. I went upstairs and into deceased's bedroom. On the right I found the furniture had been burnt and that the bed had been on fire. . . . I found the clothes of the deceased which she had worn the previous day. . . . I went through the other rooms upstairs, but found no bloodstains there. . . . I examined the honeysuckle room and found that the bed and furniture had been burnt. . . . In the dining room I discovered a quantity of charred newspaper, a portion of it being on the sofa and the remaining part on two arm chairs. It smells of paraffin. . . . I called prisoner into the hall. I said, 'I caution you to be careful what you say; your words may be made use of. What time were you home last night?' He replied, 'Eleven o'clock. We had prayers in the dining room. The other two servants and Miss Keyse were there. I went to bed about quarter past eleven.' I said, 'Did you hear any noise at all during the night or any call by the other servants?' He replied, 'No: I heard them shouting out, and I said "What's the matter?" and they said, "The house is on fire." I put on my trousers, I came out and found Jane or Eliza outside; I went into the dining room but didn't see Miss Keyse, not then.' I asked him, 'What's this blood down over your trousers?' He said, 'It's blood from my arm, I cut it in trying to open the dining room window to let the smoke out. I then went and called Mr. Gasking.' . . . From instructions received I apprehended the prisoner about ten o'clock in the forenoon. . . . I said, 'I charge you on suspicion of having committed the murder of the deceased, Miss Keyse.' He shook very much, and said, 'Oh, on suspicion, eh! All right.' I said, 'Yes, you will have to go with me to Torquay.' He said, 'All right.'

Police Superintendent, Captain Douglas Barbor:

I went to The Glen, Babbacombe, arriving there at 7 o'clock. I first went into the dining room, which I found had been on fire. I found the window opposite the door shut and barred, and I examined it, finding some panes broken. There was blood about the glass. I found the window could not be opened from outside when the shutters are closed. . . . I found all the rooms secure and I came to the conclusion that no-one had entered from the outside. I afterwards examined the outside of the dining room, and found a piece of human skin. I saw prisoner's arm dressed and the piece of flesh tallied with one of the wounds on his arm. On the door in the middle of the hall I found spots of blood; also on the handle of the hall door. There were more spots in the corridor and on the grass leading into the corridor. On the other house [Cary Arms] I saw smears of blood near the kitchen door and on the rockwork. Also on the iron gate in the path. There is a right hand thumb mark on the gate at the back of the house, and there is also an impression of a hand on Mr. Gasking's gate. I afterwards saw the body and sent for a doctor. I saw the body examined. I went into the pantry with Sergeant Nott and cautioned prisoner . . . and as he was the only man in the house he would be taken into custody.

THREATENING BEHAVIOUR OF THE ACCUSED

When a woman was seen being taken into custody (charged with drunk and disorderly behaviour on Babbacombe Beach), a rumour quickly circulated that the cook, Elizabeth Harris, had been arrested in connection with the crime. A week later, on the fourth day of the inquest, there was a sensational development when she was recalled. Earlier, at the inquest, the siblings had been seated together. On this occasion, John was not brought to court to embarrass or intimidate Elizabeth during her testimony, although the official reason given was as follows:

> There is no doubt that the morbid curiosity evinced by the public to see the prisoner had also some influence on this decision, and it has since transpired that this non-appearance prevented a grave scandal, for numbers of persons had threatened to mob him if occasion presented itself. This feeling has arisen through the defiant attitude of Lee when he has previously been at Court, for on each occasion he has amused himself while in the ante-room by looking out upon the crowd and pulling faces at them. (*Torquay Times*, 28 November 1884)

On this occasion she gave damning evidence against her brother.

Elizabeth Harris: I had a conversation with John Lee. We were talking and reading in the kitchen. I said, 'Suppose Miss Keyse won't give you a character.' He said, if she wouldn't give him a character he would level the place to ashes to the ground. I said, 'Don't burn me with it,' and he said he would let me know. He did not say anything more. On 28th October, I had another conversation with Lee in the kitchen. He came in and sat down crying. I asked him what he was crying for and he made me no answer. He afterwards said that Miss Keyse was only going to pay him 2s. a week; and I said I thought the agreement was for 2s. 6d., and he said there was no agreement. He grew very angry, and said he would not stay there another night.

Mr. Templer to the Coroner: Don't you think sir, in fairness to the prisoner, that is quite enough?

Coroner: I think I must hear any statement which will throw light on this inquiry.

Witness went on: He said before he left he would have his revenge, and on another occasion that Miss Keyse had been grumbling with him about his work, and if she had been near him, and if she had been near a cliff, he would have pushed her over. (Great sensation in Court, and cries of 'Order' from the police.) This must have taken place two months ago. Prisoner has talked with me about murder, and two should never be concerned in a murder, because one – (there witness was stopped by the Coroner). Being asked why she had not told this before, witness replied, 'I tried to screen him' (Sensation in Court). She had now told the whole truth. Being further pressed she remembered prisoner saying something about setting the house on fire and going up on the hill to look at it.

John Lee seated alongside his sweetheart, Kate Farmer, and his half-sister, Elizabeth Harris (far left), at the inquest.

The threats against Emma Keyse made by John Lee to Elizabeth Harris were reiterated by similar intentions expressed by the accused in conversation with the village postman:

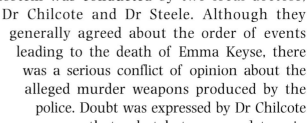

William Richards said he had known John Lee six years. A short time since, about two months, he saw Lee in the grounds of Vine Cottage – one of Miss Keyse's houses. Lee then said he was tired of his place and that if missus did not get him a good place very soon she would wish she had done so. He said, 'I will put an end to one in the house before I leave,' but he did not say who. I said, 'You had better be careful, Jack; if anyone gets hold of your words you will be locked up.' He replied, 'I don't care.'

MEDICAL EVIDENCE

Forensic science was virtually non-existent during the Victorian age, with no method of identifying fingerprints or blood types. Therefore, with limited knowledge at his disposal, government analyst Dr Stevenson examined various bloodstained items. The post-mortem was conducted by two local doctors, Dr Chilcote and Dr Steele. Although they generally agreed about the order of events leading to the death of Emma Keyse, there was a serious conflict of opinion about the alleged murder weapons produced by the police. Doubt was expressed by Dr Chilcote that a hatchet was used to rain blows on the victim's head or whether a small knife was capable of inflicting such a deep wound to the throat:

Dr. Herbert Chilcote: I am a surgeon practising at St. Marychurch. I was called between five and six o'clock on Saturday morning by a constable and went down to Miss Keyse's. I saw the body first. It was not in the house then, but in a small building close by in charge of a constable. The body was scorched and there was a wound in the throat. I made a post-mortem examination this morning with Dr. Steele, and found the skull fractured in two places. One was a cut wound at the back of the head; the other wound was on the side, more to the right. Those wounds were decidedly inflicted during life. There were no other wounds on the head except those two. There was a bruise on the left temple, but it was very slight. I then found the throat cut, all the main arteries and vessels being severed right to the very vertebrae, and even the bone was notched. The principal burns were on the feet, the right foot being very much charred. The hip, chest and hands were also burnt and scorched. All these burns were caused after death. My opinion is that death was caused by the blows on the head, either in itself was sufficient to cause death. I am most certain that the blows on the head were inflicted before the throat was cut. The instrument, which caused the wounds, must have been a round instrument, such as a hammer or knob-stick, as the fractures were depressed. It would require great force to give such blows, and a heavy instrument. In my opinion the wound in the throat was inflicted by a knife, and it must have been done with great force. (A small yellow-handled table knife, with short blade, was here produced by the police and handed to witness, but he expressed his doubt as to the throat having been cut by it. He thought, however, that the stains on the paper in which it was wrapped were those of blood). Continuing witness said: It was impossible for the deceased, to have inflicted such wounds upon herself, or for them to be caused accidentally.

P.S. Nott here produced a piece of chair covering, saturated with blood and containing congealed clots, and Dr. Chilcote gave it as his opinion that these clots were caused by a person applying the covering to the throat of the deceased after it was cut to stop the flow of blood.

Juror: How long had the deceased been dead when you saw the body?

Witness: Three or four hours, if not more. The hands were drawn up, and the fingers partly clenched. The deceased was rendered insensible by the first blow. From my examination of the body I found that there was no sign upon to show that there was any struggle before death. I think death was instantaneous.

Coroner: Did you examine the arm of John Lee?

Witness: Yes. He came to my surgery at eight o'clock the same morning. He had a small punctured wound on the right arm and two circular wounds on the left forearm, between the elbow and wrist. He had a piece of cloth wrapped round his arm, which I removed. Each wound on his left arm was about the size of a florin [large coin]. Lee said the wounds were caused by his breaking the panes of glass in a window and they were decidedly wounds which might have been occasioned in this manner. The wounds had stopped bleeding when I saw them, but they were of such a nature that they might have bled a good deal.

P.S. Nott here produced a coloured shirt of Lee's with marks of blood upon the right shoulder of the garment.

Coroner: Could a man with a wound on his arm such as you have described have got bloodstains from it on that portion of the shirt?

Witness: I should say not.

Dr. William Stott Steele: I received a letter from Mr. Chilcote asking me to come down and view the body. . . . I observed that the right foot was very much burnt, and the stocking upon it was hardly charred. The chest was burnt, and one of the sides was slightly burnt. The hair was not even singed. On the throat there was a wound extending from the angle of the jaw on the left side, across the throat and past the middle line, but not far to the right. This wound divided the muscles, arteries, the jugular vein, the windpipe, the muscles in front of the spine, and also notched one of the vertebrae. I should say that wound was inflicted before death. That is to say, I am inclined to think she was not quite dead when the wound was made. On the head I found three wounds. The smallest was the farthest behind. It was about an inch in length. There was a wound there one-and-a-half inches long, and the skull was fractured and depressed. A third wound was a large square wound, and the bones of the skull were fractured and driven in on to the brain. The membranes of the brain were torn and the brain itself lacerated. Such a wound would be fatal in a very short time. I think the immediate cause of death was the great loss of blood. The scalp wound was sufficient to cause death by itself. Why I think the wounds on the head were caused first is that if the throat had been cut while the heart was acting strongly there would have been a spurting out of blood, and the walls of the house and the dress of the person who did it, would have been covered. There was an enormous loss of blood, which must have flowed out quietly. A blunt instrument must have caused the wound on the head. It would not require a heavy instrument to inflict the injuries to the throat. I think the small knife produced (found in the butler's pantry) might have caused the wound.

Captain Barbor: You have seen this hatchet. On examining it did you find anything upon it?

Witness: I did. I discovered what I believed to be stains of blood.

The witness went on to say that the largest stain (which was discovered by employing a microscope) was found in a notch in the blade of the hatchet. He had since examined the body, and found that the wound on the right side of the head very much corresponds with the form of the hatchet.

Coroner: Does it actually fit the wound?

Witness: It does.

Dr. Steele, in the course of further evidence, said he had also examined the wound on the centre of the head and thought it might have been done by another part of the hatchet. He also thought the weapon would be capable of inflicting the third wound.

Dr. Thomas Stevenson: I live at Sandhurst Lodge, Gresham Road, Lambeth, and am a doctor of medicine, a lecturer on medical jurisprudence and surgery at Guy's Hospital, and analyst to the Home Office. I received on 21st November certain articles from Captain Barbor, superintendent of police, namely a hatchet, a knife in paper, a woman's nightdress, a man's shirt, a pair of socks and a lock of hair. On 27th November, I received from the same person, a pair of trousers and an oil can. I have examined and analysed these articles. The hatchet is marked with white plaster. On the back of the handle was a smear of blood. At the back of the iron head there is a trace of blood, and in a notch of the lower portion of the blade were a few blood corpuscles. The blood was that of a mammalian animal or a human being. . . . I am unable to say to which the blood belonged and I can't say whether it was a male or female, young or old animal or person, or whether it was arterial or venous. The blood on the handle of the hatchet had not lost the character of recent blood. I am unable to assign the date of it except that it might have been shed for any period of up to six weeks. I produce a knife in a paper. It is a table-knife. The blade is scratched, having recently been rubbed against some sharp substance, stone or earth. The handle, which is much polished from wear, is free from blood. There is a trace of blood in the deposit around the junction of the blade and the handle. There was also a trace of blood near the hilt. The rest of the knife was generally free from blood. This blood was also of a mammalian animal or of a human being. I can't assign a date to this. The condition of the instrument is not favourable to saying how long the blood has been on it. There was a little earth about the blade.

Coroner: Would the fact of the knife having been wiped prevent you from discovering traces of blood?

Witness: Simply wiping on paper I don't think would. If it were stuck in the ground, blood stains would effectually be removed from the blade.

Coroner: Would the fact of the knife being handled by persons, prevent you from tracing stains of blood?

Witness: I expect that blood stains would easily scale off from the smooth and greasy handle of a knife. I found no trace of blood colour on applying damp blotting paper. I am prepared to say I saw no traces of any.

Coroner: Is that knife a weapon which might produce a deep gash in a person's throat?

Witness: Yes; it is blunt towards the point, but a powerful man, using it on an insensitive person, might cut the throat with it. At the same time it is rather a blunt instrument. Not having seen the wound on the deceased, I cannot say whether this knife would be likely to produce it. Certainly the throat might be cut with it.

The Coroner, Sydney Hacker.

Mr. Templer pointed out to the doctor that the vertebral bone behind the wound in deceased's neck was notched.

Witness: It would be possible to cut the throat effectually with this knife, and also to notch the vertebrae. Although it is blunt it would go into a piece of wood or a table and undoubtedly make a notch in living bone.

Giving his result of his examination of the nightdress of the servant Neck, witness said: It had been worn and smelt strongly of burning oil, like a smoky lamp. The right sleeve was turned back. It was extensively bloodstained, chiefly in the upper part, below the shoulder. It was also much smeared behind over the shoulder blades. Blood is present in a lesser degree over the right dress. There was a small quantity of blood on the left sleeve, more especially behind, halfway between the wrist and the elbow. The blood was not spurted, but smeared. . . . Dr. Stevenson next gave evidence in regard to the check cotton shirt belonging to prisoner Lee. He said there were extensive bloodstains on the front and left side. The back generally and right side were free from blood. There were bloodstains on the right sleeve between the elbow and the wrist. The left sleeve was torn and was free from blood, except a spot just below the shoulder. The blood is outside the garment generally, except in the case of the right sleeve, where there was some on the inner side. The right sleeve has evidently been worn turned back. The blood was chiefly in smears, but some had been splashed on; it was that of a human being or mammalian. It had not lost the character of fairly recent blood. There was no recognisable difference between arterial or venous blood after exposure to the air, nor between that of an aged or a young person. The smell of smouldering oil was on the shirt. Dr. Stevenson next produced the socks of the prisoner. They were, he said, stained with earth and mineral oil. Several hairs were stuck on them. There were two hairs which were long and uncut; they were human hairs, like those of a woman. They were exactly like those of the deceased, a lock of which he had also examined. . . . The mass of it is a reddish tint. Flakes of blood were scaling off it. . . . There were also human hairs on the socks like the others in all respects, except that they were thinner. There was a third kind of human hairs – fine and greyish, like those of a woman; and a fourth fibre, of a reddish colour, of a vegetable nature and seemingly those of a kind of matting. On one sock was a slight trace of blood, altered by the secretions of the foot. I could not identify its source. On Lee's trousers, the witness said he found grease stains smelling of mineral oil. On the left leg, in front of the thigh, there was a bloodstain altered by the application of water. It might have had a spirit rubbed on it with a sponge. Dr. Stevenson described the appearance of a number of other stains on the trousers worn by the prisoner. On the oil can produced, near the handle, to the right of the seam, he had found a red smear, of mammalian or human blood. There were similar smears on the bottom of the can. They had not lost the character of recent soluble blood. The stains retained their red colour and he found during the course of his examination that paraffin over blood made the latter retain its bright appearance longer than when it was exposed to the air.

THE SUMMING UP

Without hearing any testimony on behalf of the man held in custody, the Coroner had used his authority to make the inquest a full-blown trial – with a jury of local men who were personally acquainted with the victim and the circumstances in which she had re-employed her manservant. Sydney Hacker summed up expecting the jurymen to put all bias aside in reaching a verdict:

During the course of his observations the Coroner said he must ask the jury to banish from their minds everything which had come before them either in newspapers or from private sources, conversations or remarks, everything except what they had heard stated by witnesses in that Court, and excepting the evidence they had received through the medium of their own eyes when they viewed the body of the deceased. They were charged to enquire how, when, where and by what means the deceased came to her death. They would without doubt find in the first instance that the deceased had been killed by some person or persons, and if, as had erroneously been suggested, their duty was only to find out the cause of death, their function would have ceased on the first day of the enquiry. But they were charged with the duty, not only of enquiring whether deceased came to her death naturally or violently, but it was also their business to find out if possible in what way the deceased was killed and whose was the hand that killed her. It seemed to him that their enquiry was now mainly directed to that point. After having referred to the circumstances that the examination of Miss Keyse's house led to the supposition that no person from the outside committed the deed, Mr. Hacker said the jury must consider who the inhabitants of the house were and the probabilities of the suspicion which lies upon John Lee. Referring to the evidence given by Dr. Stevenson, he said the jury must be cautious not to attach too much importance to the testimony connected with the hatchet. They must consider whether they had anything before them to connect that hatchet with any person, and they must also take into account the fact that the hatchet was not found in any particular place, but was brought by John Lee to the coastguard who asked for it to knock down the ceiling with. He made allusion to the statement made by prisoner Lee, directing special attention to that in which Lee says he never heard anything until the maids woke him, and to that made by P.C. Boughton of a similar nature, and pointed out their inconsistency in comparison with the evidence of one of the servants who met him when she first came downstairs. The jury were entitled to consider any menace or threats by any persons against the deceased, and there was the evidence of two witnesses on this point, which might appear important to their minds. The Coroner went on to recapitulate the testimony of the postman Richards and of the cook Elizabeth Harris, saying that it was the duty of the jury to consider whether the statements made by Lee to them were serious threats or mere idle words spoken without purpose, mentioning also that he felt when Harris first gave her evidence that she was keeping something back, a supposition proved by her subsequent evidence. In conclusion, he said that if they felt honestly and truly, that they were unable to say from the evidence that any particular person or persons caused the death of Miss Keyse, they would be justified in bringing in a verdict of wilful murder against some person or persons unknown. If, on the other hand, they felt they had sufficient evidence before them to satisfy them reasonably that any particular person caused the death of the deceased, they would not be performing their duty if they did not unflinchingly give the name of that person, remembering that they were not now trying a person for his life, but that the person whom they named, would be committed to take his trial before a jury at the Assizes. The jury retired to consider their verdict. After half-an-hour's deliberation the jury returned with the following verdict:

'We find unanimously that the deceased, Emma Ann Whitehead Keyse was murdered at her house, the Glen, Babbacombe, on the morning of the 15th of November, 1884, by the prisoner John Lee, by striking her on the head with some blunt instrument and afterwards cutting her throat with the knife found in the pantry drawer, which is stained with human blood.'

THE PRISONER BEFORE THE MAGISTRATES

The magistrate's hearing had commenced on Wednesday 19 November. Access to the proceedings was limited to people holding a pass. After taking evidence from a number of witnesses, the prisoner was remanded to reappear on Tuesday 25 November. On this date there was a misunderstanding about the starting time and the court had been cleared before Lee's solicitor, Reginald Gwynne Templer, arrived. Prosecutor Isadore Carter was half an hour late and further upset the magistrates by asking for an adjournment as he was still preparing witness depositions for the inquest. Before complying with the request, the Chairman reminded him tersely: 'You made a remark about the Coroner's investigation. We know nothing about that here – nothing at all – and you must understand that after this remand the Bench will expect to go on whether the Coroner has finished or not' (*Torquay Times*, 28 November 1884).

The court reconvened on Monday 1 December within twenty minutes of the coroner's inquiry concluding at St Marychurch. The object of the proceedings was to enable Dr Stevenson, the government analyst, to attend both the inquest and the magistrate's hearing before returning to London the same day: 'Lee's demeanour had undergone very material change since his last appearance before the magistrates. When he first came into the dock, his face was flushed, but it soon paled, and when Dr. Stevenson was giving his evidence respecting the blood stains on the oil can, it visibly blanched' (*Torquay Times*, 5 December 1884).

The following day, Isadore Carter outlined the case against the accused:

Mr. Carter said that he should best discharge his duty to the Crown by laying before the Bench the simple facts of the case. . . . In the first instance it would be shown that Lee was on the premises when this crime was committed, and the further particulars of the case were pregnant with circumstances directing suspicion to the hand of the prisoner, as being that which committed the crime. The deceased lady resided at the Glen, Babbacombe, and had done so for upwards of half a century. The Glen was well-known to everybody in this county, being famed for its beauty and marvellously endowed by nature, and wooded from the top of the hill to the beach whereupon the house stood. The household consisted of two sisters, who had been in Miss Keyse's employ for over forty years, and who were nearly 70 years of age, of another servant named Elizabeth Harris, half-sister of prisoner, and of the prisoner who did work in the house and also acted as gardener. The maids first alluded to, slept in a room on one side of the house and Elizabeth Harris occupied a room adjoining. Prisoner's bed was in the pantry, on the ground floor, near the dining room. Miss Keyse was a lady who was punctual in her household arrangements, and she was a Christian lady, having prayers twice a day. . . . It was the usual practice of Lee to go out between six and seven o'clock for the purpose of posting letters, and he usually remained away until just before prayers. One of the servants made up his bed in the pantry and on the evening of the 14th November it was made in the usual way, and prisoner retired to it shortly after prayers. Elizabeth Harris was ill on that night and went to bed early. Prisoner Lee had been in Miss Keyse's employ since January last, having been on an occasion prior to that also in her service. Mr. Carter would not then say why Miss Keyse took him back, but she engaged him at 2s. 6d. a week. On Friday night Jane Neck, one of the servants, locked up all the doors as usual, and everything was perfectly safe and sound when she retired. Miss Keyse was left in the dining room writing. In tracing what the prosecution believe to be the facts which occurred after that time, Mr. Carter said there could be no doubt that something attracted the attention of the deceased, and caused her to come downstairs after she had gone to her room with the intention of going to bed. She descended with a candle in her hand, but evidently did not suspect anything wrong, or it was improbable she would have gone down in her nightdress; nor did she alarm the servants which she could easily have done. At the bottom of the stairs she was met by someone who was either engaged in an evil purpose, or was lying in wait for her, for while she was outside the dining room door, she received two terrible blows on the head with a heavy instrument. These first two blows must have felled her to the ground, and while on the ground it was evident that she received another blow with an instrument having a square head, and which the prosecution believed was a hatchet. The first two blows rendered her unconscious, but the third was fatal, and produced violent convulsions. Then Miss Keyse had a knife drawn across her throat, and was so rendered lifeless. The body was then dragged into the dining room and an endeavour made to consume it. Evidence would be brought before their worships showing that in the dining room heaps of charred paper were found under the sofa and on an arm chair. But it was apparent that the fire could not be got to burn, and as a last resource paraffin was obtained and used, being poured over the carpet in the hall, where the pool of blood was found and over the first two stairs, which places were also set on fire. Turning to the motives which are supposed to have actuated the prisoner, Mr. Carter said that latterly Miss Keyse threatened to reduce the wages from 2s. 6d. to 2s. per week. That seemed to have caused him much dissatisfaction, and he made use of menaces against his mistress to two persons. The observations of Mr. Carter were next directed to the instruments with which prisoner is supposed to have committed the crime, and he commented first upon the fact that the hatchet, which had never been seen in the house before, was brought by Lee to a man who asked for it in order to break down the dining room ceiling, and secondly, upon the circumstances that a bloody knife was found in a drawer in the prisoner's pantry. He also said that the prosecution laid much stress on the circumstances connected with the emptying of the oil can which was kept in a cupboard in prisoner's pantry, and which could not be got at by any person without stepping over prisoner's bed. In conclusion, he asked the Bench to commit the prisoner for trial at the next assizes on the charge of murdering Miss Keyse.

The Chairman complimented Mr. Carter on the excellent manner in which he had presented the case. (*Torquay Times*, 5 December 1884)

The second committal of the prisoner took place on Thursday 4 December – the fifth day of the magistrate's hearing:

The prisoner was brought up by a police constable at 11 o'clock prompt. His left hand was still bandaged. He looked carelessly around the Court, but particularly at his half-sister, who, even now has no mourning to wear for her mistress. . . .

The Chairman then addressed the prisoner saying: John Lee, the charges against you are two-fold. The first is that you did murder Emma Ann Whitehead Keyse; and the second is that you did set fire to a house in which persons were living. You have heard the evidence?

Prisoner: Yes, sir.

Chairman: Do you wish to say anything in answer to the charge?

Prisoner: I wish to reserve my defence.

Chairman: You are committed to take your trial upon these two charges at the next Assizes to be held for the County of Devon at Exeter.

Prisoner turned around, laughed and was taken down to the cells.

'The prisoner was brought up . . . He looked carelessly around the Court . . .'

The long-drawn-out nature of the preliminary enquiries was defended in this summary of the outcome by the editor of the *Torquay Times*, 5 December 1884:

The first chapter, and the second, in the story of the Babbacombe Tragedy has been brought to a close this week. The Coroner's Inquest has resulted in a verdict of wilful murder against John Lee, who was taken into custody on the morning of Miss Keyse's death, and the Magistrates have committed him for trial at the next Assizes in the charge of murder and arson. For the third chapter in this horrible story we must wait, and what is to be its end we cannot tell. . . . There have been comments made both in conversation and the press on the conduct of the two local enquiries, which we think hardly justifiable. It has been thought that they were unduly prolonged, but it should be remembered that it was only bit by bit that the facts came to light, and several things which were at first passed by almost without notice proved afterwards to be important links in the chain of evidence which has gradually wound itself around the unhappy prisoner. Some of those links seem very slight and yet as they have one by one been put together they have produced a strong chain of circumstantial evidence which seems to bring home the crime to the prisoner, and the force of which he will certainly find it difficult to overcome. It would have been a grave scandal if an enquiry involving such important issues had been hurried over, and it is not unlikely that the completeness of these preliminary proceedings may facilitate the ultimate trial which will determine the fate of the prisoner. . . . A strong *prima facie* case has been made against him, but it remains to be seen what defence he can make; he is sure to have a fair trial when the time comes. . . .

CHAPTER 5

A foregone conclusion

In this case all the facts proved seemed to point to the one conclusion of the prisoner's guilt, while some of them seemed absolutely inconsistent with his innocence.

— Torquay Times, 6 February 1885

John Lee spent Christmas and the New Year in Exeter Prison, waiting to be tried for his life at the Devon Assizes which commenced at Exeter Castle on Friday 30 January 1885. As the witnesses prepared to travel from Torquay to Exeter for the opening of the assizes, it became apparent that, at the time of the murder, one of the household servants was concealing a dark secret: the unmarried cook, Elizabeth Harris, was carrying a child. Her condition was now plainly visible and her appearance attracted the attention of a reporter from the *Torquay Times*, 30 January 1885:

There was quite a busy scene at Torre Station this morning owing to the number of passengers who were awaiting the arrival of the first up-train. The majority were composed of the witnesses in the case of John Lee, charged with the murder of Miss Emma Ann Whitehead Keyse, at Babbacombe. Wet weather made the circumstances very disagreeable for those who had to walk to the railway station. The coastguard officer and his men were amongst the first comers, and they were soon followed by the police witnesses. Sergeant Nott of St. Marychurch had charge of the females, notably Elizabeth Harris, half-sister of Lee, who was dressed in dark clothing, but not in conventional mourning. She appeared in fairly good health and spirits, and talked gaily with her companions while in the station. The train from Dartmouth had a large number of passengers in it before it reached Torre Station, and when all waiting there had got in, the carriages were unpleasantly crowded. Sergeant Nott rode with Harris and some of the other women. . . . There was no allusion made to the prisoner or his crime in the carriage in which Harris was seated. Her demeanour did not justify the reports which have been circulated as to her depressed condition of mind. She was silent, however, for nearly the whole time of the journey, and did nothing but look contemplatively out of the window or glance askance at a reporter in the corner of the carriage as though she suspected she was the subject of his notes. Her face is rather thinner than when she appeared at the inquest room and police court, and her resemblance to the prisoner Lee is more striking than ever.

Trial Judge Mr Justice Manisty opened the Assizes and upon hearing an application on behalf of the two prosecuting counsel, Mr. Collins QC and Mr. Vigor, fixed the trial for 10.30am the following Monday. As an appeal to raise funds for a top lawyer to represent Lee had been met with indifference by the local populace, the judge then appointed Walter Molesworth St Aubyn, MP, to take charge of the defence. The circuit barrister had previously encountered Lee in court, presenting the case for the prosecution when Lee had pleaded guilty to theft. The Judge brusquely turned down the lawyer's plea for more time to acquaint himself with the case and make a visit to Babbacombe. St Aubyn moaned, 'I shall have to go down on Sunday, I suppose.' Laughter broke out in court when the unsympathetic judge replied: 'I don't say so!' (*Torquay Times*, 30 January 1885).

Trial Judge Mr Justice Manisty.

It was no laughing matter for John Lee, however, when he was informed that solicitor Reginald Gwynne Templer would not be available to instruct his newly appointed counsel. The news was broken by the solicitor's cheerfully optimistic 22-year-old brother Charles Templer: 'On the Saturday afternoon before the trial I had a visit from Mr. Templer's brother. He told me that Mr. Templer was too ill to look after my trial, but that he, the brother, would be present in court. "Shall I have anything to say, sir?" I asked him. "No," he replied. "Don't you say a word. I'll get you off all right"' (Lee, 1908).

The trial of John Lee was reported in special editions of the local newspapers:

The Trial of John Lee

The trial of John Lee (20) servant, who was indicted for the wilful murder of Emma Ann Whitehead Keyse, late of The Glen, Babbacombe, on Saturday November 15, was commenced on Monday. For an hour and a half prior to the time anounced for the opening of the Court a large crowd held possession of the Castle Yard and the approaches to the Court which were guarded by police officers. Those who had business in the Court found quite as much difficulty in entering as the general public. At ten o'clock the public parts of the Court, were filled, and the Grand Jury and Magistrates' balconies were also occupied. . . . Numerous complaints were made by barristers, solicitors and others that their space was given to bearers of private admission tickets, but their representations proved of no avail. The seats on the Judge's right hand were appropriated to ladies. Mr. Sydney Hacker, the coroner, had a seat on the benches of counsel, with Dr. Stevenson, the Government analyst. So great an interest is felt in the case that there were representatives present of all the important papers of the country, and the reporter's box was inconveniently filled. Some delay took place when the petty jury was about to be empanelled in consequence of most of the jurors having taken seats in the public gallery under the impression that they would be nothing more than spectators of the proceedings. His Lordship took his seat at 10.35. He was accompanied by the High Sheriff (Mr. Octavius Bradshaw) and the usual officials.

Prisoner, on being put up, had the charge read over to him by the Clerk of Arraigns, and answered clearly and calmly 'Not Guilty'. He was accommodated with a chair. Lee anxiously regarded the jurors as they were sworn. In general appearance he had very much improved since he had been waiting for his trial at Exeter. His beard had grown and his face become refined to a considerable extent. His demeanour was quiet, and he paid much attention to the opening statement of counsel for the prosecution. (*Torquay Times*, 6 February 1885)

Opening address for the prosecution
Mr. Collins opened the case at a very considerable length. The household consisted of the two elderly servants, Elizabeth and Jane Neck, who had been in the deceased's employ nearly fifty years, a cook named Elizabeth Harris, half-sister of the prisoner, and John Lee, the accused. Some years ago, when a boy, the prisoner had lived in Miss Keyse's service, since then he had been in several situations, but in January 1884, being out of employment, Miss Keyse took him into her service again, giving him a weekly wage of 2s. 6d. in addition to board and lodging. In November last, prisoner seemed to have been anxious to get another place in order to better his circumstances. He was in an unsettled state, and it would be shown that he uttered threats against the deceased. The house, at the Glen, consisted of two floors. Miss Keyse slept in one of the upper bedrooms, the two old servants a second, and Harris, the cook, a third.

Prisoner slept downstairs in a pantry immediately adjoining the passage leading to the kitchen. It was a material point in the case that the partition separating the pantry from the passage did not reach the ceiling, but left an open space of 1 foot 10 inches. The murder was committed early on the morning of November 15th. On the previous day the cook had gone to bed at 5 o'clock. Prisoner went out in the evening, but returned in time for prayers at eleven o'clock, and soon afterwards went to bed. Miss Keyse did not retire until after twelve o'clock. One of the servants prepared her a cup of cocoa, which, as usual, she took to her bedroom; and Jane Neck carefully bolted and fastened all the doors and windows.

At twenty minutes to one Jane Neck took a candlestick into the dining room, and she there saw Miss Keyse writing in her diary. She had some talk with her mistress, and left. Miss Keyse was never seen alive after that, except by her murderer. There could be no doubt that Miss Keyse went to her bedroom, partially undressed, putting on her nightdress and a small woollen jacket; and she drank about half of her cup of cocoa. Between three and four Elizabeth Harris – who was in delicate health, and about to become a mother – gave an alarm of fire.

Eliza Neck jumped out of bed, ran downstairs in her nightdress, and found the whole place was full of dense smoke. As she was going down she heard the prisoner's voice exclaiming 'What's the matter?' Going into the dining room she found the dead body of Miss Keyse on the floor smouldering, and the whole of one side of the room on fire – not burning quickly, but a smouldering mass. She at once called out to the prisoner, and told him to run for Mr. Gasking, of the Cary Arms. He did not seem to have gone directly, for Jane Neck – who had remained behind her sister, and had gone to Miss Keyse's room to look after his mistress – met him in the passage leading to the stairs that go down to the dining room. The smoke was then so dense that Jane Neck was unable to find her way down, and the prisoner guided her by taking hold of her right hand arm and throwing his left arm around her waist.

A most material point arose here, for marks of blood were found on her nightgown at the place where prisoner put his hand. Jane Neck next went into the dining room, opened the shutters, which were fastened on the inside, opened the window, and went out upon the lawn facing the beach to call for help. Getting no answer to her cries, she returned to the dining room. She there saw the prisoner, who told her he 'had broken the window to let out the smoke'. The window at that time, according to Jane Neck, was open. She entreated the prisoner to go for Gasking, and went out on the lawn again. She then saw that the window was broken. Gasking arrived a short time afterwards. Jane

'Jane Neck . . . saw Miss Keyse writing in her diary. . . . Miss Keyse was never seen alive after that, except by her murderer.'

DISCOVERY of THE BODY of MISS KEYSE

'Eliza Neck . . . ran downstairs in her nightdress . . . Going into the dining room she found the dead body of Miss Keyse on the floor smouldering . . .'

Neck, a little later, saw the prisoner in the colonnade. To get there he must, in all human probability, have passed the windows again, and on the spot where he was then standing were afterwards found several drops of fresh blood the significance of which would appear as he detailed the facts of the case. Jane Neck would tell the jury that when she came down and found Miss Keyse's body in the dining room the whole of the doors and windows (except one) were in the same state as when she went to bed. When Gasking arrived it was about four o'clock. As he came in he saw the prisoner standing near the water cask; and told him to smash in the top and get as much water as he could. On asking him what was the matter prisoner told him that Miss Keyse was burnt to death in the dining room. Going thither Gasking found that a quantity of paper and other things had been heaped on the body, and that judging from the hold on the fire had on the furniture and other articles he believed it was burning for a considerable time. Gasking called on the prisoner to help carry the body out; but he hesitated, and had to be spoken to a second time. He then helped to carry the body out into the passage, and it was laid on the stones near the kitchen door. The body itself was much burnt, and had begun to stiffen. They returned to the dining room to cope with the fire. Gasking called for a hatchet or something of the sort to cut away a portion of the ceiling, and it was noticed that the prisoner in a very short time brought a hatchet, which was usually kept in the woodhouse, and was never seen within the dwelling house. Gasking would say that when he called to the prisoner to help remove the body, the shutters of the dining room were closed, and as far as he observed, his arm was not then cut. Superintendent Barbor and four other constables were soon on the spot, and they made careful examination of the premises. In the hall outside the dining room they found a large pool of blood. One of the coverings of the dining room chairs had been brought out into the hall, and that was also covered with blood. A hair comb belonging to the deceased was found in the passage, and in the hall, not far from the stair-end, were spots of candle grease. There could be no doubt, he thought, that the murderer (whoever he was), attacked this unfortunate woman in the hall outside the dining room door; the medical evidence would show that the wounds were of such a nature that she could not have moved again, and, therefore, the deceased must have been dragged into the dining room, where paper and other things were piled on her body and set fire to. The paper and part of Miss Keyse's dress were found to be saturated with paraffin oil; and had also been found on the stair carpet, and an ineffectual attempt made to fire it. Separate fires had also been made in the 'Honeysuckle room' immediately above the dining room and in Miss Keyse's bedroom, the latter having apparently been kindled only a short time before the servants were aroused. The police satisfied themselves by a careful examination of the premises that no one had broken in from the outside; and if the jury believed that, it was proved that the murder must have been committed by some person in the house. The police also examined the pantry, in which the prisoner had been sleeping. Miss Keyse, it seemed, often placed a note on the little table at the foot of the bed, giving prisoner direction as to what he should do in the morning. On the Friday evening she had told him verbally to go to Compton before breakfast; but she had evidently changed her mind, for a piece of paper was found in the pantry, with these words on it in the deceased's handwriting – 'John, it will be better to do some raking of the paths before breakfast, and go to Compton after.' In a drawer in the pantry the police found a knife – an old worn, sharp table knife – which used to be kept in the hall, for gardening purposes, by Miss Keyse.

BUTLER'S PANTRY
1. WHERE THE KNIFE 2. TURN UP 3. CUPBOARD
& BLOOD STAINS   BEDSTEAD   WHERE OIL CAN
WERE FOUND   4. PASSAGE   WAS KEPT

There were marks of blood on the knife; two pieces of paper upon which it was lying were also stained; and a drop of fresh blood had trickled on to the underside of the drawer. In a cupboard on the further side of the prisoner's bed, to which no one could have access without disturbing the occupant of the bed, an oil can was found. Jane Neck would say that this can was nearly full on Friday evening. She had used it, and on putting the can back into the cupboard she had corked it and placed an inverted funnel on the cork. When the can was found by the police it was empty, the cork was out, and there were marks of blood on the can. The prosecution suggested that the contents of the can must have been used to saturate the paper and other articles in the dining room, and the carpet on the stairs. Prisoner was spoken to on the Saturday morning by several of the constables. He seemed to show great anxiety to go to Compton and actually did go there. In a conversation with P.C. Boughton he said, 'Good God, that this should have happened. I have lost my best friend.' He added: 'I was dead asleep in bed, and the

I CHARGED HIM ON SUSPICION — HE SHOOK VERY MUCH

'It was clear that whoever broke the window, broke it from the outside . . .'

servants had great trouble to wake me.' Now the learned counsel should show that this was utterly untrue, for when the servants came down, he had his trousers on, with the braces hanging down.

Superintendent Barbor thought it right to take the man into custody on suspicion of the murder of Miss Keyse, and the only words he made use of when the charge was made were, 'Oh, on suspicion, aye!' Medical men were called in and they examined the body of the deceased. They found two fearful wounds on the head, either of which was sufficient to cause death, and the jury would be told that they were such wounds as might have been caused by the round part of the hatchet. The throat was cut, in a ghastly fashion, the wound being so deep that the weapon actually notched the bone of the neck. The medical men were of the opinion that the throat must have been cut when the deceased was nearly, if not quite, dead, because under these conditions the blood would not spurt, but would slowly trickle out into a mass, such as the police found. Every drop of the poor woman's blood must have been drained out of this fearful wound. The distance from where the prisoner was sleeping to the spot where this foul murder was committed had been carefully measured; from the door of the pantry to the pool of blood was 5ft 6ins; from the bed to the pool was 8ft 9ins. The door of the pantry was usually kept open, and the jury would remember he had already told them that there was an open space over the partition of 1ft 10ins. Prisoner, when apprehended had a severe cut upon his arm.

The window of the dining room had been carefully examined. The police would say that when they opened the shutters a quantity of glass fell into the room; there were spots of blood on the outside of the glass, as well as small pieces of skin, as if a man had scraped his arm; and the prisoner's arm was scratched. It was clear that whoever broke the window, broke it from the outside, though the prisoner's statement was that he broke it from the inside to let the smoke out from the dining room. The socks which prisoner had worn that morning were sent with other things to Dr. Stevenson, the Government analyst, and they were found to be soaked in paraffin, while some hairs, similar in appearance to those of the deceased, were found adhering to them. Prisoner's trousers were stained with blood, which someone had attempted to obliterate with washing. A letter of the prisoner's, written to a sweetheart four days before this occurrence might be of some importance. In this letter he said: 'Dearest Katie, I write to tell that I am very unsettled in what I am going to do in my future life. I am tired of service, and I am going to look out for something else to do, which might not be to your liking.' A day or two before this, it appeared, his wages were reduced to 2s. a week. The letter went on to speak of the affection he felt for the young woman, and how sorry he was to part with her.

The learned counsel's statement concluded with the observation that the prisoner had the good fortune to be defended by his learned friend Mr. St. Aubyn, and it was the duty of the jury to give him the benefit of any doubt they might consider to exist in the case. (*Torquay Directory*, 4 February 1885)

For the third time, a procession of household servants, neighbours, fishermen, coastguardsmen and doctors gave their often conflicting evidence. New witnesses were members of Torquay Fire Brigade, Stephen Warren, Gilbert Palmer and Thomas Smith, who testified that they had been in conversation with Lee about the cuts on his arm. Also, fisherman Thomas Henry Stigings appeared for the first time, claiming it was he, not George Pearce, who had been handed the axe by Lee. Dr Chilcote, who had earlier expressed the view that the knife produced could not have inflicted the injury on the victim, shifted his opinion and stated that the use of 'great strength would have done it'. The evidence of the cook, somewhat tarnished by her all too obvious moral lapse, came in for particular scrutiny: 'Elizabeth Harris was then placed in the witness box and looked much careworn. Owing to her condition she was offered a chair but did not use it. While in the witness box she studiously avoided the prisoner's stare. Witness repeated her former evidence and detailed the conversations she had with the prisoner. . . . Lee looked very pale when she repeated the threats she had heard him make use of' (*Torquay Times*, 6 February 1885).

Debarred by court rules from testifying on his own behalf, the defendant was reduced to the role of a mere onlooker at his own trial. The reaction to his accusers drew this comment:

The prisoner resumed his place in the dock with the almost serene indifference which characterised him the previous day, and looked around the Court with as little concern as if he had been a mere spectator instead of the principal figure in the trial. On the previous day he seemed almost bored by the whole proceedings, and the only time he evinced anything like keen interest was on the few occasions when the witnesses slightly contradicted themselves, contradictions which drew from the prisoner something like a smile of contempt. His uneasiness, however, was manifest when allusions were made to the blood marks on his clothes, which the wound in the arm would not explain, and when reference was made to his failure to make any sign until the servants called him. (*Torquay Times*, 6 February 1885)

"BLACK·MARIA"·IN·WHICH·LEE·WAS·
·CONVEYED·FROM·GAOL·TO·ASSIZES·

Despite a staggering total of twenty-eight witnesses being called by the prosecution, the trial looked set to be completed within its allotted two days, but it was realised that a twenty-ninth, P.C. Ware, had not been summoned to appear, which unnecessarily extended the trial to a third day. His evidence was hardly worth waiting for. He had met Lee about five on the morning of the murder at the top of Beach Road and asked him where the fire was and was told, 'It's our house at the bottom of the hill. My mistress is burnt to death, and I'm going to Compton to tell her sister' (*Torquay Times*, 6 February 1885).

Closing speech for the prosecution
Mr. Collins . . . invited the jury to give weight to his observations if they thought them worthy of it, but at the same time not to let anything influence them against their better judgement. . . . There seemed no doubt that from January 1884, to the night of the murder the prisoner was in the employ of Miss Keyse at a very low wage indeed and that she was paying a boy's wages for a man's work, at which he became discontented and unsettled, as shown by his letter to the young woman with whom he was keeping company. The threats he used to his half-sister, who, as they knew, was *enceinte*, and to whose misconduct in that respect, they could attach what importance they chose, were very serious indeed. It was true she said she did not attach any importance to them because she did not believe he was in earnest, but it was also true, that threats were used and it was for the jury to consider their importance and bearing upon the case.

Mr. Collins recapitulated the threats which prisoner made use of to Elizabeth Harris and also to Richards the postman, after which he proceeded to make it clear that the glass of the dining room window was not broken until after Miss Keyse's body was seen by Gasking, suggesting that prisoner afterwards smashed the glass with the intention of cutting his arm so as to account for the blood about his clothes. In reference to the blood stains on the inside of the leg of prisoner's trousers, the learned counsel pointed out that a person dragging the body of Miss Keyse from the hall into the dining room would probably have had her head between his legs and so smear his trousers just as the prisoner had done. Mr. Collins next drew attention to that part of the evidence having relation to the oil can, saying that it was not only not feasible but quite impossible that any person could have stepped over prisoner's bed; secured the oil can, used its contents and replaced it, without Lee's knowledge. In conclusion the learned counsel pointed out that plunder could not have been the motive of the murder, and the absurdity of supposing that it could have been committed by any other person than the prisoner. (*Torquay Times*, 6 February 1885)

The hastily arranged defence team were poorly prepared and proved totally ineffectual throughout the proceedings. No one was called on behalf of the defence, and there was little attempt to cross-examine the chief prosecution witnesses: 'Sergeant Nott was under examination two hours and-a-half, and it was anticipated that he would have to undergo a severe cross-examination but Mr. St. Aubyn surprised most people by intimating that he should not ask him a single question.' It was surprising that Elizabeth Harris also escaped any probing questions about the identity of the father of her child, particularly as the defence counsel's 'able defence', in his last-ditch appeal to the jury, would be based on unestablished insinuations about her love-life. It was readily acknowledged that even 'the most brilliant speech in defence could not dissipate the black cloud of adverse testimony hanging over the prisoner' (*Torquay Times*, 6 February 1885).

Closing speech for the defence

Mr. St. Aubyn in the course of an able defence, asked the jury to dismiss all previous prejudices against the prisoner. He had heard it remarked by several persons before the prisoner was tried, 'The case is as clear as possible.' The jury must dismiss all this kind of thing from their minds. He admitted that the case was one of the gravest suspicion against the prisoner. It was a case resting on circumstantial evidence. Unless the jury were satisfied that nobody else *could* have committed the crime it would be their duty to acquit the prisoner. They all agreed that a most brutal and foul murder was committed that morning by somebody. If the prisoner was the murderer no punishment could be too severe in any shape or form. Mr. St. Aubyn then pointed out the discrepancy between the medical men's opinion whether the murder was committed with the knife or hatchet. When doctors disagreed it was hard for them to say which was right. He suggested that the instrument that caused the murder was not the hatchet which the prosecution had alleged was the weapon used. It was a most extraordinary thing that on the night before the murder – the first occasion it had ever happened – the cook went to bed at five o'clock. The jury however, must not suppose he was going to suggest that the cook – who had trouble enough – knew anything about the terrible tragedy which was about to happen. But there was the fact that the cook went to bed at five o'clock, and was the first up in the morning. The cook could not have been enceinte without a lover, and as in a terrible case of this sort, the jury had to consider the possibility of anybody else having

'Referring to the
threats, the learned
counsel contended that
when people were
going to commit
offences they did not
often speak about it.'

committed this murder, whether somebody else might have been concealed in the house
on that particular night. There might have been somebody else in the house that night,
and on going out of the house he was confronted by Miss Keyse, and then he knocked
her down with a knob of a stick. Could not this person go down to prisoner's drawer for
a knife and have taken it without waking Lee? Referring to the threats, the learned
counsel contended that when people were going to commit offences they did not often
speak about it. What motive could Lee have for the crime? Did they think the prisoner
brutally and deliberately murdered his best friend for the sake of a reduction of sixpence
a week in his wages? Did the jury think that if Lee had committed the murder he would
have put the knife back in his own drawer? Alluding to the blood on prisoner's clothes,
Mr. St. Aubyn urged that there was nothing in that against the prisoner, as the wonder
was that everybody who touched deceased had not their clothes covered with blood and
hair. . . . Mr. St. Aubyn reminded the jury that men had been convicted of murder when
they were innocent . . . In conclusion, the counsel for the defence said: When I have sat
down my responsibility will end, and when the Judge has summed up his duty will be

Counsel for the defence, W.N. Molesworth St Aubyn QC.

finished. With you (the jury) is the dreadful issue of life and death. I ask you to consider this solemn question. Having taken an oath to God in this case, am I satisfied beyond all reasonable doubt, that no other person but the prisoner, *could* have committed this crime? Further ask yourselves this question – If I am not satisfied better let 99 persons go unpunished than that one person not guilty should suffer? It is an important issue for you, and I pray God you may be guided right. (*Trewman's Exeter Flying Post*, 4 February 1885)

'The learned Judge . . . pointed to the fact that the prisoner put his hands on Jane Neck's nightgown, on which blood was found, before the breaking of glass . . .'

Summing up

The Judge proceeded to sum up the case, which he did in a most masterly manner. At this stage prisoner became more agitated and seemed to realise his critical position, more than he had hitherto done. He watched the Judge anxiously and listened to every word. He alternately looked to the Judge and nervously turned to the jury. The learned Judge said that this was one of the most important cases that had probably fallen to the lot of any man to deal with for a very long time. The case was of vital importance, both to the public and the prisoner, but especially to the prisoner. The evidence had properly been described as circumstantial evidence, but there were cases in which circumstantial evidence was more conclusive than direct evidence, because direct evidence was subject to suspicion. Having referred minutely to the condition of the house on the night before the horrible affair, the Judge closely dealt with the theory of the defence, upon which he said everything rested. If the jury thought it was possible – if it was reasonably possible – that the murder could have been committed by a person other than the prisoner, and all that had occurred could take place without the prisoner knowing it, prisoner was entitled to this doubt. Of course, if the jury thought there was a reasonable possibility of this, they would require overwhelming evidence to say prisoner committed the crime. This was the very foundation of the case and having regard to all the circumstances of this case there was no reasonable ground to suspect that anybody committed the murder but the prisoner. The theory was that Elizabeth Harris might have a lover. He did not know that Mr. St. Aubyn directly insinuated that Elizabeth Harris's condition had anything to do with the case. It would not have done to suggest that the crime was the act of a robber and the object was plunder, because there was no trace of anything like an intention to plunder. Whoever committed the murder evidently had endeavoured to burn the house to conceal the crime. The jury must, as men of reason and sound judgement, give weight to the theory for the defence, but he was bound to say it was a very 'far-fetched' idea to suppose that any person committed the murder if he had not a grudge or spite against the lady. The learned Judge, in analysing the evidence, pointed to the fact that the prisoner put his hands on Jane Neck's night gown, on which blood was found, before the breaking of glass, which prisoner alleged cut his arm. If that blood did not come from Lee's arm, it was for the jury to say where the blood came from. It was evident that whoever committed the murder endeavoured to conceal it by setting fire to the house. It was also for the jury to consider whether the fact that prisoner described the affair as Miss Keyse being 'burnt to death,' and making no mention of the 'murder,' was for or against the prisoner. The suggestion of the prosecution that prisoner, to account for the blood on his person and clothes, inflicted the wound on his arm, was quite consistent with the design of setting fire to the body. With reference to the knife having been put in the drawer by some other person, the learned Judge admitted that this would have been a strong fact but for the other circumstances. They could not sever the fact of the knife in the drawer from the fire, because if the fire had been effectual, as was intended, all traces of blood on the knife would have been destroyed. As to whether the blood on the knife came from prisoner's arm or deceased's body was not important, the material point was who placed the knife in the drawer. In conclusion, the learned Judge said the case was deduced to the one point suggested, whether or not, beginning with the theory that the murder was committed by some other person, you can make all these facts fit in with that, and consistent with that theory, having regard to the position in which prisoner was, and the place where he was, his conduct at the time, and his statements before and after the occurrence. If there is any reasonable doubt, you must give prisoner the benefit of it, but if not, you will be bound to find him guilty. (*Trewman's Exeter Flying Post*, 4 February 1885)

Verdict and sentence
The jury retired at five minutes after one to consider their verdict, and after an absence of half-an-hour they returned into Court, and the foreman announced the verdict of 'GUILTY OF MURDER.'

The Judge then assumed the black cap, and solemn silence was enjoined on the Court. The prisoner standing appeared more composed than ever, and to the enquiry of the Court official answered, 'I am innocent, sir.'

The Judge then said: John Lee you have been found guilty of a crime as barbarous as was ever committed, and this jury have found you guilty of the murder upon evidence so clear to my mind, and so absolutely conclusive, that I am sorry to say I cannot entertain a doubt of the correctness of their verdict. It is not my habit to dwell on the details of a case so painful, nor do I think it would be good for the public or yourself. You say you are innocent; I wish I could believe it. You have throughout the case maintained a calm appearance, but I need not say the jury having found you guilty of the crime of this

'My Lord, the reason I am so calm is because I trust in my Lord, who knows I am innocent.'

murder, I am not surprised to see you maintain such a calm appearance. I have one public duty to perform. The law imposes it upon me, and I must perform it – it is to pass the awful sentence of death. You have broken the law – Divine and human – and by that law – most Divine and human – you must suffer the penalty. The sentence is that you be taken from the place where you are now to the prison whence you came, and on a day appointed be taken thence to the place of execution there to be hanged by the neck until your body be dead, and it then be taken down and buried in the precincts of the prison in which you were last confined. I cannot hold out any hope, so far as I am concerned, of any mercy being extended to you. I advise you during the short time that remains to listen to the good advice which will be given to you, and avail yourself of the little comfort that can be afforded you in this world in preparing for the next. And may God have mercy on you.

Before the prisoner was removed he said: 'My Lord, the reason I am so calm is because I trust in my Lord, who knows I am innocent.'

Prisoner was then removed, and left the Court in a bold and seemingly defiant attitude. (*Trewman's Exeter Flying Post*, 4 February 1885)

A correspondent observed the scene at the close of the trial: 'The Castle was soon deserted after the sentence had been passed, but in the Yard a group stood outside the window of the apartment set aside for the use of witnesses gazing at those who had been connected in any way with the case. Kate Farmer, the prisoner's sweetheart, was present, and was the cynosure of all eyes. Elizabeth Harris, prisoner's half-sister, was much affected, crying bitterly, but absorbing coffee and bun withal' (*Torquay Times*, 6 February 1885).

Public opinion on the verdict was summed up in the *Western Morning News*, 5 February 1885:

> The trial of John Lee for the murder of Miss Emma Ann Whitehead Keyse November last terminated yesterday in a verdict of guilty. It is difficult to contemplate without a shudder the guilt which was brought home with absolute conclusiveness against him.
>
> There is scarcely a phase of his crime which does not represent a special element of horror. He was the only man in a lonely house occupied by women. He used his position to slay one of them unobserved: that was cowardly to say the least. He was kept in the house partly for the purpose of protection: he gravely abused the trust. He had been taken from prison in order to earn a character, to murder his friend was the sort of gratitude he displayed.
>
> When the dread sentence was passed his lordship made the customary pious ejaculation 'and may the Lord have mercy on your soul', greeted with a fervent 'amen', and the penultimate scene of the Babbacombe tragedy ended.

CHAPTER 6

On the brink of eternity

The condemned man John Lee was executed at Exeter this morning. Berry, who was the executioner, gave a seven foot drop. The culprit died easily.

– Dartmouth and Brixham Chronicle, 23 February 1885

After the trial, in accordance with the custom of the day, there was a period of three clear Sundays before the dread sentence of the law could be carried out:

> It is always said that these three weeks waiting for death are more terrible than the actual execution. It may be so in some cases, it certainly was not so in mine. If anything I felt relieved. All the suspense was over. I knew now what to expect, and I made up my mind to face it cheerfully as I could.
>
> My only anxiety was to know when the sentence was to be carried out. This news I received two days after I had been sentenced. About half-past seven in the morning, the governor came into my cell. . . . 'Lee,' he said, 'your sentence will be carried out on the 23rd.' I turned round and smiled. I suppose I horrified him, for he said in a very shocked voice: 'It is nothing to laugh at.'
>
> Neither was it. But I was happy. His news did not at all frighten me. I was no murderer. I was innocent. What had I to fear. (Lee, 1908)

With the ultimate sentence of the law approaching, Lee's religious needs were now addressed by the Reverend John Pitkin, who must have felt some remorse at having recommended that John Lee be taken back at The Glen by Emma Keyse. The condemned man was urged to confess all, but resolutely reiterated his innocence and demonstrated in a letter to his parents, published in the newspapers, that he was prepared to meet his maker:

HM Prison, Exeter
6 February, 1885

Dear Father and Mother,
    A few lines hoping this will find you much better after the first shock. I hope you will bear up as well as you can. I am quite happy and well, and I am quite prepared for my home above. You must trust in God the same as I have. You see how I have borne it up.

I do not know whenever I was happier than I am now, because I know where I am going to. It is a pity you should have stopped to hear the sentence passed. I heard you crying behind. I hope you got home alright. I know you feel it more than I do, but you must not think of things in this world, you must pray to God to meet me in heaven. I will pray for you the little time I have to live, you must pray to God to help you. Do not think I am unhappy, you do not know how happy I am, you would be surprised to see me. Do trust in God and you will see the difference in the worldly man and the spiritual man. Dear Mother, if you think you would like to see me before I die you must write and tell the Governor of the Prison, and tell him the day you will come up, or else you cannot see me. You can write to me at any time. Give my love to Milly and tell her I have trusted in the Lord, and she must do the same and meet me in heaven. I am happier than I should be if I was out. What does it matter about a few hours in this world? We must all leave it sometime. You can all come and see me, only let the Governor know. I cannot think of anything more to say at present, so I must say good-bye, and we must trust in God.

From your affectionate son,
J.H. Lee

P.S. The day is fixed for the 23rd of this month. Good-bye.

In the following letter sent to his sister Amelia, Lee made it clear that the blame for the crime for which he was condemned lay elsewhere. The newspaper reports censored the use of people's names mentioned by Lee, although 'KF' obviously refers to his sweetheart, Katie Farmer:

HM Prison, Exeter
11 February 1885

Dear Sister,

Your letter to hand this morning was received with much pleasure, and gave me great comfort to see that you are still the same kind and loving sister, who is always willing to do anyone any good. I have always noticed that you have not trusted the world altogether. I think you said Miss Keyse taught us to look above for help. I think she gave us both very good counsel. She never went to bed without praying for us, and I hope we shall meet her in heaven. We shall know the truth of this case; it is the same as you say, it is hard to be punished when one knows that he did not do it, but I will trust in the Lord and ask Him to give me strength to bear it all. This world's punishment it is nothing after all for a better home above. Dear sister, I hope we shall meet in heaven, we must trust in the Lord, and ask His forgiveness for all our sins. Dear sister, I shall be very glad to see you and father when you please to come. I was very glad to hear mother got home alright. It's a very heavy blow for you all, you must help mother and father. Though Mr. St. Aubyn worked very hard for me, but there is no doubt that the truth will come out after I am dead. It must be some very hard-hearted persons for to let me die for nothing. All the witnesses will and must appear before our Saviour for what they have said against me and to answer for my life, they little think of it now, but the time will soon come for them, and I hope they will be prepared to meet our Saviour. I thank God I am not blind so as not to know what I have seen and what I done. They have not told six words truth, that is, the servants and that lovely step-sister, who carries her character with her. Give my love to mother and father and yourself; we must trust in the Lord, he will help us through all our trouble, he has helped me so far, and he will help me to the end. Have you heard from K.F., or seen them, you know who I mean. Good-bye, my dear sister for the present.

> From your affectionate brother, who is dead to the world.
> J.H. LEE

In a last desperate move by family sympathisers, an appeal was made to the Home Secretary for a stay of execution. The details were revealed in the Lee family's local paper, the *East and South Devon Advertiser*, 23 February 1885:

As a last resource to save the prisoner from the gallows, the following petition was drawn up:

To the Right Honourable Sir William Vernon Harcourt, M.P., P.C.
    Her Majesty's Chief Secretary for the Home Department.
The humble petition of us the undersigned sheweth as follows:-

1. John Lee was tried before the Hon. Mr. Justice Manisty at the Assizes, held at Exeter, on the second, third, and fourth inst., for the wilful murder of Miss Emma Ann Whitehead Keyse, was convicted, and sentenced to be hanged.

'P.S. The day is fixed for the 23rd of this month. Good-bye.'

2. Lee is only 20 years of age, and has protested his innocence all through his trial. The only motive that could be assigned for the crime was a supposed ill-feeling toward his mistress in consequences of her having reduced his wages from 2s. 6d. to 2s. a week. His parents, who are respectable people living at Abbotskerswell, in the county of Devon, consider that he is suffering from a deranged state of mind, he having from his youth upwards shewn at times symptoms of temporary insanity.

Your petitioners therefore pray that, taking the above circumstances into consideration, especially Lee's extreme youth, you will be pleased to commute the sentence passed upon him to one of penal servitude for life. And your petitioners will ever pray, &c.

This petition has been signed by the Rev. Veysey Hine, vicar of Abbotskerswell, who knew the prisoner from his youth upwards, and a large number of other influential and highly respectable persons; and owing to a variety of incidents coming to light, and the eccentricities the prisoner was known to indulge in from time to time, many people consider that his right state of mind is very questionable. His parents assert most positively that from his youth upward he acted at times 'as though he was not right', but that they never divulged their suspicions lest it should affect him in getting his living. The father had an interview with the condemned man a few days ago, when he assumed the same indifferent demeanour as to the doom that awaits him as he has ever since he has been in custody. He told his father he was perfectly innocent of having committed the murder, that he knew he should be hanged, and that he was resigned to meet his fate, and was in every way prepared to meet his God.

It also emerged that Lee had broken his silence to make a late statement to the Vicar of Abbotskerswell, alleging that 'a man in a mask' had visited his half-sister on the night of the murder – a story confirmed by *Trewman's Exeter Flying Post*, 25 February 1885:

Rumours have been freely circulated that Lee made a statement or confession to the Vicar of Abbotskerswell, not altogether exculpating himself from guilt but implicating another person whom he alleged was the actual murderer. It is a fact that the reverend gentleman visited the unfortunate man on Wednesday last [18th February], and we understand that Lee made a statement to the above effect. Whatever the statement was it was deemed of sufficient importance to be sent to the Home Secretary, presumably with the view of having the execution postponed pending inquiry whether a person not yet known was the actual murderer. Sir William Harcourt, however, discredited the allegations, and accordingly the day appointed for the execution was not altered.
 Whilst Lee has stoutly protested his innocence of the actual crime since his incarceration, he has not denied all knowledge of the affair. He has not, however, appeared to be desirous of incriminating anyone on his account, although he has said that before he has been dead twelve months the real murderer will confess the crime.

The signed petition and the condemned man's statement failed to sway the Home Secretary and Lee prepared for his last night on earth and wrote letters to his parents, sister and sweetheart, although as he explained later, only two reached their destination:

'I put a lock of hair in each. I don't think Miss Farmer ever received her letter. I imagine it was kept back in case it might be useful after the execution, for I think I told her that I deserved hanging for being so foolish as "to let things go" as I had done. This is what has been called a "confession," I believe!' (Lee, 1908).

Details of the condemned man's farewell letters to his family were released to the press:

HM Prison, Exeter
23 February 1885

Dear Mother and Father,

I am now taking my pen to write you a few lines before leaving this world and I hope you are well after your journey last Saturday. I hope you got home all right. I know this is a great trial for you to bear. I know it is harder for you than for me but we must trust in the Lord Jesus Christ and ask Him to help us through this great trouble. We must forgive our enemies and ask God to forgive them. I forgive them all, and the Lord will forgive me and my sins which are a great many. We must pray to help us in this great trial. There is a nice Christian lady living at the Rooklands, Torre, Torquay [Lydia Sparke, wife of Morton Sparke, J.P., Deacon of Belgrave Congregational Church, Torquay], she has been so kind to me in sending books, lovely flower-cards and letters, and I am sure I have learned much from them, and I hope the Lord will reward her for it. Dear Mother and Father, I hope we shall all meet in heaven. There are a lot of friends offering prayers to our Lord for me, and I hope their prayers and mine will be answered. Please pray to God and ask Him to help you, and He will; we must not stick so fast to worldly things. We must put our trust in God. I am quite happy, and hope the Lord will give me strength to meet my doom, which I deserve for not opening my mouth, and for all my other sins. I am a great sinner, and hope the Lord will pardon my sins, which are many. I am only sorry I did not know the Lord before, but I thank God He has shown me my sins now.

My dear Father and Mother, I hope these lines will give you comfort. It is all I can give you in this world, and I hope you will pray to God to meet me in the next world. I do not see that I need write any more, as it will do no more good. Give my kind love to all and to yourselves, so I think I must say 'Goodbye' forever in this world, but I hope to meet you in the next. So I must say 'Goodbye.'

Your affectionate son,
John Lee

Dear Sister,

Your letter to hand, and it gave me so much pleasure. It was a very nice letter, and I hope this will find you quite well. I am very happy and I hope the Lord will give me strength to meet my doom, and I hope we shall meet in heaven. We must pray to God to help us in this great trail; and to forgive us our sins, and help us to forgive our enemies. We must forgive all those that hate us, and ask God to forgive them. Dear sister, you must forgive Lizzie, I do forgive her. I have had kind friends to send me letters and books and offer up prayers to the Lord for me, a great sinner, and to forgive me all my sins, which are great and many, and I hope the Lord will forgive me and receive my soul into heaven, where I hope to meet you, mother, father, and all my friends. Dear sister, you must pray to God and ask him to help you through all your trouble. . . . Dear sister, these are a few lines before I leave this world as my time is short and I hope they will give you comfort. It is all I can give you in this world, but I hope we shall meet in the next. You must help mother and father to bear up as well as you can. It is a great trial to you all, but, dear sister, it is my own fault. I ought to have opened my mouth before. I deserve hanging for my other sins and keeping my mouth shut, so I hope to meet you in heaven, and I think I must say my good-bye to you in this world, and you must pray to God to forgive you your sins and not care so much after the worldly things as I did. So good-bye, dear sister.

From your affectionate brother,
John Lee

As it turned out, John Lee's relatives hadn't heard the last from him, and the crowds of people who poured through the city gates to see the black flag raised over the prison were to be disappointed as the condemned man cheated death on the scaffold in sensational fashion.

The editor of the *Dartmouth and Brixham Chronicle* was acutely embarrassed when he prematurely published the outcome: 'The condemned man John Lee was executed at Exeter this morning. Berry, who was the executioner, gave a seven foot drop. The culprit died easily.' Recollections in other journals varied as to how many separate attempts were made to carry out the sentence of the law. The general consensus among the ten reporters who were admitted to the prison was three, while James Berry, the executioner, believed it was only twice; others, including Gerald de Courcy Hamilton, Chief Constable of Devon, thought that Lee was placed on the scaffold four times – an opinion shared in this brilliantly written, though possibly flawed observation of events published in the *Western Morning News*, Tuesday 24 February 1885:

What under ordinary circumstances would have proved the closing scene in the Babbacombe tragedy was enacted in the Devon County Prison yesterday morning, when John Lee . . . was brought to the scaffold to undergo the dread sentence of the law. The details of the scene which accompanied the official efforts to deprive Lee of the life he had forfeited were of a most harrowing description, and are, probably, without a parallel in the history of such events in this country. . . .

The execution was fixed for eight o'clock. At 7.30 the approaches to the exterior of the gaol were barred to all but the representatives of the Press, who were admitted by ticket and ushered one by one into a large room immediately within the portals of the main entrance to the building. Here and at every stage of the proceedings every arrangement was made for their convenience, thanks to the kindly solicitude of the Governor (Captain Cowtan). At five minutes to eight the reporters, ten in number, were stationed within the main corridor of the building at a point to be passed by the culprit on his passage from the condemned cell to the place of execution. A few seconds later the procession, headed by the Chief Warder (Mr. Rainford), entered the corridor. The Chaplain (Rev. J. Pitkin) and the Schoolmaster (Mr. Libby) came next and were immediately followed by Lee, who walked with pinioned hands between a couple of warders. The Prison Surgeon (Mr. Caird) and the Governor (Mr. Cowtan) also accompanied the procession, while other

Exeter, the 'Ever Faithful' city: 'the crowds of people who poured through the city gates to see the black flag raised over the prison were to be disappointed . . .'

warders, and beside them Berry, the executioner, brought up the rear. The slow and deliberate tread of Lee and his companions, the tolling of the prison bell, added to the impressive tones of the chaplain as he repeated portions of the burial service, combined to make the occasion one of deep solemnity. The look of the doomed man during what was literally regarded as his march to the grave, bore no signs of anything like fear. He walked with firmness and with head erect, but beneath the assumed indifference which he carried even to the gallows there were not wanting indications of an imperfectly concealed realisation of the terrible fate which seemed to await him.

The scaffold, which was the same as that employed in the execution of Annie Took about five years ago, had been removed to another part of the building. It was sunk into the ground and formed, in fact, the flooring of a small brick shed ordinarily used for sheltering the prisoner's van, which vehicle, for the occasion had been removed outside. The small enclosure which accommodates this vehicle is situated at the north-west end of the gaol, and abuts on a small garden. From a beam across the interior of the shed the hangman's rope depended, immediately beneath and in the same centre of the floor being the trap from which it was intended to drop the prisoner. The advantage of this arrangement in ordinary cases would be obvious in the fact that it necessitated no ascent, which in the case of culprits prostrated by fear is often so painful an ordeal. The gloomy and repulsive character of the gallows was, if possible, intensified by its enclosure

'By this time the convict had become an object of the supreme sympathy of every man present.'

within brick walls. As Lee walked into the building and, by the direction of the executioner, placed himself on the fatal planks, there was no faltering or sign of fear. He cast a glance at the rope above him as if to assure himself that its fastenings were perfectly secured, and then inaudibly muttered something to Berry as the latter functionary adjusted the noose around the culprit's neck. There was even a dash of bravado in the unhappy man's demeanour as he glanced at the ghastly paraphernalia of death. A white cap was, in the usual manner, placed over the head and face of the convict, and as the closing words of the burial service died away on the chaplain's lips, Berry, at a given signal, drew the lever. The only response was a grating sound and a slight movement of the trap upon which the culprit stood. A second and third attempt were made to draw the bolt, but with no more success than attended the first effort. Something was evidently wrong, and Berry, assisted by some of the warders, made an examination of the apparatus, having in the meantime, withdrawn the rope and the cap from the culprit's neck and face and moved him a little forward. In this terrible position Lee never flinched, but stood erect as before, his countenance having undergone no visible change. But not so with the officials, whose hurried movements and pale faces betrayed signs of deep anxiety and even terror. The apparatus having again been prepared, Lee's legs were once more pinioned and the rope and cap adjusted. Again the fatal signal was given, and the loud click of the lever once more startled the witnesses to this terrible scene. The bolt having once more defied the repeated efforts of the hangman, Lee was freed from the fatal noose and removed, this time to the back of the building in full view of a further trial to put right the stubborn machinery. By this time the convict had become an object of the supreme sympathy of every man present. Still, seemingly unmoved by the lingering torture thus added to his terrible fate, the condemned man surveyed the preparations which were going on before him. After a suspense of several seconds he was once more placed, and Berry ran hurriedly to the back of the shed to drop him. As the bolt again and again refused to yield, Berry made a desperate effort to force the trap by stamping it with his feet. Fortunately for himself the effort was unsuccessful, otherwise in all probability the executioner would have fallen with his victim. As the convict had once more to be set aside, a feeling of inexpressible horror plainly depicted on their countenances, seemed to seize every one present. After a hurried conference of the officials Lee was conducted to the interior of the prison. In the meantime the services of a carpenter were procured, and by the process of planing it was sought to remedy the cause of previous failures. This occupied something like five minutes, when for the fourth time the condemned man was placed in readiness for execution. The hope that every possibility of failure had this time been averted was quickly removed, for the apparatus seemed, if possible, more rigid than ever. The impossibility of proceeding with the execution under the circumstances was too obvious to require further thought, and Lee was accordingly returned to the cell from which he had been taken. In the absence of instructions to the effect that it would not be required further efforts were made to reduce the apparatus to a workable condition. The governor held a consultation with the chaplain and surgeon of the gaol, and a mutual feeling was expressed that the unhappy convict had already expiated the terrible crime of which he had been convicted. The circumstances, at least, did not seem to justify any further attempt to carry out the dread sentence of the law before the Home Secretary had been appealed to. The under sheriff (Mr. James) afterwards had an interview with the representatives of the Press, in the course of which he intimated that the proceedings having been brought to a close in consequence of the apparatus not working as it ought to work he had decided, acting under the advice of the surgeon and chaplain, to defer the execution, and intended going at once to London for the purpose of obtaining an interview with the Home Secretary and taking his instructions as to further action in the matter. Mr. James added that it was only fair to the executioner to say that he could not be held in any way responsible for the failure of the apparatus, which was duly examined and submitted to a successful experiment on Saturday last. The failure was attributed to the supposition that the woodwork must have become swollen as the result of the damp produced by the heavy rain of Saturday night. The incident, however, serves to show the importance of a trial of the apparatus as near as possible to the time of execution, a practice which Marwood [former public executioner] invariably observed. . . .

After the successive attempts to hang Lee had proved a failure, and he was removed to his cell, the great strain upon him throughout the terrible ordeal was followed by a certain amount of physical prostation. The Governor assisted him to his cell and offered him stimulants, but he pointedly refused and repudiated the necessity for anything. He soon recovered his full vigour and wonted composure, and no bad results are apprehended from what to many would have proved a serious, if not fatal, shock to the nervous system. . . . The terrible anguish to which Lee must have been subjected is matter of general comment, and has had the effect of rendering him an object of general sympathy.

The under sheriff proceeded to London by an early train yesterday morning, and an official notification from the Home Secretary of a respite was received by the governor of the gaol at five o'clock last evening. In answer to an inquiry in the House of Commons yesterday Sir William Harcourt, in confirming the report that Lee had been respited, said that in consequence of the prisoner having twice undergone the pangs of imminent death at Exeter he had obtained the consent of the Queen to a respite.

Headlines in the national press were still reflecting the country's horror at news of the recent loss of General Gordon at Khartoum, but this stinging attack on home affairs appeared in an editorial of *The Times*, 24 February 1885:

We greatly regret to have to report this morning one of those occurrences which, from time to time, discredit the administration of justice and, we are bound to add, the Government of the country.

The Babbacombe murderer, John Lee, who on the 15th of last November, cruelly slew his aged mistress, Miss Keyse, was to have been executed yesterday morning. He had been convicted on the clearest evidence, which his Counsel scarcely attempted to refute, of what the Judge called 'as cruel and barbarous a murder as was ever committed.' A scantily signed petition had been presented in favour of a reprieve, and the Home Secretary had very properly replied that he saw no reason for interfering with the sentence. Accordingly Lee prepared for death, and at eight o'clock yesterday morning he was to be executed in Exeter Gaol. Berry was the executioner, and the preparations had been made under his supervision. . . . The drop would not work; and the culprit with the

Sir William Harcourt: 'it would shock the feelings of every one if a man had twice to incur
the pangs of imminent death . . .'

rope around his neck and the words of the Burial Service in his ears was suddenly made aware that the attempt to hang him had failed.

He was removed and the prison officials tried to remedy the defect in the drop. Again the horrible experience was gone through, with no result, and yet a third time it was tried in vain. Then the Sheriff ordered the execution to be stopped pending consultation with the Home Secretary. The result of that communication was made known later by Sir William Harcourt in the House of Commons, and, we regret to say, that it revealed on the Home Secretary's part a lamentable tendency to prefer sentiment to justice. Because the rain had swollen the drop on which the criminal stood, therefore Sir William Harcourt has advised Her Majesty to grant him his life. After hearing the facts of the case he considered 'that it would shock the feelings of every one if a man had twice to incur the pangs of imminent death and he had, therefore, signed a respite to continue during Her Majesty's pleasure.' This was a truly miserable conclusion of a wretched case. The bungling of executioner, Sheriff and Prison Governor was scandalous indeed, tending – as much of the history of executions since Marwood's death has tended – to discredit the whole machinery of Justice in this country. It is a shocking and grievous thing that even such a criminal as Lee should have been tortured by three attempts to hang him and those responsible ought to be visited with severe penalties.

Lord Cowper has given notice that he will ask a question tonight in the House of Lords relating to the case and will suggest, as is reasonable, the appointment of a Public Executioner under the control of the Secretary of State. But whatever steps may be taken to put executions on a satisfactory footing the immediate concern is with this particular criminal Lee. We cannot but think that the Home Secretary's action singularly ill-advised and likely to have the worst effect; that it will encourage superstitious and foolish people to believe, in spite of evidence as clear as noonday, that Lee was wrongly convicted and that the failure of the executioner was Providential is a comparatively slight matter. The real harm it will do is by substituting a false standard for the true standard by which these things ought to be judged. Sir William Harcourt thinks that a second execution would shock people's feelings and, therefore, he commutes the murderer's sentence.

We submit that the question of whether people's feelings are shocked or not is of secondary importance. The essential thing is to show that the sentence of the law shall be carried out, and that, though untoward events may delay, they cannot be allowed to defeat it.

We are not surprised to learn from Exeter that 'the decision of the Home Secretary meets with general approval.' For the moment, no doubt, it will have done so. People are naturally given to sentiment and superstition.

But tomorrow will bring reflection. They will remember that the man whose life has been spared is the author of one of the most cold-blooded, the most unprovoked and the most dastardly murders of the day, and they will ask themselves whether it is right that an executioner's blunder should restore to such a being the life that he has lawfully forfeited.

Meanwhile, John Lee seemed the least affected person in the prison as this terrible drama was played out. Newspaper reports described how he had stumbled, on the point of collapse, as he was taken from the scaffold, but he later explained that this was

'Lord Cowper . . . will suggest . . . the appointment of a Public Executioner under the control of the Secretary of State.'

because the authorities had almost taken his life by unintended means: 'The cap on my head was slowly smothering me, so I tried to push it off my mouth by bending down my head and raising my manacled hands. . . . Apparently my action was misunderstood. The officials thought I was fainting.' Upon reaching his cell, the prisoner turned down the offer of a glass of brandy, but the morning's trauma had seemingly not affected his appetite. When told by the doctor that he could eat anything he desired, he was then disappointed to learn that prison rules forbade it: 'I ordered ham and eggs for breakfast, and a beefsteak with half a pint of port for dinner. As I had already had breakfast, such as it was, the ham and eggs had to be put off till the following morning' (Lee, 1908).

In letters released to the press it was clear that Lee and his sister Amelia firmly believed that God had interceded on his behalf:

The Accused
John Lee

'I had a dream on Sunday night . . .
I did not think it was coming true –
but it did.'

HM Prison, Exeter
24 February 1885

Dear Sister,

Your letter to hand this morning was received with much pleasure, and I was glad to hear from you. . . .

Dear sister, the last letter I wrote to you I thought would be my last, and I did not expect to ever have the pleasure of writing this letter. It was the Lord's will that I should not die yesterday at the time appointed by man. Everything was all right, and in working order; and it was no fault of anyone. Everything was done in order to carry out the orders of the country; but it was the Lord's hand that would not let the law be carried out.

Dear sister, I did not fear to walk unto death with a firm foot, because I knew the Lord was with me; and had I passed through the shadow of death, I should have went into that home which the Blessed Lord has prepared for all that believe in Him.

Dear sister, I have had attention shown me, and, dear sister, I was at the brink of death three times. Dear sister, it was my will to die; and I hope to yet. I hope that the next time I go to the scaffold I shall pass from this life to that home above.

Dear sister, it was my wish to die. I am tired of this world, and am waiting for the time to come. Dear sister, I have been dead to the world three times; and I give myself to the

Lord that whatever His will is, His will be done! I leave it all in the Lord's hands; and, dear sister, I believe this was a miracle worked by the Lord. Dear sister, I am respited. The sentence of death is put off for a day or two. Dear sister, I hope mother and father are bearing up as well as they can. I know they feel it more than I do. I fear no evil while the Lord is with me. Dear sister, give my love to all. I wrote to Miss F. [Farmer] before I went to meet my doom.

Dear sister, we must not forget to pray to the Lord, and give thanks to Him for His mercy. Dear sister, I had a dream on Sunday night that the scaffold was not ready, and that they had to make another. And I told the officers that were on watch over me the dream at 6am. I did not think it was coming true – but it did.

Dear sister, I must bring this letter to a close.

Goodbye, my dear sister. From your affectionate brother,

John Lee

Amelia Lee immediately replied giving the reaction of family and friends to Lee's unbelievable good fortune:

Newton Abbot
25 February 1885

My Poor Dear Brother,

Many, many thanks for your most welcome letter. It was such a great pleasure to mother, father, and myself to see you are so happy. What a blessing it is to feel the same as you do! Oh, it is a blessing! I only wish I did; but I will pray the same as you have done. . . . Dear brother, I saw by the papers that it was no fault of anyone. It was the will of God, and seems very much like Daniel in the lions' den; only yours is of another nature. My mistress gave me leave from Sunday until Tuesday. We were grieving over your death, and in another way thinking you were with your blessed Saviour, when Dick Taylor [a neighbour of Mr and Mrs Lee] walked over from Newton to Abbotskerswell to tell us of the joyful news. I should like to see you again, dear brother. . . . I hope you are still praying, and I will pray for you, as we have been praying all along. I have heard from K.F. [Katie Farmer] this morning. Could you read it if I was to send it to you?

Love from all. Hoping you are quite well.

Your affectionate sister,
A. Lee

P.S. There was one of the reporters out to see mother on Monday afternoon that was up there [at the execution].

Details of John Lee's prophetic dream were revealed by *Trewman's Exeter Flying Post*, 25 February 1885:

It appears that on the night previous or on the morning of the execution Lee had a remarkable dream, which is in keeping with the whole circumstances of this extraordinary affair. On Monday morning Lee awoke at six o'clock, and told the two warders in charge that he had had a dream, and he did not think he should be executed that day. He then communicated to them a dream which he had, and which turned out to be an exact portrayal of what really transpired within a few hours afterwards. He said he saw himself being taken to the place of execution, and that when he got to the scaffold the machinery would not work. He was removed and put back until a new scaffold was erected. After the actual attempts had been made, and Lee again found himself in his cell, he told his dream to the Chaplain, and also mentioned the fact that he informed the warders of it at six o'clock on Monday morning – two hours before the time for execution.

The outcome of Lee's trial had been little more than a formality, but, surprisingly, in a letter to the prison chaplain, the barrister, Walter Molesworth St Aubyn, who had conducted a somewhat half-hearted defence of Lee, displayed a sense of relief when news reached him about the failure of the execution:

February 24th, 1885

Dear Mr Pitkin,

What a terrible time you must have had of it with Lee! I am one of those who was never fully satisfied of his guilt. What a marvellous thing if he turns out to be innocent! At any rate he must have a nerve like iron. What will become of him now, I wonder? (Pitkin, 1918)

CHAPTER 7

Imprisonment for life?

I did not know that the living death I was about to endure was more terrible than anything the grave can inflict.

– John Lee, 1908

Despite being personally acquainted with the victim, Queen Victoria made her feelings clear about the condemned man's ordeal. Within hours of the sensational news breaking she sent a telegram to the Home Secretary, Sir William Harcourt: 'I am horrified at the disgraceful scenes at Exeter at Lee's execution. Surely Lee cannot now be executed. It would be too cruel. Imprisonment for life seems the only alternative' (Royal Archives, Windsor Castle).

Sir William concurred, although a month passed before Lee, labouring under the mistaken belief that the respite was temporary, was officially informed that the death sentence had been commuted to life imprisonment. The Governor of Exeter Prison assured him that in his case 'penal servitude for life means twenty years'; however, unbeknown to the prisoner, the Home Secretary had recommended that he should never be released. Oblivious to this fact, John Lee reflected on his fortuitous escape from death and looked forward to freedom: 'I wondered what I would be like when release came. I tried to think of all the changes that would probably take place whilst I was in prison: "The time", I said to myself, "will soon pass"' (Lee, 1908).

Queen
Victoria.

As was customary at the time, Lee had to serve a period of solitary confinement at the outset of his sentence. This was spent in two London prisons, Pentonville from 23 March to 10 June 1885 and Wormwood Scrubs from 10 June to 28 October 1885:

'In all my experience of prison life these eight months were the worst. The authorities presumably have reasons for everything they do, but why they should leave a man alone with his thoughts for eight months I cannot possible conceive. Perhaps the object of the solitary confinement is to break the man's spirit' (Lee, 1908).

Transferred to Portsmouth Prison, Lee was employed briefly making hammocks and also laboured on the construction of new docks in the seaport, before spending six and a half years in the prison laundry. Throughout this period of incarceration, rumours were frequently circulated around the globe, alleging that the authorities had acknowledged a miscarriage of justice and secretly freed John Lee. This is a typical example relating the mischievous nonsense telegraphed to Australia by the London correspondent of the *South Australian Advertiser*, which then boomeranged back to England and was regurgitated via the *Pall Mall Gazette* in the *Gloucester Journal*, 6 August 1887:

> A rumour of a most extraordinary and sensational character, which, if true, would seriously shake public confidence in sentences pronounced on circumstantial evidence, is being whispered among the clerks at the Home Office. Some years ago, a young man, a butler named Lee, was sentenced to death for murdering his mistress and benefactress, an elderly maiden lady residing at Babbicombe, near Taunton. The case attracted a lot of attention at the time, and your readers will probably remember the facts well. I may remind them, however, that the lad, all through, stuck firmly to his innocence. . . .
>
> Mark the sequel. It is now said that some months ago one of Lee's fellow servants – the girl who at the trial was suspected of having an illicit lover – confessed to the crime on her deathbed, and satisfied the authorities of Lee's innocence. The unfortunate young man was subsequently released, and pensioned off for life at 30s a week, but not till he had given a solemn undertaking to the prison chaplain not to reveal the truth. The Home Office justify their extraordinary action in the matter on the ground that, if the facts were known, circumstantial evidence in capital cases would practically become a dead letter; and that it is most undesirable, as in ninety cases out of a hundred, conclusions deduced therefore are correct.

Two days before this latest article was published, the new Home Secretary, Henry Matthews, had faced questions in the House of Commons from a member of parliament about the current whereabouts of John Lee, which brought the following weary comment from the *Torquay Times*, 5 August 1887:

> John Lee once more! When are false reports about the Babbacombe murder and its perpetrator to have an end? On Wednesday evening a story was circulated in London to the effect that John Lee had been liberated by the authorities, who had become convinced of his innocence of the crime of which he was convicted. Last evening the Home Secretary was questioned on the subject by Mr. Pickersgill, member for a London constituency. Mr. Matthews, in reply, said that the story was without foundation in fact; Lee is still undergoing his sentence in the convict prison at Portsmouth. Mr. Pickersgill further asked whether the Home Secretary had any information of another person having, under circumstances of peculiar solemnity, confessed to having committed the murder. The Home Secretary replied: 'No, sir; I have no such information as that.'

Henry Matthews 'asked whether [he] had any information of another person having, under circumstances of peculiar solemnity, confessed to having committed the murder. The Home Secretary replied: "No, Sir; I have no such information as that."'

Mr. Pickersgill: 'Is the case of John Lee under consideration at all?' The Home Secretary: 'It is not, sir.' It is much to be desired that forgers of falsehoods on the subject of the Babbacombe tragedy will now 'give it a rest.'

Following the closure of the prison at Portsmouth in 1892, John Lee made a final move to Portland Prison, Dorset. Known as the 'Prison on the Cliffs', inmates laboured in the local quarries and cutting sheds producing the world-famous Portland stone used for buildings and monuments. Discipline was harsh and Portland had a fearsome reputation among convicts, second only to Dartmoor, as the most reviled prison in the country. For many years, John Lee was punishment orderly and witnessed at first hand the inhumane birchings and floggings meted out to prisoners: 'I have seen some terrible objects of bleeding humanity brought back to the punishment cells. Their faces alone – I could hardly look at them – bore testimony to the awful agony they had suffered' (Lee, 1908).

Lee himself avoided such a terrible fate and had an exemplary record during his incarceration. He hoped his good behaviour would reduce his sentence to fifteen years, but he was to be sorely disappointed. He petitioned the Home Secretary annually throughout his sentence, persistently proclaiming his innocence, citing the inadequate arrangements for his defence and recounting his ordeal on the scaffold as extenuating circumstances in his favour. His pleas were always dismissed with the same curt reply, 'No grounds'.

Approaching the twentieth anniversary of the Babbacombe Murder, the London correspondent of the *Washington Post*, 11 October 1904, prematurely anticipated the imminent release of John Lee: 'Dramatic as anything in fiction, not only as a whole, but in every detail, is the story of John Lee, whom men condemned to die, but who is soon to walk the earth in freedom – Providence itself having apparently intervened in his behalf. . . . Lee who is now forty, will come from confinement in good health, except for the nervous attacks from which he has suffered ever since the third attempt to hang him. At Portland Prison he is known as "the man they could not hang" and is quite a hero among his fellow-convicts.'

Although Lee had spent over twenty years in custody since his arrest, it was generally expected that he would be released twenty years to the day sentence had been passed, and a number of articles appeared discussing the prospect. A fellow inmate revealed Lee's plans to write a book in an article which was reproduced in the *Torquay Directory*, 4 January 1905:

Lloyd's Weekly News publishes what purports to be an account of the experiences of an ex-convict recently discharged from Portland Prison. He says:
'One of the first men I spoke to on my arrival from Dartmoor, where I served ten months, was John Lee. We were in the building party together, and we stood together in the ranks to be searched on commencing and leaving off work. He told me he was innocent, and I asked him if it was true that he thought that God had interfered especially on his behalf, and he replied "Yes". I thought to myself at the moment that if ever I should be in such a terrible position I would rather the law took its course, for this man has tasted the bitterness of death three times, and on top of all suffered a living

death for just on twenty years. He seemed to guess the bent of my thoughts, for he said, "I suppose you wonder why He did not get me released?" "Exactly," I replied. "Ah! I shall explain all that in my book," he answered.

'The date of his release will be on January 21st, 1905; or rather, I understand he will have completed twenty years on that day. The regulations say that "a prisoner doing "life" must not hope for release before the expiration of twenty years, when his case will be considered on its merits." . . . Convicts advance the fact of Lee's exceptionally good conduct in prison, and his sister confessing the crime on her death-bed, as circumstances in his favour; but a man's conduct in prison is no guarantee for his behaviour outside it. He is a man who is spoken well of among his fellow-prisoners as being civil and obliging, and they all hope he will be released – a hope which is shared by myself. He seems to think he has the sympathy of the public; in fact, he thinks all sorts of strange things, for I remember a man telling him the best way to lay out ten shillings in enjoyment on his release and his reply was to touch his forehead, and then touch his knickers, where his money ought to be. From this he would lead one to infer that he was the possessor of a huge sagacity, and that he had financial tact.

'He expects to make a vast sum of money by giving lectures and by the sale of his book. He speaks as if he had some tremendous revelations to make, but the only complaint I have heard him utter was that "some ten years ago prisoners were punished for covering their faces up while in bed asleep." God would show him mercy. All he wanted was justice.'

Some further developments, including an interview with John Lee's mother, were discussed in the *Torquay Directory*, 25 January 1905:

John Lee, who was convicted of the murder of Miss Keyse, of The Glen, Babbacombe, in 1884, will this week complete twenty years' imprisonment, and inasmuch as numerous life-sentence prisoners have been released upon the expiration of twenty years' incarceration, it has been fairly generally assumed that Lee would be granted his liberty this week. It was reported a week ago that the release would take place at Exeter on Monday, and in anticipation of the fact London daily papers despatched special representatives to the 'Ever Faithful' city. Others were sent to Portland, where Lee has been confined. Lee's release is however, a matter of doubt and indecision. The only point which appears to be certain is that if he is released at all it will be when the public least expect it. The probabilities are that Lee will never regain absolute personal freedom.

'He expects to make a vast sum of money . . .'

On Saturday the *Daily Mirror* gave a portrait of Lee and an interview which a correspondent had had with his mother, who lives at Abbotskerswell, near Torquay. Mrs Lee told her story – the long waiting, and almost hope of a re-union – with quiet simplicity:

'I have not seen my son for five years, but I have had a letter from him once a month. In the last one, which was dated December 1st, he wrote that the twenty years would be up in January, and then he would petition the Home Secretary for his release. Yet, I do not know. It will be twenty years come the 23rd of February since my son John stood upon the scaffold and escaped death three times. All the folks believe he is coming out on Monday, and I hope it is true, but I have my doubts. When my husband died two years ago, I placed all the photographs we had of our children and ourselves in the coffin with his body. It was agreed between us that whoever died first the survivor was to put all the relics of the family in the coffin, so that they would not fall into the hands of strangers. I do not think he will ever come back here, she concluded. He might appear in public to earn a little money for us to live upon, but too much money is bad for poor folks.'

Meanwhile there comes from York the news, through an interview with Datas, the wonderful 'memory man,' that definite negotiations are being made with John Lee to appear on the stage with Berry, the ex-hangman, who could not hang him.

'The offer has been made on behalf of Mr Graydon, of the Middlesex Music Hall, and myself. The salary we are prepared to offer him is £100 a week.'

The prospect that John Lee might become part of a popular music-hall act was greeted with alarm in some quarters and this 'warning' to the Home Office appeared in the *Star*, 20 January 1905:

The circumstances that the approaching release from serval penitude of John Lee, the Babbacombe murderer who escaped hanging twenty years ago because the gallows three times failed to work, has been first notified to a provincial music-hall performer may be merely the latest instance of Home Office nascensce, but it has the promise of something like a public scandal. It is rumoured that Lee, whose approaching release has been heralded by the publication of fictions about 'the little white bird' which hovered over him on the gallows, is to be exploited on the music-hall stage – whether as hero or martyr does not appear. In these matters of good taste and public decorum we are accustomed to congratulate ourselves on the advance of enlightenment, but we do not remember that the famous 'Half-hanged Smith', who was cut down and resuscitated at Tyburn Tree two centuries ago, was permitted, even in that lax age, to make a public exhibition of himself for money. John Lee has served a term of imprisonment, and if the prison authorities consider it fitting to release him we have nothing to say. But we do protest against his entrepreneurs being permitted to parade him in public in any capacity. In London the L.C.C. [London County Council] supervision of the music-halls, of which so much has been written by the enemies of that body, will make such an exhibition impossible, but in the provinces the local authorities cannot always be depended upon to take similar action. It is for the Home Office then to see that the conditions of John Lee's license absolutely prohibits him – under pain of its revocation – from being exploited in any such indecent manner. That department has been denounced for lack of energy in ordering the release of the innocent; it can surely bestir itself to ensure that the guilty do not trade upon their guilt. We do not grudge John Lee his freedom – or his recollections – but his place is in private life, and not in the limelight.

Rumours of John Lee's imminent release proved unfounded, and the general public's disappointment was recorded by the *News of the World*, 29 January 1905:

> Despite the fact that John Lee, the Babbacombe murderer, who survived three attempted executions, has completed his twentieth year of imprisonment, he was not released from Portland Prison. His release was generally expected in the district, and large crowds assembled at Weymouth Railway Station to meet the Portland trains, and more than one unfortunate man was mistaken for the convict. But Lee himself did not arrive. He is at present working on the scaffolding of a new building in the prison. He ranks as a first-class prisoner, and has recently been an assistant librarian. When not so engaged, he was either acting as prison barber, or serving out tools to his fellow-prisoners. As his period of deliverance draws near, Lee, who himself expects to be liberated on the 28th, grows more melancholy. His long separation from the world has made him almost dread his return to the busy haunts of men. When he will regain liberty is unknown. A high official recalled the case of Ruddiford, who was sentenced to death for shooting a gamekeeper in Gloucestershire, and served a commuted sentence of 24 years. It is quite possible, he added, that Lee will not be liberated for some time.

When denied his freedom, Lee was bitterly disappointed and in a letter to Stephen Bryan, a sympathiser, blamed the article which had appeared in *Lloyd's Weekly News* written by a former Portland inmate, L226 Walker. This intimated, Lee wrote, that 'I intended to exhibit myself and show up the authorities, which was false, I never spoke six words to the man. He did ask me the day before he went home, if he could do anything for me and I told him no. I told him that I should be outside myself in a few weeks. Of course, he did this for money and I have to suffer for what another does or says' (Bryan Letters, Exeter Prison Museum).

John Lee now launched an orchestrated campaign for his release. This was not without its difficulties in Edwardian days. Communication with the outside world was particularly difficult. Prisoners did not have the modern conveniences of radio, television or telephone cards. Newspapers were prohibited, and inmates had access only to selected magazines, with articles deemed unsuitable reading material removed by the prison authorities. Letter writing was severely restricted and heavily censored. Prisoners were allowed few visitors and conversations were always monitored. For years, Lee's parents made the long journey to Portland. They were permitted to see their son once every three months and allowed to stay for a period of only thirty minutes. In June 1894, John Lee's father wrote to Charles Seale-Hayne, explaining that he was a poor man and the cost of the prison visits was prohibitive. He asked the MP's assistance in obtaining permission to visit the prison just once a year and remain for one hour. The letter was passed to the Home Secretary, who flatly turned down the request.

It was a bitter blow to Lee when first his sister Amelia, then his father did not survive to see him freed, but his widowed mother fought on alone for her son's cause and gave

Charles Seale-Hayne. The MP's assistance was sought by John Lee's parents over prison visits.

her cooperation to the Manchester *Sunday Chronicle* for a sympathetic series of articles lasting four weeks. The final instalment on 5 March 1905 published an extract from a letter (surprisingly unsuppressed) written by Lee to his mother on 23 February – the twentieth anniversary of the day he had been supposed to die:

Ask a member of Parliament to ask the Home Secretary in Parliament when I am going to be released from prison. He is bound to give the member an answer. He cannot say he does not know.

I wish you would write to all the newspapers, and also get up a public petition for me. I am sure there are hundreds and thousands of people in England and Ireland would sign it, because they believe that I am innocent of the crime. It is a great consolation to me to know that most people believe in my innocence.

I don't suppose there has been a man in any country made to go through, and suffer, the same as they have made me go through. This is some of it:– Nearly three months waiting trial; sentence of death passed upon me; three weeks under that awful sentence;

three times led to the gallows (each of these times the trap did drop and left me standing upon my heels and toes); taken back to my cell. That same and the following days I was taken out and made to exercise in the sight of the grave dug to receive my body.

For four weeks I was kept in the terrible suspense of being put to it again at any hour during that time, before the Governor of Exeter Prison came and told me that Her Majesty the Queen had been pleased to commute my sentence to penal servitude for life. He told me that it was twenty years. I have done twenty years with good character, and now they think that I have not suffered enough. They will not release me, nor hold out any hopes of release. Twenty years today it pleased God to save me from a horrible death, but death is preferable to twenty years in prison.

John Lee, L150

Harry Eve MP.

In response to this plea, the Home Office received correspondence from several members of parliament who had been urged by the public to campaign for Lee's release. Officials were clearly rattled and an enigmatic internal memo noted: 'There seems to be a frail canvas about this man. I have had at least twenty members inquiring . . .'. However, Harry Eve, the member for the prisoner's home constituency, responded apologetically after receiving a request on behalf of Mary Lee from solicitor Herbert Armstrong Rowse:

13 March 1905

Dear Mr Home Secretary,

I am sorry to trouble you but in my constituency lives the mother & some other relatives of the convict John Lee who was sentenced some 20 years or so ago for the murder of Miss Keyse at Babbacombe. I believe three attempts were made to carry out the sentence at Exeter Gaol but without success.

Would you please read the enclosed communication which has reached me from the solicitor who has been writing for the mother & tell me if anything can be done in the matter.

I feel it is too bad to bother you but I am in rather an awkward position as Miss Keyse was an acquaintance of me & my family & if I do nothing it will perhaps be said that I am influenced by prejudice against the convict.

So I venture to trouble you & will apologise for so doing.

I remain
Yours faithfully
Harry T. Eve

(HO 144/1712//A60789/33)

Charles Fenwick MP was told by the Home Secretary that 'this convict had constantly repeated threats against the lives of many now living'.

Eventually, questions about Lee were raised in the House of Commons and reported in *The Times*, 28 March 1905:

Mr. FENWICK . . . asked the Home Secretary whether his attention had been called to the case of John Lee, who was convicted in February, 1885, for the Babbicombe murder and sentenced to death, which sentence was afterwards commuted to one of penal servitude for life; and whether, having regard to the fact that Lee had now served a period of 20 years' imprisonment, he could see his way to advise that the clemency of the Crown could be exercised in favour of this man's release.

Mr. ACKERS-DOUGLAS . . . I have fully considered the facts of this case; but I regret that, having regard to the character of Lee's crime, and to the circumstances under which the capital sentence was respited, I cannot advise any exercise of the Royal Prerogative in the convict's favour. Perhaps I may say that, while persons under original sentence of penal servitude for life are as a general rule released on licence when they have served 20 years, this practice does not necessarily apply to cases where a death sentence for murder has been commuted to penal servitude for life; but each case is considered independently on its merits. . . .

Mr. ACKERS-DOUGLAS added that the case had been brought up for consideration from time to time. Sir W. Harcourt considered it a very bad case indeed. Other predecessors in the Home Office all agreed with the Secretary of State who originally considered the case. Besides considering the original facts of the case, he had to consider that this convict had constantly repeated threats against the lives of many now living.

This last point by the Home Secretary concerning alleged 'threats' was completely unjustified, and when Lee was told about the comments by a friendly prison warder, he raised the matter with the visiting Board of Magistrates and was totally exonerated of the charge – although the result of the inquiry was not made public. The real reason for Lee's continued incarceration, overlooked by the prisoner himself, was addressed by the parliamentary correspondent of the *Daily Mail*, 28 March 1905: 'People forget that the case is all together different from those of other murderers. Lee was not reprieved because the merits of his case justified the step, but because of the miserable bungle which was made in attempting to hang him.'

When a further appeal for release was turned down in 1906, Lee naturally became despondent and hinted at suicide. Concerned, the authorities summoned Dr Brayn, Superintendent, Broadmoor Criminal Lunatic Asylum, and Dr Smalley, Medical Inspector of Prisons, to assess his mental state, which they duly reported to the Home Office, 26 September 1906:

In accordance with your instructions we have the honour to report that we visited Portland Prison on the 24th September and examined the convict John Lee, with reference to his present mental and physical condition.

We carefully went into the notes of his history during the period of his detention in Portland and fully discussed his case with the Governor and Medical Officer of the Prison.

With regard to his bodily health he made no special complaint, and physical examination revealed no evidence of active organic disease. His body weight is well maintained and his general health appears to be now satisfactory.

As regards his mental condition, he entered readily into conversation respecting his prison life and occupation, displaying considerable intelligence and shrewdness in his remarks. We were unable to elicit any sign or indication of mental derangement. He was cheerful in demeanour, exhibiting no undue emotion or symptom of depression.

Both the Governor and Medical Officer informed us that the prisoner is now more contented and decidedly less morose than he was a few months ago.

From what these Officers told us we think that Lee felt thoroughly convinced in his own mind that he would obtain his release on completing 20 years' imprisonment, and that he was (naturally we venture to think) much disappointed, depressed and somewhat irritable at finding his hopes were not realised. This state of mind appears to have, to a great extent, now passed away, but the Governor is of the opinion that the improvement is partially due to the revival of his hopes of his ultimate release, more especially since his last interview with the Board of Visitors.

As a result of our examination and enquiry, we have come to the conclusion there is no reason to suppose that imprisonment has, up to the present time, injuriously affected John Lee's bodily or mental health. Should, however, he come to the conclusion that it is intended to detain him for the period of his natural life and thereby lose all hope of ever regaining his liberty he might give in to despair, and such morbid condition would doubtless increase the risk of mental depression which, if unrelieved, might possibly develop into actual melancholia. We would observe that even in the event of such mental deterioration or depression setting in, it is unlikely to arise suddenly; it would probably be of slow and gradual development, giving sufficient warning of its approach to enable its being called attention to and dealt with.

The prisoner expressed himself as being quite satisfied with his prison treatment, but seemed to feel his being cut off from seeing his Mother and stated he would be happier and more contented if he could be transferred to Dartmoor where his Mother could visit him occasionally. (PCOM 8/87 – XC12455)

Earlier that month, Lee was informed that permission had been granted to Stephen Bryan, of Leigh, near Manchester, to write to him. The correspondent had petitioned the King, the Home Secretary and several members of parliament on the prisoner's behalf since reading about his plight in the *Sunday Chronicle*. After an exchange of letters Lee thanked his ally for his considerable efforts:

Portland Prison
28 March 1907

Dear Sir,

I am very thankful to have the pleasure of answering your most kind and welcome letter that I received on the 7th February. I thank you Sir, very much for all your kindness to my Dear Mother and myself. My Dear Mother tells me in her letters that you are so kind as to write to her every week. I am sure that is most kind and noble of you to take such an interest. Also, your kindness in that you have kept petitioning to the Home Secretary for my release. Dear Sir, I gleaned from your beautiful letters that whatever rank of life you hold at present, that you did rise from the noble British Workman which is the backbone of the English Nation. And I must say Dear Sir, that it is very noble of you to come forward and to intercede for my Dear Mother and myself in our hour of need, both to His Majesty King Edward and Mr. Gladstone, the Home Secretary. Whether you succeed or not in my release from prison, you may rest assured Dear Sir, the God Almighty will remember it. I shall be forty-three years of age in August next, so that there is not much difference in our ages. You are Dear Sir, comparatively speaking, quite a young man yet. But I am afraid that the trouble and the long sentence which I have done in prison will make me appear more of a man of fifty years of age than forty-three.

My Dear Mother is about the same age as your own Dear Mother. Dear Sir, I hope that it will please Almighty God to keep your Dear Mother in good health and to spare her to you for many years to come yet. If it pleases God that I am released, I must come and visit you and thank you for all that you have done for me and mine. And I should like to have a good talk with you and your Dear Mother. As I do not see any sign yet of being released, I have asked my Dear Mother to come and see me when the weather is warm enough to do so comfortably. You see, life is so very uncertain that we do not know whether we shall have the pleasure of meeting again on Earth. My Dear Father & Mother both wanted to come and visit me in 1901, but I would not let them, because everyone thought that I would have been released in 1902. And as I was not, my Dear Father died in September 1902. After living so long he was not spared to see me out. And if I do not see my Dear Mother this summer, I may not see her again on Earth. I wrote to my Dear Mother the twenty-first of this month. I have not heard from Mr. Howell [another sympathiser, said by Lee to be an adviser to the King, who prompted Mr Fenwick to raise the case in Parliament] and I do not know his address. I thank you again Dear Sir, for all that you have done for me and my Dear Mother.

I wish to remain your most humble and obedient servant,

John Lee

(Bryan Letters, Exeter Prison Museum)

Inmate Fred Farmer, a trusted confidant of John Lee, left prison with instructions to join the campaign and he immediately made contact with Stephen Bryan:

Portland Prison – the 'Prison on the Cliffs'.

22 Wesley Road, Leyton, Essex
5 May 1907

Mr Stephen Bryan,

I thank you very much for your nice long letter and also all you have done for poor John Lee.

I do not think that any petition to the Home Secretary is any use. He has refused every one that has been sent to him. Someone has said that John used threats, but he told me he had never done so. However, the Home Office evidently believes he has. Some wicked person has made a false statement about him and so the authorities are keeping him in prison. It is a great shame after all he has gone through. He has completed 22 years of imprisonment last January besides going through the awful suffering of trying to hang him three times. He maintains he is an innocent man, but of course, very few people believe him. However, even if he is guilty, he has surely been punished enough. He has borne an excellent character all the time he has been in prison and that ought to have got him out. Other murderers are released after 15 years if their conduct has been good. And why not John Lee?

I think if we could get a good paper to take his case up and get a lot of petitions from the public for his release it would help him most. For any one person to write to the Home Secretary or the Queen is clearly of no use. That has been tried, as you know, many times and has failed. Or, if some strong Member of Parliament would take his case up it would be of great help. I have tried one or two London papers but they won't.

We also want a good solicitor to work for him in getting petitions from the public, but that of course wants money, and we have none. I am still out of work myself unfortunately. It is almost impossible for a convicted man to get on again – such is the world. I have written tonight to poor Mrs Lee and sent her your letter to me to read. Mr Howell has not answered my last letter to him. I shall be very pleased to hear from you again.

Yours respectfully,
Fred Farmer

(Bryan Letters, Exeter Prison Museum)

Stephen Bryan published a letter from John Lee in his local paper and sent a copy of the article to Fred Farmer before receiving the following reply:

London, June 1907

Dear Sir,

I have been very much interested in reading the paragraphs which appeared in the *Leigh Journal* on May 23 last about John Lee in connection with the Babbicombe murder, and also in reading John Lee's letter to you, which was published in the same paper. Poor Lee seems very grateful to you for all you have done for him, and I hope you will be able to continue to work on his behalf until his release has been obtained. It is very gratifying that an influential paper like the *Leigh Journal* should concern itself about him.

I know John Lee well, having been with him in Portland in the same working party, and am acquainted with the full history of his case. As you are aware, he completed 22 years of continuous imprisonment on January 28th last, and when you consider the three attempts to hang him, and what terrible punishment that was itself, apart from the imprisonment, I am sure you and all reasonable people will admit that he has fully expiated his crime and ought to be released. I am quite sure that there are many thousands in England who would sign a petition on his behalf, if it were put before them. And in no part of the country could such a petition be more successfully launched than in Lancashire with its thousands of warm hearted and outspoken people. If you could induce your Editor to take the case up in earnest I am sure it would meet with hearty response from all his readers.

John Lee's case cries aloud for Justice. Other men and women convicted of murder have been released after 15 years. And why not Lee? Then think of the awful fiasco of the hanging. He has described his sufferings to me at that time. If your fellow citizens saw a man making such a bungle over hanging a cat and causing it such pain they would lynch him, I am sure. Let people realise, if they can, what it is to be led to the scaffold three times. When Lee was taken down after the third failure, he was more dead than alive.

He has all along been a most exemplary character in prison and has the sympathy and good wishes of everyone in Portland.

Believe me, yours respectfully,

Fred Farmer

(Bryan Letters, Exeter Prison Museum)

Following the collapse of the Conservative government under Arthur Balfour in December 1905, the Liberal Party swept to power and incoming Prime Minister Sir Henry Campbell-Bannerman appointed Herbert Gladstone as Home Secretary. He was the son of William Gladstone, who had been premier at the time of the execution debacle of Lee. The incoming Secretary of State received a well-researched document (dated 16 March 1906) on the case from Charles Nicholson, newly elected MP for the Doncaster division of the Yorkshire West Riding, which concluded:

If John Lee is innocent he is the most ill-used man on earth. . . . If he is guilty is it not right that the exceptional agonies he was made to suffer should be taken into consideration as grounds for mercy at this eleventh hour? He was a boy then. After twenty-one years of imprisonment he is 41. What is the use of keeping him longer until he is too old to make a start of any kind whatever in the outside world? He is now in good health and may live to be eighty. Is he to be kept in prison till he dies? If not the sooner he is liberated, the better for himself and for Society. . . . It is hoped that the new Home Secretary will go into the case apart altogether from previous decisions of the department. . . . (HO 144/1712//A60789/64)

After deliberating long and hard, Herbert Gladstone eventually agreed with Charles Nicholson's assessment and addressed the following decision to Sir Mackenzie Chambers, Under-Secretary for Home Affairs:

Herbert Gladstone: 'If it is decided that he shall be released, it is best to do it at once.'

15 August 1907

Sir,

Mr Chambers – Lee's case has now been under my close consideration for more than a year. It is true that he was guilty of a most abominable crime. It is also true that 'he has received a tremendous punishment.' Had he been executed it would have been a speedy release. As it was, he underwent the terms of death three times. And subsequent to the third time there was a period of suspense when his life hung in the balance. He did not know whether he should not face death a fourth time. At the close of this year he will have served 23 years penal servitude.

The view expressed by Sir William Harcourt must be treated with the utmost care for the reason that the decision to respite was in a sense conditional on Lee's imprisonment being maintained for the period of his life. At the same time I do not consider that such a decision can necessarily bind Sir William Harcourt's successors twenty years later. I can understand that the horror in the public mind of Lee's crime made ordinary remission difficult even under the extraordinary circumstances which occurred. Again, such a decision could be adhered to if opinion and practice, as regards very long sentences, underwent alteration. I consider therefore, that I am entitled to exercise my own judgement on the case by the light of present facts and views.

Lee is now 43. Imprisonment for the rest of his life would inevitably mean sooner or later – and from recent reports probably soon – mental and bodily decay. Then perhaps a decision to release him would be arrived at. And he would leave prison a wreck of a man. I cannot think this would be right. If that being so it becomes merely a question as to when he should be released before that stage of final decay sets in. It seems to me rather useless to decide in a compute period of time of 25 or 30 years. If it is decided that he shall be released, it is best to do it at once. I have today consulted Mr. Asquith [Deputy Leader of the Commons] on the case and he agrees with the view that I have formed that he may be discharged on licence at the end of the year, say, before Christmas.

It may be well to transfer him from Portland to Dartmoor at once. As to when he should be informed, this depends on the opinion and advice of Prison Authorities. Clearly strict conditions must be made, otherwise the press and music halls will get hold of him. It may be impossible to prevent the press from making use of him but he can be stopped from making public appearances should he be tempted by offers sure to be made to him.

– H.J. Gladstone

(HO 144/1712//A60789/100)

It was decided to allow Lee to sell his story, which the Home Office believed would be nothing more than 'a passing sensation'. However, although James Berry and the Reverend Pitkin were in great demand to lecture on their experiences at the infamous execution, Lee, under the terms of his licence, faced the prospect of losing his liberty unless he observed four standard conditions and a fifth added specifically to prevent him from trading on his notoriety:

1. The Holder shall preserve his Licence, and produce it when called upon to do so by a Magistrate or Police Officer.
2. He shall abstain from any violation of the Law.
3. He shall not habitually associate with notoriously bad characters, such as reputed thieves and prostitutes.
4. He shall not lead an idle and dissolute life, without visible means of obtaining an honest livelihood.
5. He shall not take part in any public performances or deliver any lectures or speech, or in any way exhibit himself at any meeting, assembly or place of entertainment.

If his Licence is forfeited or revoked in consequence of a conviction for any Offence, he will be liable to undergo a Term of Penal Servitude for Life.

(HO144/1712//A60.789/100)

Lee was informed that release was imminent, and he was now allowed to let his hair grow. He had recently had dentures fitted to replace the eleven teeth he had lost in prison. As Christmas approached he sent a cautious message to his mother:

21 November 1907

Dear Mother,
I hope I shall be home soon. I do not know how or when. Keep up a good heart. Do not tell anyone. Goodbye.
John Lee (L150)

(Lee, 1908)

'a strange, middle-aged man . . . entered a cottage kept by an elderly woman named Lee'.

In utmost secrecy, John Lee was released on 18 December, escorted by a chief warder and his wife who were travelling to spend Christmas in Torquay. Although he would later claim that the prison authorities prevented him from letting his mother know in advance, he in fact chose to turn up unannounced to spring a surprise on her. Rumours quickly circulated about his homecoming and pressmen gathered outside the family home in Abbotskerswell. News of his arrival was reported in the *Torquay Directory*, 25 December 1907:

> Wednesday afternoon there drove in a cab to the South Devon Village of Abbotskerswell, obviously from Newton Abbot, a strange, middle-aged man, who entered a cottage kept by an elderly woman named Lee. Ere evening there arrived in Torquay the news that the stranger was no other than John Lee, who, in 1885, was sentenced to death for the murder of Miss Keyse at Babbacombe. Lee was not hung, though he ascended the scaffold at Exeter. The fact is that he lives today, in a commonly-expressed term, as 'the man the hangman could not hang'. The circumstances of the abortive execution have rendered Lee's case notorious in the annals of crime. Now, after existing in prison from young manhood to middle-age, he is free, and with his delighted and thankful mother at Abbotskerswell. On Wednesday night and on Thursday a little army of journalists from Torquay, Newton Abbot, Plymouth, Exeter and London invaded Abbotskerswell, to interview either Mrs Lee or her son or both, but even when Mrs Lee could be seen she refused to have anything to say.
>
> 'Well, Mrs Lee, what can you tell me?' queried a London pressman,
> 'Nothing,' replied Mrs Lee.
> 'Nothing?'
> 'Nothing'
> 'Sure?'
> 'Sure.'
>
> So it was to all as to one – save to the representative of one London newspaper, which it is said, despatched to Abbotskerswell post haste an emissary to 'buy' Lee's exclusive story. If the rumour be true, the silence of Mrs Lee and her son is easily understandable.

CHAPTER 8

Lady killer

I have dozens of sweethearts [aged] from fifteen to forty.
– John Lee, 1908

Within hours of arriving home, Lee was locked in negotiations to relate 'the story of the Babbacombe Murder, his awful experiences on the scaffold, and his 23 years' prison life', which, beginning on 29 December 1907, was serialised in weekly episodes by a mass-circulation Sunday newspaper, *Lloyd's Weekly News*. After spending only one full day at his mother's cottage, he was whisked away to London by the paper's representative and did not return to Abbotskerswell until Christmas Eve.

Apart from a brief account of his early life and a telling insight into the oppressive regime conducted in English prisons, Lee made no startling revelations about the crime he had been accused of in his published account. He simply reiterated his innocence, insisting that he had neither heard nor seen anything on the night of the murder: 'I say again that I slept soundly whilst every blow in that terrible murder was being struck, whilst all the other deeds that were afterwards discovered were being done' (Lee, 1908).

For anyone who had difficulty believing that he had been totally unaware of the attack on Emma Keyse, he cited a recent case, which had been reported in his local paper, the *East and South Devon Advertiser*, 28 December 1907: 'Gunner Charles Billington, a native of Bristol, was found lying partially on his bed in a barrack-room in Dover Castle with his head nearly severed from his body, as if by a razor. Companions were sleeping on each side of him, but they heard nothing during the night.'

The prospects for Lee's future were addressed in the *Western Morning News*, 20 December 1907:

> Lee is described as looking very well. He is clean-shaven, and has a very mild demeanour. Those who have spoken to him describe him as in good spirits and revealing a somewhat religious frame of mind. How long he is likely to remain at home with his mother and what are his prospects or intentions for the future, in regard to earning a livelihood, is being kept more or less a secret; but, although an air of mystery is being maintained in this respect, there is every reason to believe Lee has had a number of tempting offers made to him to appear on public platforms and relate some of his prison experiences. That he is a keen businessman is evident from the hard bargains which he is understood to have driven with certain people who flocked to the cottage yesterday. . . .

'How long he is likely to remain at home with his mother and what are his prospects or intentions for the future . . . is being kept more or less a secret . . .'

The deal struck by Lee with *Lloyd's* was revealed by the *East and South Devon Advertiser*, 21 December 1907: 'We hear that John Lee has sold the copyright to publish his experience in prison, for a large sum of money – said to be £240.'

Having received an advance which would take an average worker four or five years to earn, there was no immediate need for Lee to seek employment, especially after enduring so many years 'hard labour' in the stone quarries of Portland. The fee made him a man of means and an eligible bachelor. However, any hopes of a romantic reunion with his former fiancée Katie Farmer were crushed when she made the following announcement to the press:

He has suffered. I hope his future life will be happy. His way will not be my way, for I am now settled in life after my vicissitudes. I hope he may be able to prove his innocence . . .

Before I go on with my story this week I want to express my heartfelt thanks to "Lloyd's News" and its readers for all that is being done in my interests.

Since last Sunday I have received hundreds of Christmas Cards, Letters, and gifts from all parts of the Country. I am astonished at the kindly Sympathy with which the simple narrative of my sufferings has been received

How I would like to take all those dear people by the hand! I am only a poor unhappy man. But I have a heart and it is overflowing with gratitude.

God bless you all in 1908

John Lee.

John Lee's gratitude to readers of *Lloyd's*.

I was then a silly sentimental girl, and did not know my own mind. I am wiser now . . . I remember most vividly the last time I saw him. It was at the inquest. I recall he walked with his head in the air, although he was in such deadly peril. He recognised me and smiled, and said, 'Goodbye, my dear.' Those words were the last words I heard him utter. He never sent a letter from prison to me, and never asked me to visit him in Portland. . . . My friends told me that Lee would be kept in prison as long as he lived, and a life's devotion would be thrown away. So I put him out of my heart. (Honeycombe, 1993)

Kate Pomeroy: 'I was then a silly sentimental girl . . . I am wiser now . . .'.

Katie's 'vicissitudes' had continued a little over a year after the trial of John Lee, when she married James Parrish, a former seaman, who had set up in business as a mineral water manufacturer in St Marychurch. The marriage took place in May 1886, but lasted barely five years before ending with a touch of scandal reported by the *Totnes Times and Gazette*, 2 May 1891:

Interest in the Babbacombe murder of 1884 is, says a correspondent, being revived by the disappearance from St. Marychurch of a married woman named Parrish, the whilom sweetheart of John Lee, who was condemned to death for the murder, but whose sentence was commuted to one of imprisonment during her Majesty's pleasure, after several attempts had been made to carry out the capital sentence. A smack of romance is given to the case by the fact that simultaneously with the disappearance of Mrs Parrish, a painter named Pomeroy, of the same place was missed, and that neither has since returned. Not unnaturally, the names of the two are now generally associated, although there is little evidence to support the theory of an elopement. It is believed that the missing woman is at present located at Plymouth. Her husband was, strange to say, a witness in the case of the murder of James Carey, the informer in the Phoenix Park tragedy [the murder of the British chief secretary of Ireland and his deputy, 6 May 1882].

Further details of the doomed marriage appeared in this 'extract from a Torquay paper', reproduced in the memoirs of the Reverend John Pitkin:

Her husband, James Parrish, like herself, had been an important witness in a startling murder trial. The case against the Irish Invincibles [a nationalist group], for the assassination of Lord Frederick Cavendish and Mr. Burke in Phoenix Park, Dublin, was practically affirmed by the statement of James Carey, who belonged to them, and turned Queen's evidence. After the trial the government sent Carey to South Africa to try and save his life, but when the vessel which carried Carey was near the Cape, a man named

Donald, assassinated him. Parrish, being one of the ship's crew, helped to disarm Donald, and returned to Ireland to give evidence against him. After this, Parrish renounced the seafaring life and, marrying Kate Farmer, settled down at West Hill, St Marychurch, where he got a living by doing odd jobs and attending to a skittle-alley, etc. They seemed to live a fairly happy life, but on a certain Friday, just as the funeral knell was being tolled for Jane Neck, one of the chief witnesses against Lee, who had died aged seventy-seven, it was reported in St Marychurch that Mrs Parrish had disappeared. The husband, on his return home on the Friday, found a note from his wife awaiting him, informing him that she had left him and gone far away. (Pitkin, 1918)

Katie fled to Plymouth, the birthplace of her new love, painter and decorator Frederick Pomeroy, and three years later she gave birth to their daughter, named Daisy.

James Parrish gave evidence at a murder trial.

Happily remarried, she had no wish to rekindle a relationship with her old sweetheart. However, Lee soon found there was no shortage of females willing to make an 'honest man' of a convicted lady killer. Far from being shunned by the public as a reviled murderer, he was treated like a celebrity, particularly by women. One man who got to know Lee well during this period was Frank Wood, a tailor who owned a shop in Queen Street, Newton Abbot. Many years later, he recounted his memories of 'the strangest customer he ever had' in an interview with the *Torquay Times*, 13 March 1936:

Everywhere he went a crowd followed him – a crowd largely composed of women, who almost went mad with excitement when they saw the tall figure in the streets. Young girls rushed to kiss his hand, while others begged for a handshake or a smile. . . . His fascination for women was enormous.

On one occasion . . . he called Mr Wood on one side and produced a bundle of fifty or sixty letters from a cupboard. All the letters were from women, married, unmarried, middle-aged matrons, and young girls who sympathised with him.

Lee was by no means adverse to their advances and would often return after a trip and recount in his boasting way of the good time he had had.

In Newton Abbot, tradesmen's wives, milliners' assistants, and stolid country milkmaids, were all under his spell and fought with each other to get closer to him.

In February 1908, Stephen Bryan read newspaper reports claiming that John Lee owned a tobacconist's shop in Newton Abbot and had become engaged to be married and wrote to Lee asking if these developments were true. In reply, he obtained an insight into the attraction Lee had for the fair sex despite being convicted of murdering a woman:

Abbotskerswell
3 March 1908

As regards what you saw in the paper about my being engaged, to tell the truth I am writing to a young lady 250 miles away from my home and we may become engaged later on. But I write to dozens of Ladies, Widows and all. It was all over town that I was marrying a Widow. I only went to Tea once with her, she is a very nice person but still I do not take a fancy yet to Widows. One Widow has written and offered me six acres of land and six children and says marriages are made in heaven and we are made for one another. I have dozens of sweethearts [aged] from fifteen to forty but my young lady is only 22 years of age. It is wrong about my taking a Tobacconists Shop. I have been offered a job in one with good pay. I do not know whether I shall accept it yet or not.

John Lee
(Bryan Letters, Exeter Prison Museum)

John Lee's 'report card' at Newton Abbot police station.

Despite this admission that he had good prospects of marriage and had turned down a good offer of employment, Lee presented another version of his circumstances to the Home Secretary. Taking exception to continually having to report his whereabouts to the police, he attempted to be excused from this procedure by exaggerating his struggle to support himself and his 'poor old Mother':

Abbotskerswell
16 March 1908

Sir,

I beg of you in your well known clemency. To kindly remove those obligations of my release from prison off me. On these grounds I ask for their removal. That for the last six years of my imprisonment my poor old Mother was on the parish pay. And as soon I came home I got a few pounds. And I took her off the parish.

Now so long as I am a Ticket of Leave man, no-one will employ me, and my money will soon be all gone. I am forced to give a Newton Abbot photographer permission to sell postcard photo's of myself now to get money. And if those obligations are not removed I shall be forced to break my conditions and go Lecturing to get a living for my poor old Mother and myself.

I hope that you in your clemency will in your well known humanity & power see fit to remove the Ticket of Leave. That I may be able to get employment. And your petitioner will ever pray.

John Lee

(HO 144/1712//A60789/108)

Home Office officials were wary of Lee's cynical ploy, and on his failure to find work an internal memo commented 'how hard has he tried'. Lee's submission was branded 'implausible' as he 'entirely ignores the possibility of reporting by letter', but nevertheless, aware that 'the case requires most careful handling' to avoid a 'predictable outcry', they decided upon a cautious response by instructing the Chief Constable of Devon, Captain Herbert Reginald Vyvian, to see Lee and 'ascertain what efforts he is making to obtain employment and whether there is any real reason to think that the requirement as to reporting stands in his way' (HO 144/1712//A60789/108).

The Chief Constable telegraphed details of the outcome of his subsequent meeting with Lee to Home Secretary Herbert Gladstone:

Chief Constable's Office, Exeter
31 March 1908

I interviewed John Lee personally yesterday and informed that while wishing to give him every opportunity of getting good employment his liberty would probably be curtailed in the event of his breaking the terms of his licence. The man appears to me to be rather imbued with an exalted opinion of his power of rights, which he has no doubt received from a number of people from all parts, who have written to him on the subject of his release. He hinted to me that he was shortly going to bring pressure to bear on yourself for the purpose of having his ticket of leave revoked and be made a free man.

I do not in any way trust this man, he tells me he refused two offers of work as he would not accept them while still being a ticket of leave man. I do not believe him and am of the opinion that his idea is to go lecturing on his own innocence & the sins of others – as an easy means of livelihood. (HO 144/1712//A60789/110)

As Lee had mentioned in his letter to the Home Office on 16 March, he had initiated a small enterprise, marketing postcards of himself. Despite being incarcerated for more than half his life, he displayed a surprising amount of business acumen when Stephen Bryan informed him that Herbert Norris, the professional photographer engaged on his behalf, was breaking their agreement:

HERBERT NORRIS,

PRACTICAL PORTRAIT, LANDSCAPE, and ARCHITECTURAL PHOTOGRAPHER,

18, Queen Street, NEWTON ABBOT.

Group Specialist.

At Home Photography.

Artist in Water Colours and Monochrome.

Composite Photography of Business Premises for Note Headings and Billheads.

Awards :—Gold Medal Diploma, 1901 ; Diploma of Merit, 1905 ; V.H.C., Grantham, 1906 ; 3rd Prize, Plymouth, 1908.

Established 20 years (1912).

Abbotskerswell
8 April 1908

Dear Mr. Bryan,

I am sorry to say after reading Mr. Norris' letter which he has written to you, I shall stop all sales of my photos, both at Newton Abbot and all the world. Because I do not think that Mr. Norris is straight forward. He wrote to me some four weeks ago to know if I would allow him to sell Cabinet size photos of myself. And I wrote back and told him no. Now I find he has offered to do you Cabinet size for 1 shilling each. That looks very much like underhand work and that sort of thing I detest. I am straight forward myself and like other people to be. I am going in to Mr. Norris this morning and stop all sale of my photos. He also says that the copyright belongs to him on his letter to you. But they belong to me, I have paid for them at Stationers Hall. I am sorry that this should have happened because I know you are a straight forward man and I would like to do you a good turn for your great kindness. But I have finished with Mr. Norris. And I shall put in an advertisement in the News of the World – any person found selling the photo of John Lee 'The Man They Could Not Hang' will be prosecuted after the 11 April, and any persons giving information of the same will be rewarded. I am going and see Mr. Norris today and speak very plainly about his conduct. (Bryan Letters, Exeter Prison Museum)

Although profiting from his criminal infamy, the 'straight forward' Lee was not about to tolerate transgressions in others and Stephen Bryan was soon informed that Herbert Norris's underhand activities had been brought to a halt:

Abbotskerswell
9 May 1908

Mr. Norris was in a way when I stopped him selling any photos. He should have acted straight forward. He wrote to me and said he had written to the solicitor at Stationers Hall to see if the copyright was mine and I was not to do anything until he had consulted his solicitor. So I went straight to mine and he soon put a stop to Mr. Norris and made him destroy the negatives so that he could not take any more photos. (Bryan Letters, Exeter Prison Museum)

Lee also told Bryan that he had spent the previous two weeks in Brighton. This time had been spent in the company of the unnamed 22-year-old young lady, whom he had referred to three months earlier, when discussing his marriage prospects. When the wedding plans were finalised, Lee notified the Home Secretary:

Abbotskerswell
20 May 1908

Sir

I have been offered marriage by a lady who has sufficient means to live independently. If you will be so kind as to remove the Ticket Of Leave. So that we can live quietly without going to report myself to the police. I do not want for all the street looking at me

John Lee: 'I have been offered marriage by a lady who has sufficient means to live independently.'

and coming to shake hands. We shall be living out of Devonshire and if it would be legal, I would like to change my name after marriage to the name of Harris, my mother's maiden name. And I would inform you of my place of residence so that you can send a confidential official to see that everything was correct. Your petitioner would humbly ask you to keep this matter private. And if you would be so kind as to give him an early reply to the above petition. (HO 144/1712//A60789/112)

Herbert Gladstone welcomed this news but, sensibly, waited to see some positive proof of Lee's matrimonial intentions before acceding to the bridegroom's request:

> Home Office
> 29 May 1908

> If it is a fact that Lee is about to marry, I think he should be relieved of the obligation to report. Marriage is a better substance of conduct and may well be given the best start. Ask the Chief Constable to inform Lee that if and when he marries I will favourably consider his application. (HO 144/1712//A60789/112)

However, the Home Office did not hear from Lee again until August when he wrote 'asking to be relieved of the obligation of his licence' as he had been at liberty for a period of eight months and 'did not visit any public house' or 'keep low company'. Puzzled, the Home Office decided to 'enquire confidentially of the Chief Constable of Devon whether he [Lee] is yet married and ask for report of his conduct and mode of living generally'. The Chief Constable soon discovered that Lee's marriage plans had fallen through, although he appeared to have quickly recovered from the setback:

> Chief Constable's Office, Exeter
> 16 August 1908

> I have the honour to acknowledge the receipt of your letter of the 13th instant re: licence holder, John Lee, and to inform you that Lee is not yet married and gives as his reason that the lady would not marry him in consequence of Mr Gladstone not having taken off his ticket of leave after six months.
>
> About two months since I gave Lee permission to go to Brighton to get married without reporting himself to the Brighton Police and informed him that has soon as he posted his marriage certificate to me I would communicate with you when, no doubt you would exempt him from reporting and I would then post him your order of exemption. This you will see, would not bring him into contact with the Police in any way after his marriage, so I think his excuse for not marrying is frivolous.
>
> He is not following any occupation at present, his conduct is good, regular in reporting, and keeps himself respectable. He is at present keeping company with a nurse at the Newton Abbot Union. (HO 144/1712//A60789/115)

The latest object of Lee's affections was Jessie Bulled, possibly a distant relative of Lee, as her father was a retired chief coastguard officer named John Lee Bulled. It became clear that the couple were planning a future together when Lee, somewhat optimistically, wrote to Herbert Gladstone asking him to provide a character reference to help him to obtain employment at a London Workhouse:

Abbotskerswell
2 September 1908

Sir,

Your petitioner is petitioning to you. Asking you if you [will] be so kind, as to use your great influence with the Guardians of St. Giles Workhouse, Endell Street, W.C.

As your petitioner has made application to the above mentioned Guardians for the appointment of Attendant on Male Insane. In conjunction with Miss Jessie Bulled, the Head Attendant of the Female Mental Wards at the Newton Abbot Workhouse. If your petitioner can get the appointment to the above named Workhouse or any other where he can settle down to a quiet life. He intends marrying the above mentioned young Lady. Your petitioner would be very thankful if you could see your way clear to use your great influence on his behalf. As he is afraid he will [have] a very poor chance of getting honest work without some Great Persons Influence to help him. Of course your petitioner gets plenty of offers to come to exhibit himself and to recite his life. And also plenty of the different denominations of chapel people has written to your petitioner asking him to come to their places of worship. And speak to the congregations of the Great Power of Almighty God, and his son, Jesus Christ. Your petitioner knows that it is your wish that he should not go to these places. Therefore your petitioner appeals to you to use your great influence to get him a post where he can earn a honest living for himself & to settle down quietly and also support his aged mother.

P.S. Your petitioner has also written to Major Briscoe, Inspector of HM Prisons, asking him to give your petitioner a reference. (HO 144/1712//A60789/56)

The Home Secretary expressed his regrets that he was unable to assist Lee in his job-hunting endeavours. A letter to Stephen Bryan revealed that Lee's career aspirations had not found favour with the Guardians of St Giles Workhouse, but he consoled himself by trading on his celebrity status to accept an offer of hospitality:

Abbotskerswell
18 September 1908

I did not get the post with the young Lady, we have not heard anything yet.

I had a letter this morning from a Gentleman who lives at Bristol asking me if I would come with him to South Wales tomorrow, Saturday the 19th of September. So I wrote back and told him I would come with him just to see the country. It will be a change, he is going to pay all expenses. I shall see a little of the world going about shall I not. I wish I could come up and see you all, I shall some day. I must be back by the 29th to see a gentleman from Dorset who wants to see both my dear Mother and myself. It is very wet down here. Mr. Briscoe the Governor that was at Portland has given me a good reference. (Bryan Letters, Exeter Prison Museum)

Upon his return from Bristol, Lee made his real intentions clear to the Home Secretary in a determined effort to be allowed to address religious meetings:

Abbotskerswell
27 September 1908

Sir,

Your petitioner humbly begs your permission to be allowed to speak to the people of Great Britain. In churches & chapels. The power and the love of our Lord & Saviour Jesus Christ and to win souls to God (your petitioner will not speak of his imprisonment or about his life in prison after leaving Exeter Prison the 23rd March 1885). Your petitioner is a Christian and he knows the power of God to save precious souls. I am asking this request in the name of Almighty God.

I know I have a power to appeal to the people. Thousand[s] are waiting your answer. Give me a month trial and you will see how God works. Sir, you can do a great work for the Almighty God by granting my request. You yourself being a Christian gentleman.

I know I am laying a great responsibility on your shoulders by asking you to grant me what I feel God has put in my heart to do. Your petitioner is praying for a favourable answer. (HO 144/1712//A60789/116)

The Home Office dismissed the request and concluded that: 'He ought not to be allowed to exhibit himself in chapels anymore than in Music Halls.' Not to be outdone, Lee then enlisted help from the gentleman he had stayed with in Bristol to achieve his aim:

Withleigh Road, Bristol
5 October 1908

To Hon. Herbert Gladstone M.P.

Honourable and Dear Sir,

Having had a spiritual interest in Mr. John Lee from Abbotskerswell from the first day of his release, I have been anxious that he could come under Divine Influence, viz 'Perfect Love,' and in due time become a witness for his Lord and Master.

Now I feel confident by personal contact with him days together, that his spiritual advancement is such that would commend itself to the government and the country, if you would allow such liberty in witnessing to the Grace of Almighty God. I am herewith willing with utmost caution, to conduct him as a test trial in a month's mission.

To prove the truth of my statement.

Thirty and seven years experience I have had among the classes, and my only motive, as before the living God, is that of improving society, socially, morally and spiritually.

Your earliest possible reply will oblige.
Stephen Thomas Crocker

P.S. It is at Mr Lee's request that I write you. He says:–

'Dear Mr Crocker,

Will you be so kind as to write to Mr Gladstone the Home Secretary for me to speak in church (missions) or chapels (of the love and power of God)'

I am sending a copy of my letter to you, to John Lee, so that he will see conditions of such liberty granted in mercy. (HO 144/1712//A60789/118)

Lee's 'ever so 'umble' approach to the Home Office was starting to closely resemble Charles Dickens's odious character Uriah Heep, particularly when his requests took on a more threatening nature:

Abbotskerswell
4 October 1908

Sir,

Your petitioner begs permission to ask you if you can secure him a situation in a Government post of some kind where he can earn an honest living for his aged mother and himself. Your petitioner has tried to get a post under poor law, but did not succeed. Thousands of people as [sic] asked him to devote his life to Almighty God's service. Your petitioner does not want to appeal to the country against your decision or to do anything to offend. But your petitioner will have to give an account to Almighty God & by the tallent [sic] God has given him.

Your petitioner must do something as soon as possible for a living. If it is to write another book of his prison life & photos an officer kept some papers for your petitioner which he did at Portland Prison. The officer sent them to your petitioner after his release from prison. But your prisoner did not let Lloyd's have them or tell Lloyd's half he knew about prison so that he should offend no-one. Your petitioner would like to settle down quiet if he can but he must live. Would you be so kind as to help him get a honest living. He lost several places when he first came home by having to report himself and also a marriage.

As your petitioner is situated it is as well for him to be in prison. Your [petitioner] has been persecuted more than any other man. The country at large believes in his innocence and he must appeal to the whole world to help him if he cannot get a post of some sort. Your petitioner is free is he not to publish his petitions to you and your answer as he keeps a copy of them. Your petitioner is waiting anxiously for a favourable answer to this petition. (HO 144/1712//A60789/117)

A meeting at the Home Office concluded in the minutes: 'He threatens to publish another book, if the S of S does not find work for him and says that he has materials kept back from his contribution to Lloyd's which he will use to portray his life in prison. His desire is doubtless to live by a mixture of sensation & religion, rather than by work. It is not likely that he would get much for a book now, as the novelty of his case has evaporated' (HO 144/1712//A60789/117).

The Home Secretary excused himself from using his influence to find Lee a situation by agreeing to remove the obstacle which Lee claimed was preventing him from obtaining employment – his obligation to report to the police. Lee, however, was still not satisfied:

'I am going to write The Sequel to my unparalleled story John Lee.'

Abbotskerswell
15 October 1908

Sir,

Not having my freedom in England to earn an honest living for my dear Mother and myself by witnesses the pure love and power of our Lord Jesus Christ to save precious souls I am denied that freedom by the Home Office. I am going to write The Sequel to my unparalleled story John Lee. I have given Lloyd's notice of the fact. I shall print them myself with photo and travel the country & sell them. My solicitor will compare it with the one Lloyd's has published and see that it is not the same. I shall travel to different countries. I believe that if I leave the British Shores, I am at liberty to say what I like about English convict prisons am I not? I know I have the public sympathy on my side, the greatest part believe that I am an innocent man unjustly punished, in fact I am a living monument of English justice. Being an innocent man I hope before many weeks to get the confession of my stepsister Elizabeth Harris, the cook who confessed to the crime on her death bed to Major Pearson, a Salvation Army officer. The Salvation Army promised to help me get it but they did nothing, but God is on my side, I shall get it very soon now. If I had only myself to get a living for I should not care but I have a dear Old Mother who was receiving parish relief when I came home. But I took her off and now she is debarred from Old Age Pension because she received it the 2nd January.

Kindly tell me if I am driven from my dear old mother to a foreign country by the Home Office. If I am a free man to speak what I like about prisons. (HO 144/1712// A60789/120)

Lee's reference to Elizabeth Harris was in response to syndicated articles published during his imprisonment that were brought to his attention by several correspondents. The Home Office contacted the Salvation Army and learned that Major Pearson had died six years earlier and it had no knowledge of a deathbed 'confession'. A Home Office committee responded to Lee's threats about selling his story abroad with a curt 'better take no notice', which stemmed the flow of letters from the aggrieved job seeker as he concentrated on settling down and making a fresh start with his future bride Jessie Bulled. In an attempt to avoid unwanted publicity, the wedding ceremony was shrouded in secrecy. No family members were invited, not even Lee's beloved mother. One of the few people in the know was Lee's tailor, Frank Wood, who made the bride's wedding dress and the bridegroom's suit. Wood later revealed that when Jessie Bulled fell under Lee's spell, many people tried to dissuade her from getting involved with him: 'An old doctor friend . . . spent hours begging her to forsake him, but in spite of her parents who were almost broken-hearted at the loss, the two were married . . . ' (*Torquay Times*, 13 March 1936)

A report of the big day appeared in the *Torquay Directory*, Wednesday 27 January 1909:

John Lee – 'the man they could not hang' for the murder of Miss Keyse, at Babbacombe twenty-three years ago – was married, by special licence at Newton Abbot on Friday. It was in December 1907, that, after serving twenty-two years in prison, Lee was released from Portland gaol. He at once proceeded to the home of his mother at Abbotskerswell, and there he has continued to reside. His visits to Torquay were frequent. More frequent have been his journeys from the village of Abbotskerswell to Newton Abbot, especially since he began to woo a Miss Bulled, who for four or five years has been the chief mental attendant in the female wards in Newton Workhouse. The courtship of the twain was not a secret, but secret was the date they fixed for their marriage. Not even the officials of the Workhouse were aware of the fact that Friday was the selected day. Miss Bulled was a member of the Newton Congregational Church, and there the ceremony was conducted by the pastor on Friday morning, in the presence of the registrar, the treasurer of the church, and the caretaker. A special licence had been procured, and on it Lee was described as 'John Henry George Lee, bachelor, proprietor of general stores, 44 years, Three Towns' Cottage, Abbotskerswell'. The description of the bride was:– 'Jessie Augusta Bulled, spinster, 33 years, head attendant in female mental wards, 68 East Street, Newton Abbot'. The latter is the registered address of Newton Workhouse. The bride wore a blue cloth travelling dress, and Lee a grey suit, with a white carnation in his buttonhole. Lee gave the responses with a confident air, but the bride was somewhat nervous. When the benediction had been pronounced, Lee drew the pastor aside, and enquired if he might ask a blessing himself. The minister concurred, and remained at the altar whilst Lee and his bride knelt for two or three minutes in silent prayer. After the register had been signed the pastor wished the couple a happy married life, and they left the church by the main entrance, amid showers of confetti thrown by a few friends who had gathered outside. They went direct to the railway station and booked for Bristol, en route for Durham, where it is stated, they have taken a business, but they kept that a secret also, and even their closest friends cannot furnish any information as to their future place of residence. It appears that soon after Lee was released from prison he visited some friends at Newton Abbot and was entertained by them. Miss Bulled was also on friendly terms with the people, and meeting at the same place, an engagement between them speedily resulted.

When seen after the ceremony, Lee's mother would not even admit that her son had been married. She maintained a cryptic silence. Her only remark was, 'People say so, but they said so once before'.

Later that year, Lee returned to Abbotskerswell to stay with his mother. During his visit, he gave a rare interview to the *Mid-Devon and Newton Times*, 14 August 1909:

John Lee, the leading figure in the Babbacombe murder drama, has been spending a short holiday in the neighbourhood of Newton Abbot. It is six months since he was quietly married in the early morning at the Congregational Church to Miss Jessie Augusta Bulled, who was an official under the Newton Board of Guardians. The affair had been kept such a profound secret that it came as a surprise even to Mr. and Mrs. Lee's most intimate friends. Immediately after the ceremony they left Newton by rail, very few being aware in what part of the country they intended to settle. Since then, Mr Lee informed a representative of the 'Mid-Devon Times,' who had a brief interview with him, they have been living at Newcastle, and have already succeeded in building up a prosperous little business. Mr Lee said he had no wish ever to come to this part of the country again – it had too many sad and unpleasant memories for him, but his mother still lived near Newton, and he felt he must run down and see her as soon as he got the chance. He had been staying with her whilst he had been here, he added. He would have liked for her to come away to the North, but there were so many associations which connected her with the place where she had lived for so many years, that she could not leave it. The breaking of old ties at her age was not what it would be to younger folk. 'How have you been getting on since you left?' asked our representative. 'Very well, indeed,' replied Mr. Lee. 'Fortune has been very kind to me in every way. I have done better than ever I could have expected in business, and I have been jogging along very comfortably. I have been glad to meet some of my old friends here at Newton, but I shall not come back to this part of the country again if I can help it – not to live anyway. You can't beat Devonshire scenery, of course, especially at this time of year – but there's more money in the North. I can earn my £7 a week there easily, as many of the workers do – and they don't mind spending it either. You can make headway there, and I feel quite at home. The North-country people, too, are a very fair-minded lot. They look at both sides of a question before coming to a conclusion. We have got on well with them ever since we have been living at Newcastle, and I and my wife have many kindnesses to thank them for.'

Despite his optimism, Mr. Lee is not looking as well as when he left Newton with his young bride that early morning in January. His health has not been of the best, but his tall figure is still as upright as ever, and he walks with the buoyant step of a youth. He is now 45 years of age.

In fact, it was John Lee's forty-fifth birthday the day after the article was published, and he had something else to celebrate, for he was about to become a father. Jessie gave birth to a son, John Aubrey Maurice, born in Newcastle upon Tyne on 10 January 1910. If, as stated on his marriage licence, Lee had been a 'proprietor of general stores', it had been an extremely short-lived venture, for his child's birth certificate revealed that he was employed in a public house. Under the terms of his release, Lee was not allowed to appear in public, so to sidestep this restriction, he was employed nominally as a 'barman', although he was paid several times more than the average wage for this occupation. The son of his employer spoke of Lee's popularity in an article published in the *Newcastle Evening Chronicle*, 5 May 1969:

A tale of strange happenings in Newcastle just after the turn of the century has been recalled for me by Mr. Edwin Wears who was then a very young boy. . . . At the time, his father owned the Chancellor's Head and the Bull and Mouth in Newgate Street and employed John Lee – better known as 'the man they couldn't hang.'

'I remember him well and as a boy would hold him in great awe,' says Mr. Wears. . . . Mr. Wears says that while working for his father, Lee was paid £8 a week. 'It was quite a sum then, but his drawing power was enormous and people came from far and near to see him, and, as a special favour, shake his hand.'

They came mostly on Saturdays when 'hoying' (bowling or throwing the ball) was played on the Town Moor. The matches were usually made in the Chancellor's Head and many hundreds of pounds were wagered on them.

'After the match, many people came to see Lee who was a slimly-built man, very sallow complexion (known, I think as "prison tan") and with hard, piercing eyes.'

'He was very kind to me,' says Mr. Wears. 'But my mother was terrified of the poor man. She only met him once and she nearly fainted.'

It seems that after the meeting, Mrs. Wears told her husband it was the look in the man's eyes that frightened her. His reply was: 'No wonder after 21 years in jail and standing on the scaffold to hang, that his eyes are so unusual.'

Mary Lee saw her son for what appears to be the last time in September 1910. Scotland Yard's Black Museum holds a memento of this holiday in South Devon – a postcard Lee sent to London from Torquay to a Miss A. Gibb, residing at Ye Olde King's Head, a public house in the Borough High Street, Southwark, where he was now working. On 19 February 1911, Lee boarded the German-built liner *Kronprinz Frederick Wilhelm* at Southampton and travelled in a second-class cabin to New York, arriving on 28 February. The ship's record preserved at Ellis Island shows that Lee had emigrated and gained entry to the USA, despite a ban on anyone with a criminal conviction. According to the list of 'alien passengers', he was accompanied by his wife 'Jessie Lee', although their one-year-old son was not travelling to a new life with his parents. The Reverend Pitkin revealed in his memoirs that Lee had in fact left his wife and gone abroad 'with the young woman who accompanied him in the bar'. With callous disregard for the welfare of his family, Lee had abandoned them in the knowledge that Jessie was expecting a second child. A daughter, Eveline Victoria Mary Lee, was born in London on 10 August 1911. The Reverend Pitkin commented: 'He left his poor wife, who was very courageous to marry a man with so black a record, without any sort of maintenance, and she was obliged to apply to the Lambeth Guardians for assistance' (Pitkin, 1918).

This was an ironic turn of events for Jessie, who had once held a high position in a workhouse and was now compelled to throw herself upon the mercy of the Poor Law. On St Valentine's Day 1912, while her husband was across the Atlantic with his lover, Jessie's humiliation became complete when she appeared before the Guardians. The outcome was reported the following day in the *Daily Mail*:

> The wife of John Lee, who, convicted for the murder of an old lady at Babbacombe over twenty years ago, was reprieved after three attempts to hang him, applied to the Lambeth Guardians yesterday for relief. Mrs Lee stated that she married Lee after his liberation from prison in 1908, on the completion of twenty years penal servitude. There were two children at a public house in the borough. Lee received a good salary for exhibiting himself, but in February last year he left for America and, after sending her help for some weeks wrote stating that he was out of work and could send no more money. The board left the matter with the relieving officer.

According to the ship's log, Lee and his 'wife' had been residing at 117 Copenhagen Street, Kings Cross, London, and were going to stay in New York with a friend, Mr E. Dingle of 625 Vanderbilt Avenue, Brooklyn. Despite concealing the fact that he had a criminal past and his female companion was carrying a false passport, the couple evidently gained entry via the strict vetting procedure at Ellis Island. They may have avoided close scrutiny by having the means to travel 'cabin' class in contrast to the vast majority of impoverished immigrants usually holed up below decks in the 'steerage' compartment of the ship.

What became of John Lee after reaching New York poses another mystery and has been the subject of much conjecture. He had always claimed that he was an innocent man who had been saved by the intervention of God, yet where or when he eventually met his Maker took on an international dimension when conflicting reports of his death emerged from Australia, Canada and the USA.

CHAPTER 9

More lives than a cat

The only man to survive three attempts to hang him. . . . Lee emigrated to the United States in 1917, married, and lived until 1933.

– *Guinness Book of Records*, 1970

After sailing to New York in 1911, subsequent reports of Lee's whereabouts emerged simultaneously from four countries on three continents. Following up numerous sightings without actual proof of existence has been rather like trying to track down Big Foot or the Loch Ness monster. It seems more than likely that other people bearing the not uncommon name of John Lee passed themselves off as their infamous namesake.

John Lee's serialised life story enjoyed worldwide exposure when it was reproduced in book form. In May 1908, he told Stephen Bryan of the encouraging response received from well-wishers overseas: 'I still get a lot of letters from Canada, Australia & New Zealand.' Despite earning a good living at home in public houses, he was clearly considering making a new start abroad and eventually decided to make a move to the USA.

When his mother made her will in January 1915, Lee was evidently still out of the country. She made small bequests to her deserted daughter-in-law Jessie Lee, two nieces and landlord before mentioning her errant son:

> This is the last Will and Testament of me Mary Lee of Number 3 Town Cottages Abbotskerswell in the County of Devon Widow. I give my silver plated Tea Pot and six China Cups and saucers with flowers on the border my family bible and contents and half of my Clothes to my daughter in law Jessie Lee. I give the rest of my Clothes and my Album and contents to my niece Mary Sanders of Kingsteignton. I give my two Pictures in the Window of Ships to my niece Maggie Lee of Abbotskerswell. I give my China Plates over the mantel-piece to my Landlord Isaac Carr. I give all the rest of my property subject to the payment of my just debts funeral and testamentary expenses to my son John Henry George Lee but if he shall be abroad at the time of my death then I direct that the same shall be sold and the proceeds forwarded to him but in case of my said Son shall predecease me then I give the same unto his son Albert Maurice John Lee absolutely. I appoint Mary Jane Bond the wife of George Bond of Abbotskerswell aforesaid Labourer, William John Windsor of Denbury Devon Agent and Gerald Douglas Woollcombe of Newton Abbot Devon Solicitors to be my Executors and I direct that the

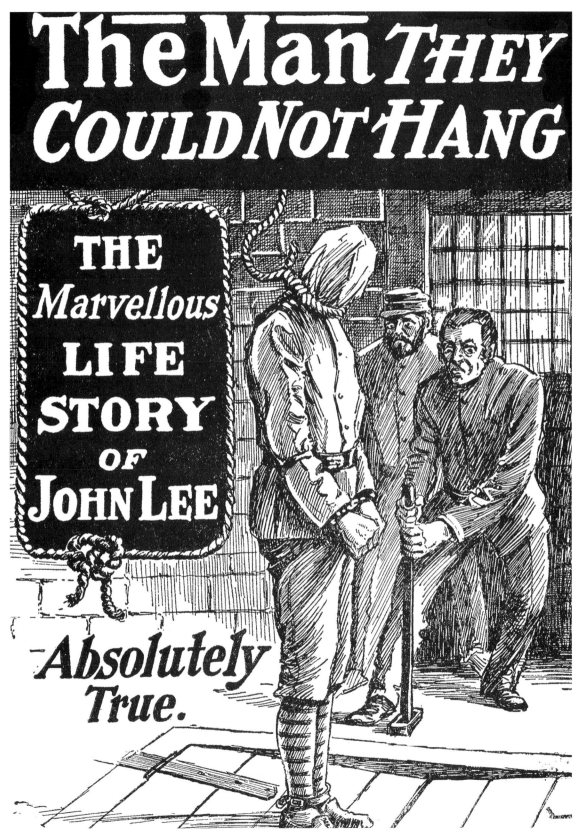

A US edition of John Lee's autobiography.

said Gerald Douglas Woollcombe shall be entitled to charge his usual professional charges out of my Estate. In witness whereof I have herewith set my hand this fifth day of January One Thousand Nine Hundred and Fifteen.

The mark of X Mary Lee

In the event of Mary Lee's son predeceasing her, his share of the estate was to go to her grandson, Albert Maurice John, although the eldest child of the marriage between John and Jessie was named John Aubrey Maurice. This was evidently a mistake by the elderly illiterate old lady who had to dictate her wishes. The gross value of Mary Lee's estate when probate was granted in April 1918 was £33 5s. 11d. A month earlier she had been found dead in bed by a neighbour, and her funeral was reported by the *East and*

Mary Lee: 'I give all the rest of my property . . . to my son John Henry George Lee but if he shall be abroad at the time of my death then I direct that the same shall be sold and the proceeds forwarded to him . . .'

South Devon Advertiser, 16 March 1918: 'On Saturday afternoon [9 March] the body of Mrs John Lee was laid to rest in the village churchyard. Deceased had reached the advanced age of 86 years. She was much respected by the parishioners, as was shown by the number who were present to pay their last tribute of respect to her memory.'

Of the twenty-five mourners named in the report, the closest relatives of the deceased were two of her nieces. Ten wreaths were laid at her grave – none of them delivered on behalf of her son. Confirmation that John Lee had not been in attendance came in 1925. A book called *The Babbicombe Tragedy* by Reginald Jones had just been published in Manchester, probably rekindling the interest of Stephen Bryan. He wrote to John Lee's old address in Abbotskerswell, which was now the home of Mary Bond, niece and executor of Mary Lee's will, to enquire about the whereabouts of Lee and received this reply from Mrs Bond's son:

3 Town Cottages
Abbotskerswell

Dear Sir,

I am writing on behalf of my mother the present occupier of the above address, in reply to your letter of the 6th inst. . . . In reference to John Lee, he left England in 1911 and according to accounts in the newspapers he is dead. He did not attend his mother's funeral. This is all the information we can give you. (Bryan Letters, Exeter Prison Museum)

By this time accounts of Lee's death had surfaced from Australia in 1918, Canada in 1921 and would emerge from America in 1929 and 1933. Although they doubtless exist, our research has failed to turn up a single contemporary newspaper report covering any of the emigrant's multiple deaths. There are also numerous unsubstantiated stories that he returned to England, where he was supposedly living during the First and Second World Wars. We look at some of these stories below.

AUSTRALIA

In the same year that Mary Lee was laid to rest, the Reverend John Pitkin published his memoirs. In a chapter devoted to the life of John Lee, he concluded: 'The newspapers have recently stated that this extraordinary criminal adventurer died a natural death in Australia, quite contrary to my expectations. I quite believed that he would have been executed for some other horrible crime' (Pitkin, 1918).

John Lee had certainly considered the prospect of life 'down under'. In July 1908, he told Stephen Bryan, 'I should like to go to Australia if I had my way. There is plenty of work and good wages, 22 to 30 shillings a week and all found in Queensland' (Bryan Letters, Exeter Prison Museum).

His popularity in Australia was boosted significantly by a silent film, *The Man They Could Not Hang*, made in Sydney in late 1912. Based on an earlier stage play, with a storyline loosely culled from Lee's autobiography, the film was considered to be technically crude even by early cinematic standards and shelved by its producer,

The Life Story of John Lee, as portrayed on the silver screen with 'Not One Gruesome Moment in the Picture'.

theatrical entrepreneur Phillip Lytton. He later passed it on as a gift to a long-serving employee, Arthur W. Sterry, who, with his partner Frederick Haldane, went on to make a fortune touring with the film. Much to the critics' amazement, who were unanimous in their condemnation of its overt sentimentality, this minor epic enjoyed huge success in Australia and New Zealand between 1914 and 1921. There has been speculation about whether John Lee was in the country during the production of the film and acted as an advisor, but there is absolutely no evidence to support this. On the contrary, the director Robert Scott told a royal commission enquiry into the Australian film industry in 1927 that his main memory of this melodramatic tale was that it was shot on an extremely low budget in a far from exotic location: 'It was really only a room, fitted out like a photographer's studio.'

It is generally claimed that the death of Lee occurred in Melbourne in 1918. The index of deaths for the whole state of Victoria for that year reveals only one possibility, the discovery of a body on the outskirts of the city which was reported in the *Bacchus Marsh Express*, 23 February 1918:

> On Saturday last, whilst some city picnickers were searching for shady dells (and incidentally fruit) under the large hedge which surrounds Mr A.C. Simon's orchard at Maddingley, they came across the dead body of a man. The police were notified who removed the body to the police station, where it was identified as that of a man named John Lee, about 60 years of age, believed to be a native of Goldsborough, near Dunnolly; and his only relative is said to be a brother in the railway service. He had been working in this district for some time, and lately at Greystones, Rowsley. Lee had been seen in the town a week previously, 'breaking down' his cheque, and had been camped under the hedge where his body was found, death having taken place some days before. Dr Pollock held a post-mortem examination and found death due to heart failure, emaciation and exposure.

Although John Lee would have been only fifty-three years old at this time, prison life might certainly have left him looking 'about 60 years of age', but the fact that the deceased was 'a native of Goldsborough' and had 'a brother in the railway service' precludes this 'suspect' from the investigation.

CANADA

It has been said that Lee went prospecting for gold in Canada before joining the armed forces during the First World War, after which he died in an unspecified area of the country in 1921. Following the announcement that the BBC were making a television programme about John Lee, a Mr Dunn of Crediton, near Exeter, related a story told by his mother about Lee coming back to England with the Canadian Forces. His letter appeared in the *Express and Echo*, 19 August 1974: 'My mother, during the war, was staying with her friend, whose father was proprietor of 'The White Swan,' Wendover, Bucks. One evening a Canadian soldier came into the bar and had a few words over a drink with the proprietor. 'That soldier was John Lee and the proprietor had been his warder at Exeter Prison at the time of his imprisonment. Lee never went into the pub again.'

When considering John Lee's alleged military exploits, it must be remembered that at the outset of the First World War, he was fifty years old. Even if a recruiting officer had been prepared to believe that he was much younger, Lee was in poor physical condition and would never have passed an army medical. At the age of eighteen, he had been invalided out of the Royal Navy with pneumonia. This illness was linked to a bout of bronchitis which confined him in the prison hospital for a month in 1906. The medical report described his lungs as having traces of an old complaint – 'probably of Tuberculosis origin'. Also, an injury suffered in prison had left him far from 'fighting fit'. In August 1905, Lee ruptured himself while lifting a trolley and was thereafter compelled to wear a surgical truss.

AMERICA

John Lee gained a place in the *Guinness Book of Records* where his death was recorded as having occurred in the USA in 1933. This is the most popularly believed version of Lee's demise, but it has never been substantiated. According to the ship's log, when Lee travelled to New York in 1911, he was going to stay with a Mr E. Dingle of 625 Vanderbilt Avenue, Brooklyn, but this person does not appear in the 1910 Census for that area of New York, nor is he listed in the Brooklyn City directories for the years 1910 and 1912. An account of Lee's movements across the Atlantic appeared in the *Torquay Times*, 15 September 1922:

> A few days since a writer, in showing up the idiosyncrasies and weakness of character of certain men who have 'done time', referred to the fact of Lee's marriage with a respectable young woman, not long after his arrival from Portland, and his deserting her and her two children. Lee then went to America, and the last that was heard about John of the very chequered career was that he was somewhere in the neighbourhood of Buffalo, U.S.

The US Census for 1920 shows more than one John Lee living in Buffalo City, and elsewhere in the State of New York, but none match the profile of an Englishman born in 1864. Likewise, the limited information in the Buffalo City directories from 1920–5 cannot help differentiate between individuals listed with this name. Of course, Buffalo might have provided a brief stopover for Lee. The city is a short distance from Niagara Falls and the border with Canada, where, as discussed earlier, Lee was said to be heading to try his luck in the goldfields.

Milwaukee is widely quoted as the place where Lee died in 1933. However, an article called 'The Man They Couldn't Hang' written by an American judge, Marcus Kavanagh, makes interesting reading. Although there are glaring inaccuracies about aspects of the murder and the attempted execution, it would be thought that the author had far more reliable sources at his disposal to make this comment about Lee's final days: 'He married, left his wife, wandered to America, and died in 1929.' Elsewhere in the article, the period of this event is given as autumn of that year. What is particularly intriguing about this information is that Kavanagh's story was published in the September edition of *Mind* in 1931, predating similar reports by two years. In common with the later version he also states that Lee died a 'natural death'.

Judge Marcus Kavanagh also claimed that Lee became an evangelist. Having been banned from addressing religious societies in Britain, it is certain that Lee would have been attracted by such a proposition in America, although such a career move would have alerted the immigration authorities to the fact that he was an 'undesirable alien'. The judge does not give the source of the text but quotes Lee's sermon relating his 'miraculous' experience on the scaffold:

> 'Well, Sirs,' he would say, 'as we stumbled along down the corridor past the other prisoners in their cells, the words of the litany kept knocking inside my heart; but I wouldn't join answering them, for, you see, I knew I wasn't going to die and it was inappropriate.
>
> 'Then, too, the noise from the street outside the walls dazed me a bit. It was like the rise and fall of waves in a storm breaking up against the rocks at Babbacombe. Every second or so a laugh or a shout darted up like a sea-gull above the roar. When I was up on the gallows I could hear the mob outside screeching at me. It was awful!
>
> 'I kept going on dazed like, Berry pushing me forward to make me go faster, till all at once we came to the barn where the scaffold stood with two or three men waiting on it and a score of others loitering at its foot. When I climbed up and faced them I said: "Lord, you're keeping me in unnatural suspense. Why don't you hurry with my saving?"
>
> 'They pushed me on the trapdoor and strapped my knees together. I looked at the people below me in the yard. There were a dozen I had known all my life. Not one of them looked sorry for me or even friendly. Some of them looked sober, some sneered up at me, and one or two grinned.
>
> 'That gave me an awful, desolate, sick feeling in my heart. Still I wasn't afraid. But I must admit that when Berry fastened the knot of the rope under my ear my teeth began knocking together in spite of myself and my heart barely fluttered. For one moment I lost hope. God forgive me for that insult! That minute was when they pulled the black cap down over my face. "Lord," I says, "have you gone back on your word?"
>
> 'In the next second what was going to happen? I wondered, terribly scared. Would I be tossing in the roaring flames of hell, as my sins deserved, or listening to the music of heaven, as we are promised? I stood suffocating for air because of the cap.

'Suddenly I realised something had gone wrong with the gallows, Berry and the others were kicking and twisting at the trapdoor I was standing on. They kept muttering excited orders to each other. Presently the crowd down below began talking and shouting. I was pushed off the trapdoor while someone worked on it.

'I shouted: "I'm smothering! Take off this cap!" Then I heard the sheriff say: "Take off the cap and send him back to his cell. We have a right to take his life by hanging, not by smothering." So they unstrapped my legs and I stumbled back into the prison. My ears were throbbing and my brain was twisting around and around. My, but I was glad! The Lord had kept His promise. When I got back to my cell I lay down all of a tremble, my face white like snow and all covered with icy sweat.'

Kavanagh was a circuit judge of Cook County, Chicago. Had he read of Lee's death occurring in his own state, Illinois, or at Milwaukee in the neighbouring state of Wisconsin? A search of the records turned up no convincing evidence of Lee's death occurring in either state between the years 1929 and 1933. The state archives of Illinois show that two men named John Lee died in Cook County and one in Edwardsville in the autumn of 1929. However, their ages were not recorded and none of the deceased men warranted a mention in the local newspapers. Similarly, a search of the state archives of Wisconsin reveal that the death of a John Lee occurred in Milwaukee on New Year's Day 1931, but his country of origin was Norway.

ENGLAND

A number of people claimed to know people who had seen John Lee in England during the First World War. The first of these sightings based on hearsay evidence occurred in June 1916. A gentleman from Sydney, Australia, having been impressed with Lee's autobiography, wrote to the Home Office with a number of queries regarding the prisoner's treatment. The official dealing with the matter made a note about the criminal celebrity: 'John Lee was recently pointed out to a friend of mine at Brighton! He was wearing a top hat and appeared in easy circumstances!' (HO 144/1712// A60789/123).

In 1932, Henry Mackinnon Walbrook, a former editor of the *Brighton Guardian* and theatre critic of the *Pall Mall Gazette*, who resided at Hove, Brighton, recalled the following tale in his book *Murders and Murder Trials, 1812–1912*:

During the years of the Great War one of my occasional duties as a special constable was that of taking charge of a small extra-mural police station between the hours of eight o'clock and midnight. . . . On arriving for these vigils I was always received by an officer of the regular constabulary, who would impart any 'instructions' that happened to be necessary. . . . One evening in the November of 1917 he informed me that I might have a visitor in the course of the night. I asked him who it might be. 'Did you ever hear of the Babbacombe murder, and of the man they couldn't hang?' came his exhilarating reply. I said that I had heard of the story, but that my recollections of it were vague. 'Well', he said, '. . . he is at present residing in this neighbourhood. Now and then he drops in for a little chat friendly-like and talks of his experience. . . . It's a nice evening, and he's quite likely to drop in to-night.' . . . As it happened . . . neither then nor on any subsequent occasion did I meet the man who had so strangely survived the scaffold.

During the making of the BBC television documentary *The Man They Could Not Hang*, the producers heard that Lee had committed suicide in Plymouth. This possibility was backed up by this story from a Mr Shearing, who claimed that Lee was in Devon during the First World War. His letter appeared in the *Radio Times*, 20 February 1975:

> I viewed *The Man They Could Not Hang* with much interest, as when I came to Plymouth in 1917 to join the Royal Marines, I quickly heard that John Lee took over a used furniture shop after release in King Street, Plymouth, near to where I lived when I married in 1920.
>
> The shop was opposite the Salvation Army Hostel, which still stands. Flats now occupy the space on which there were eight or ten shops.
>
> John Lee's shop was very sleazy. I passed it often, but never entered, but it was common knowledge in the district that Lee was the owner.

Kelly's Directory of Devonshire 1919 lists four furniture shops in King Street, none of which were occupied by the elusive John Lee. If he had been in the county during this period, it is hard to believe that he was not in contact with his mother before her death, and surely he would have attended her funeral.

In August 1959, a former colliery manager, Mr W.C. Wright, wrote to Torquay local historian John Pike with the following account of receiving a call from the vagrant John Lee at his home near Derby: 'In 1920 John Lee made a tour of the Midlands maintaining himself by doing odd jobs for people cutting hedges etc. & often sleeping out in sheds etc. I employed him to cut my hedge . . . Where he went afterwards I cannot say.'

Cinema-goers in the 'Roaring Twenties' claimed that John Lee made personal appearances wherever a new production of *The Man They Could Not Hang* was shown in Britain. It was an expanded version of the silent film owned by Arthur Sterry and Frederick Haldane. Made in 1921, it features a flock of Pre-Raphaelite angels hovering over the gallows to save a wrongly accused man. The murder is attributed to a brutish-looking 'mysterious stranger' who is having a secret liaison with a female servant of Miss Keyse. The hero John Lee emerges from prison to be reunited with his devoted sweetheart, Katie Farmer. Settling down, they live happily ever and in the final scene their child thanks God for saving her father. Its appeal to audiences was certainly lost on the reviewer of the Australian film magazine *Everyones*, 28 December 1921: 'Giving it the benefit of everything favourable that can be said [of Australian film production], there is no comparison, as regards quantity or story, with other current releases.'

Despite this criticism, the film emulated its predecessor and enjoyed huge commercial success in Australia and New Zealand. It also received a rapturous reception in Britain when Haldane toured with the film from 1923 to 1926. Early in 1972, the *Lancashire Evening Telegraph* invited readers to send in their memories of the early days of cinema and heard from several correspondents, recalling how they had been greeted at theatres

United Kingdom Rights Controlled by　-　-　-　H. A. WHINCUP, LTD., LEEDS

A Pictorial Visualisation of the most miraculous escape from death upon the Gallows.

THE LIFE STORY OF JOHN LEE

Known the World Over as

A STORY
FOUNDED
ON FACT

The STORY
OF A
BROKEN
HEART

THE PROCESSION TO THE SCAFFOLD.

"The loftiest place is that seat of grace
For which all worldings try :
But who would stand in hempen band
Upon a scaffold high,
And through a murderer's collar take
His last look at the sky ? "

JOHN LEE AWAITING THE FATAL DAY.

"With sudden shock the prison clock
Smote on the quivering air,
And from all the gaol rose up a wail
Of impotent despair."

THE MAN THEY COULD NOT HANG

THE PICTURE
WILL BE
GRAPHICALLY
DESCRIBED BY

VOCAL ITEMS
INCIDENTAL TO
THE PICTURE

FREDERICK HALDANE
OR ANOTHER
EXPERIENCED RACONTEUR

□ □

SHOULD A MAN
BE CONDEMNED
TO DEATH UPON
CIRCUMSTANTIAL
EVIDENCE ?

□ □

WAS IT AN
ACT OF GOD?

THE PICTURE IS
PRECEDED BY AN
ATMOSPHERIC PROLOGUE
IN WHICH MRS. LEE PLEADS FOR
HER SON THE EVENING BEFORE
THE FATAL DAY.

THE WHOLE STORY OF JOHN
LEE'S EARLY MANHOOD AND THE
EVENTS THAT LED UP TO HIS
BEING FOUND GUILTY, THE UN-
SWERVING FAITH OF HIS SWEET-
HEART, ETC, ARE ALL DEPICTED,
AND FURTHER YOU WILL HEAR
THE STORY WHICH SYNCHRONIZES
WITH EVERY CHARACTER AND DETAIL
OF THE PICTURE.

SPECIALLY
ARRANGED
ORCHESTRAL
MUSIC

THOUGH THE TITLE OF THE
PICTURE IS, AT FIRST SIGHT SOME-
WHAT FORBIDDING TO SENSITIVE
NATURES, THE CIRCUMSTANCES SUR-
ROUNDING THE ATTEMPTED EXECU-
TION OF JOHN LEE WERE OF SUCH
A SUBLIME CHARACTER AND THE
RESPONSIBILITY OF AUTHORITY IS
SO GREAT IN THUS LAUNCHING ONE
OF GOD'S CREATURES BACK INTO
HIS PRESENCE, THAT IT CANNOT
FAIL TO ARREST THE ATTENTION
OF THE MOST DELICATE MINDS.

KATE FARMER, JOHN LEE'S FIANCEE.
WAITED FOR HIM FOR 23 YEARS.

THREE ATTEMPTS WERE MADE TO HANG JOHN LEE
BUT EACH ONE FAILED.

Was the Almighty Power intervening for an Innocent Man?

Not One Gruesome Moment in the Picture

A film poster of the Australian production, which toured the UK.

by John Lee dressed in prison uniform. A similar recollection from John Blunford of London appeared in the *Radio Times*, 20 February 1975:

> I was watching the programme with my mother when she suddenly remembered that she had seen the film of *The Man They Could Not Hang* when it was first shown. She was living in Goodmayes, Essex, at the time, and the film was being shown at the Seven Kings Cinema, now long since gone. That was in 1921.
>
> Apparently, she said, after the film was shown John Lee himself came onto the stage in front of the screen and talked to the audience about his experience on the gallows. He was dressed in a convict's outfit, not of the broad arrow type but with broad blue bands.
>
> Although my mother was only nine or ten at the time, seeing the clips from the film brought it back to her.

The solution to these mistaken sightings of John Lee is easy to explain. An actor (Frederick Haldane or W.J. Mackay) played the part of John Lee and delivered an impassioned lecture from the stage. During the screening, he was joined by an actress

EMPIRE

NEWTON ABBOT

☞ Whit-Week, May 21st. For Six Days. ☜
TWICE DAILY AT 3 AND 7·45.

THE LIFE STORY OF JOHN LEE

The Man they could not hang

The Picture will be Graphically described by
FREDERICK HALDANE or **W. J. MACKAY.**
VOCAL ITEMS by
LOUIE FARNDON or **ELOISE MILLER**

Specially arranged Orchestral Music and Effects.

Special Prices : 1/10, 1/3, 1/- (Tax included)

The first 'Speaking, Moving, Picture' was seen by John Lee's relatives at the Empire cinema, Newton Abbot.

(Louie Farndon or Eloise Miller) and they simulated the voices of the characters, claiming in the advertising to be presenting the first 'Speaking, Moving, Picture'. Therefore, children grew up believing that they had witnessed John Lee himself presenting this 'cinema oratorio'. Many of Lee's relatives saw the film when it was shown at the Empire Cinema, Newton Abbot, where a local reviewer summarised the life of the film's subject and concluded: 'Then he went to America, and drifted to Australia, where this film was taken. He died subsequently.' The writer went on to discuss the merits of the film in the *Mid-Devon Advertiser*, 19 May 1923:

> Naturally the visualisation of this world-famous tragedy in the vicinity where it was played in grim reality has aroused considerable discussion and argument, and a resuscitation of much of the lore which surrounds the most sensational story in criminology. . . .
>
> The film is undoubtedly one of the most dramatic ever screened. Lee's life is traced from his earlier years, when he had a love affair with Kate Farmer, up to, and including the crime itself, his subsequent trial: his old mother's frantic appeal and the tense scaffold scenes when the 'drop' mysteriously refused again and again to act. Few people entertain any doubt about Lee's guiltiness of the crime, for which he was sentenced to be hung – but in the picture he is depicted as the innocent victim of a malign fate. Anyway it makes for a thundering good film story, and all who are in search of a few thrills should certainly go and see it. . . .
>
> On Wednesday I had the pleasure of accompanying Mr. Frederick Haldane and Mr. Chas. Poole [proprietor of the Empire Cinema] to some of the places in the district connected with the tragedy. Mr. Haldane was keenly interested, for he has a big financial stake in the film and rights, and was naturally anxious to see the scenes of the actual happenings. Only the ruins of the front-door of the cottage where Miss Keyse was murdered remain standing at Babbacombe. What an opportunity somebody missed in omitting to preserve the cottage as a showplace for visitors!

If Haldane had ever met John Lee, or known of any involvement he might have had with the production of the picture, he certainly did not impart this information to the reporter during the course of the day.

Further sightings of John Lee continued during the Second World War, and this story was recalled by David Green of Exeter in the *Express and Echo*, 19 August 1974:

> During World War II, my father and I went fishing at the sandpits outside London and fell into conversation with an older man fishing next to us.
>
> We thought nothing of the old man, until after he left and the owner of the fishing pit said to us: 'Do you know who that was . . . the man who could not hang, John Lee.'
>
> The pit owner then told Mr. Green and his father about the famous John Lee: After Lee was released from Exeter Prison – where three times on his day of execution the trap door failed to open – he went to Canada during the gold rush.
>
> He did not find any gold, however, and decided to return to England. He opened an antique shop in Praed Street, Paddington, London, and was moderately successful until the London bombings of the war.

A bomb exploded next to his shop and John Lee jumped to the floor as the building collapsed over him.

The emergency squad were called in and rescued him from almost certain death. As Lee was being helped out of the chaos a policeman said to him: 'I bet that is the closest you have ever come to the grim reaper.'

At the outbreak of war, the electoral roll lists only a Mr F.S.J. Lee residing in Praed Street at the Terminus Hotel. If John Lee was living and working in the area at this time, his daughter Eveline was certainly unaware of the fact. Up to September 1939, she was working as a servant in London at Clarendon Court, before marrying a house painter named Benjamin James Truman at Paddington Register Office. On the marriage certificate, her father is dismissed as 'John Lee – occupation not known'.

The search for John Lee's final resting place has long been hampered by the absence of a death certificate, a task made even more difficult by the common nature of the name. However, an exciting prospect was unearthed by co-author Ian Waugh and reported in the *Tavistock Times Gazette*, 31 January 2002:

> Torbay historian Ian Waugh, who lived and went to school in Tavistock in the 1960s & 70s, has been researching the John Lee story for several years. He has traced a death certificate of a John Lee who died in Tavistock Workhouse in February 1941 and was buried in Tavistock Cemetry. The man was also known as George Walters.
>
> Mr Waugh said: 'Reading this certificate and seeing this pseudonym struck me as extremely suspicious. John Lee was in the limelight until the beginning of World War I. After the war interest in him was largely lost, and my feeling is that John Lee wanted to fade into the background. There has been a lot of speculation about him dying abroad, but I don't think he had enough funds for that – I think he just died in obscurity.'
>
> Mr Waugh said John Lee's death certificate showed he was a 'journeyman/painter' and that he died aged 74 of heart disease. . . .
>
> Mr Waugh said: 'If these investigations turn out to be true, it will put to rest extensive speculation surrounding John Lee's final years.'

This line of inquiry had been initiated by a chapter on the 'Man They Couldn't Hang' in the book *Murders and Mysteries in Devon* written in 1996 by Ann James, which stated: 'It has also been suggested that his last years were spent in the workhouse at Tavistock, on the edge of Dartmoor, where he is purported to have died. I made a brief, far from thorough search of the cemetery at Dolvin Road in that town but did not find his grave.' The publisher of the book, Chips Barber of Obelisk Publications, in the course of giving a talk on local history, had obtained the first important clue from a gentleman claiming to be the grandson of a part-time undertaker responsible for laying John Lee to rest.

In 1999, Ian Waugh utilised his local knowledge and turned his attention to another Tavistock Cemetery in Plymouth Road. A search by the cemetery superintendent duly found the record of the burial. Incredibly, the death certificate gave two names, 'John Lee otherwise George Walters'. It was signed by Dr Watt, Medical Officer to the Tavistock Guardians, and William T. Stacey, Master of the Tavistock Institute. The deceased's age was given as seventy-four, whereas Lee would have been two years older, although such mistakes are not uncommon. During the course of our subsequent research we heard from two former gravediggers who had been told by a cemetery supervisor that this was indeed the last resting place of the infamous 'Man They Could Not Hang'.

Further information could not be obtained as the details of the workhouse records held at the Devon Record Office are subject to a hundred-year access ban. A discussion with Chips Barber threw some more light on the story. According to his informant, the homeless Lee had been seeking somewhere to rest late at night, and, finding the gates of the workhouse locked, attempted to gain access by scaling the railings. In doing so, he impaled himself, fell, then lay injured in the mud on a cold winter's night, as a result of which hypothermia contributed towards a rather ignominious end.

Although the death made a large front-page headline – 'Septuagenarian's Death at Tavistock' – almost four weeks had passed before the following report appeared in the *Tavistock Times*, 28 February 1941: 'The death has taken place in Bannawell-street, Tavistock, of Mr. John Lee, who, we understand, went in the name of George Walters. Mr. Lee, who was 74 years old, had lived at Tavistock for several years, and died as the result of a "stroke."' This innocuous coverage by the local press finally quashed our faith in the story as the report states absolutely nothing to support the tale that 'The Man They Could Not Hang' had perished after accidentally 'hanging' from the railings of a workhouse.

WHAT MADE MILWAUKEE INFAMOUS?

With the publisher's deadline rapidly approaching, there was just time to retrace our steps and investigate where John Lee's travels had taken him after the proven fact that he had travelled to New York in 1911. If Lee had remained in the USA, he would have qualified for citizenship after a residential qualifying period of five years. Co-author Mike Holgate stumbled across a press cutting at the West Country Studies Library, Exeter, claiming that this option had been chosen: 'It is reported that John Lee, who served a long sentence of penal servitude after being convicted of the murder of Miss Keyse at Babbacombe, and is now living at Milwaukee, U.S.A., is about to become a naturalised American. He has been in the States five years' (*Express and Echo*, 14 October 1916).

The Wisconsin Historical Society conducted a search on our behalf with spectacular results. A record was found – not from 1916 as we had barely dared to hope – but 1939 when John Lee was alive and well at the age of seventy-five. For some reason, he had left it very late in life before making a Declaration of Intention – the first stage of the legal process in becoming an American citizen. His application confirmed his name as John Henry Lee, born at Abbotskerswell, 15 August 1864, who had entered into marriage at Newton Abbot in 1909 – the date of his wedding to Jessie Bulled. However, he named his 'wife' as Adelina, born on 24 December 1874, at Canterbury, Kent. This lady friend was Adelina Gibbs – the Miss A. Gibb [*sic*] to whom Lee had sent a Torquay postcard when their love affair was developing while they were working together at the London public house Ye Olde Kings Head. The declaration recorded that there were no children from the 'marriage' although at the time of the US 1930 Census, John and Adelina had a fifteen-year-old daughter named Evelyn – a similar name to that given by Jessie Lee to the child born after she had been deserted by her husband. Coincidentally, Londoner

John Lee settled in America and suffered a family tragedy in 1933.

Eveline Lee was married early in September 1939, and her name was misspelt on the licence as 'Evelyn'. Later that month the father she had never known made his Declaration of Intention to the Milwaukee County Circuit Court. The American-born Evelyn was seemingly named after Adelina's mother, for Lee's partner was the third eldest of nine children born to brewer's cashier William Gibbs and his wife, Evelyn. At the time of the UK 1901 Census, the Gibbs family were living in the London Borough of Croydon.

The economic depression of the 1930s seemingly had little impact on John Lee, who, at an advanced age, was employed throughout the decade as a shipping clerk for a motor vehicle company. According to the 1930 Census returns, he owned a home in Milwaukee valued at $2,300. A terrible tragedy befell the family three years later when Evelyn Lee died on 12 October 1933. The incident was reported the following day on the front page of the *Milwaukee Sentinel*:

> Fumes from naphtha with which she was cleaning draperies in the apartment of Dr. Arthur Kovacs, at 1803 W. Wisconsin Avenue, are believed to have caused the death of Evelyn Lee, 19, a maid, whose body was found in the apartment late yesterday by the physician.
>
> The girl, whose home was at 922, S. Tenth Street and who was engaged by the Kovacs only last Friday, was found on the floor of the apartment bathroom, where she had been cleaning the material.
>
> Dr. Kovacs summoned police and himself determined that Miss Lee was dead. The body was removed to the morgue and her parents, Mr. and Mrs. John H. Lee, were notified. An autopsy may be held.
>
> Police were told the maid was using naphtha for cleaning Wednesday, and that Wednesday night she complained of nausea.
>
> Dr. Kovacs found the body Thursday when he returned about 5.40p.m. The bathroom was still redolent with naphtha fumes, police were told.

An inquest was held and reported in the *Milwaukee Sentinel*, 18 October 1933:

> Asphyxiation by naphtha fumes caused the death of Evelyn Lee, 19, a maid in the apartment of Dr. and Mrs. Kovacs at 1803 W. Wisconsin Avenue, Dr. Frank J. Schultz, coroner, decided after an inquest late yesterday.
>
> Miss Lee, who lived at 922 S. Tenth Street, was found dead last Thursday in the bathroom of the apartment, where she had been cleaning drapes with naphtha. She had been alone in the apartment most of the day, while Dr. and Mrs. Kovacs were at the physician's office.
>
> Dr. F.F. Dollert, who performed two post mortem examinations said he is convinced the naphtha fumes caused the death. Burns found on Miss Lee's body were probably caused by the chemical action of the fluid – which saturated parts of her clothing, Dr. Dollert testified.
>
> Other witnesses were Mr. and Mrs. John Lee, the girl's parents; Detective Lawrence Bailey, who investigated, and Mrs. Kovacs. Mrs. Lee said her daughter had been in excellent health. Mrs. Kovacs testified to finding the body when she returned home with her husband.

Evelyn Lee.

The death certificate states that Evelyn Lee's birth occurred in Milwaukee on 1 August 1914, although no official record could be found to confirm this.

Reports of John Lee's demise in Milwaukee in 1933 had been somewhat premature. Perhaps the untimely end of his daughter that year had been somehow misconstrued by sections of the press? At the time of their bereavement, John and Adelina were living in the city at 922 South 10th Street, where they still resided in 1939. Lee did not follow up his Declaration of Intention by formally applying for citizenship – as he was entitled to do a minimum of two years later. This led us to assume that he had not survived this period, but the street directories of Milwaukee show that the couple had moved to 454 East Holt Avenue by 1941. Curiously, they were listed with slight name changes as James and Adeline Lee. In 1947, 'Adeline' was living alone at the same address as the 'widow of John H'. Disappointingly, a search of the records by the staff of the Wisconsin Department of Health and Family Services failed to turn up a death certificate, and our quarry seemed to have eluded us once again. However, the 1920 Census for Milwaukee revealed that five-year-old Evelyn's parents had adopted the aliases 'James and Adeline' – perhaps to cover their tracks and avoid deportation, as they had entered the USA under false pretences. At long last our search came to a successful conclusion when a death certificate was unearthed for James Lee.

'James' Lee had cardiac problems. Ten days after receiving a visit from his doctor he succumbed to heart failure at his home on 19 March 1945. He was eighty years old and had survived sixty years more than anyone could have predicted when he was placed on the scaffold at Exeter Prison. His 'widow', 'Adeline', survived until the grand old age of ninety-four and passed away at Elm Row Nursing Home on 9 January 1969. There is absolutely no doubt that 'James and Adeline' are the same couple as 'John and Adelina'. The death certificates of the former give their birth dates, which tally exactly with the information on the Declaration of Intention bearing the names of the latter. 'Adeline' also confirmed her identity by naming a sister, Grace Gibbs of Surrey, England, in her will. John Lee made no will and there was no obituary or funeral report to give a detailed insight into his long association with Milwaukee. In an effort to disassociate himself from his lurid past, he had evidently craved anonymity. In keeping with the mysteries that had been a feature of an eventful life, his death certificate and death notice in the local newspaper name him as 'James' Lee, although he lies buried in a grave marked 'John' Lee alongside his common-law wife and daughter in a family plot at Forest Home Cemetery, Milwaukee. 'The Man They Could Not Hang' became, until now, 'The Man They Could not Trace'.

CHAPTER 10

The bungle on the scaffold

I regret that ever I was fated to take part in the ghastly business, and I only hope that some day the lesson of it may sink home and be a powerful factor for the abolition of capital punishment.
— James Berry, *Thomson's Weekly News*, 19 February 1927

John Lee was by no means the first man to walk away unscathed from the scaffold, and nor was he the first to survive three attempts. The original 'man they could not hang' was Joseph Samuel, who gained a remarkable reprieve in Australia in 1803. A cart supported his weight until the moment of execution, when it was driven away from under him. Two ropes broke and a third slowly unravelled, rendering him unconscious. Lee, however, remains the only prisoner to survive the method whereby the condemned man was executed by releasing a trap beneath his feet. Following the unique failure of such a mechanism to act, a legend was born, spawning numerous theories as to why Lee's life had been spared.

PROVIDENCE

Given that Lee had resolutely refused to admit any culpability, many God-fearing people naturally assumed that a miracle had occurred to save an innocent man from the gallows. This belief was bolstered by fanciful tales of a white dove hovering over the scaffold and the undeniable fact that on the morning of the appointed execution, the prisoner had related a prophetic dream to his two warders. Following the failure of the execution, they duly reported the incident to the prison governor:

> At 6am, when John Lee rose from his bed, he said, 'Mr. Bennett, I have dreamed a very singular and strange dream. I thought the time was come, and I was led down through the reception out into the hanging place, but when they placed me on the drop. They then took me off from the drop and took me (instead of the way I had come) around the A Wing, and back through the A Ward to my cell.'

> Samuel Bennett, Assistant Warder
> James Milford, Superior Officer

> (Norton File, Exeter Prison Museum)

A peculiar aspect of Lee's dream highlighted the route taken to and from the scaffold – a decision criticised by the Reverend John Pitkin: 'For some reason, unknown to anyone but himself, the Governor ordered the procession to pass down some awkward stairs, which led to the reception basement and through a door in the reception ward, which opened directly opposite the scaffold-house. It was an unfortunate way, and was never used before nor since' (Pitkin, 1918).

In answer to a request from Lord Clinton, Chairman of the Exeter Quarter Sessions, the details of Lee's dream were confirmed by the prison chaplain:

> After the attempted execution on February 23rd 1885 I went to his cell and spoke to him about the extraordinary event that had happened to him. He replied that on the night before his execution he had a dream which had shown him what would happen. At my request he relayed it to me. He said that in his dream he saw himself being led from his cell down through the reception basement to the scaffold which was just outside the basement door. He saw himself placed upon the scaffold and efforts being made to force the drop, which, however, would not work. He then saw himself led away from the place of execution, since it was decided that a new scaffold would have to be built before the sentence of the law could be carried out. He told me that when he awoke at six o'clock on the morning fixed for his execution he had mentioned the dream to two officers who were in the cell with him. (Pitkin, 1918)

John Lee revealed that his parents had also experienced a supernatural happening on the eve of the execution: 'All night long there were strange rappings on the bedroom wall. A table by the bedside shook. A candlestick on the table fell down, and the candle was broken in two pieces. In spite of that it remained alight. When at last my mother did get to sleep she had a strange dream. She thought she saw me on the scaffold. The bolt was drawn, but the rope broke, and I was thrown to the bottom of the pit!' (Lee, 1908).

All the officials involved in the failed execution were required to submit reports to Henry James, the Under Sheriff of Devon, which were then passed to the Home Office (HO 144/148//A38492). In his submission, the Reverend Pitkin evidently did not share Lee's view that his prayers for deliverance had been answered. He contended that far from being an act of God, it was an act of common humanity by the medical officer and himself which had brought the proceedings to a halt:

HM Prison, Exeter
9 March 1885

> My dear Sir,
>
> I beg to report to you that I attended at the condemned cell at 7.55 on the morning of the 23rd February to read the Burial Service at the execution of John Lee. I commenced the service outside the cell, and preceded the condemned man to the scaffold, reading the service meanwhile.
>
> Having reached the place of execution, I took up my position on the right of the building; I expected to hear the fall of the drop while I was concluding with the grace.

Having concluded the service, I found the man had not been executed. I then turned to the Psalms appointed for the burial of the dead.

While these were being read Lee was taken off the drop by the executioner, and when he tried the drop, which seemed to work, Lee was placed on the second time; I had nearly read through the service the second time before the second attempt was abandoned. During this time there seemed to be much confusion among the officers, and I felt that I ought to go on reading to keep the painful scene as quiet and orderly as possible.

After the second attempt the Governor removed Lee to the 'A' basement. I followed; no-one uttered a word. In about two minutes the executioner summoned us to the scaffold. When the rope had been again placed on Lee's neck a great noise was made in attempting to move the bolts of the drop, but the effort failed.

With this third attempt I began the service at the Lord's Prayer, and when I had finished I asked the Governor if the execution had been performed, and having a negative reply, I began the service for the fourth time.

For some minutes this third effort was tried, and when I saw that the condemned man was again removed from the drop I appealed to the Governor to stop all proceedings.

The Governor said that the Sheriff was responsible.

More than 30 minutes had elapsed since I first began the service at the condemned cell. Then, when I saw the helpless confusion that prevailed, the great mental suffering through which the culprit had passed, and the improbability of the scaffold working, I joined with the medical officer in an appeal to the Under Sheriff to postpone the execution for that day. Great cruelty would have characterised further effort to carry out the sentence that day.

Lee suffered much, and seemed to be almost unconscious of what was going on. He would rather have died, I verily believe, and the first words he uttered after he had been led back to his cell, and recovered from his state of apparent semi-unconsciousness, were 'Why am I not to die?' On looking back upon the events as they happened, one cannot help deploring them; and one is driven to the conclusion that if only thoughtful care and supervision had been exercised in the erection of the drop, and in its examination prior to the attempted execution, all this public scandal would have been avoided.

The prison chaplain was supported in his action by the medical officer, T. Wilson Caird:

I have the honour to state, with regard to what transpired at the attempted execution of the condemned prisoner John Lee, that on the morning of 23rd ultimo, in compliance with an Act of Parliament known as the Private Execution Act, I attended the place appointed for the said execution; that I did not actually witness the original proceeding, but that on finding that a failure had taken place, I at once went to the front, placing myself by the side of the Chaplain, to encourage that officer in my presence; that I beheld the prisoner at the back of the coach-house, pinioned, a white cap over his face, and with the rope around his neck, while the prison officials and the executioner were trying the flap of the drop.

That Lee was again placed on the drop; that another attempt failed; that I then said he should be withdrawn; that a scene of confusion ensued. A hatchet being sent for, a chipping of the woodwork took place; that the prisoner was again put on the platform, the noose etc., being re-adjusted. That this third attempt having failed, I ordered him to be removed to a cell near, myself attempting to take him into my reception ward through which he had previously passed. That I am reported to have said to the prison officials, 'You may experiment as much as you like on a sack of flour, but you shall not experiment on this man any longer.'

That he was accordingly taken into a passage near; that presently the Governor informed the Chaplain and myself that the apparatus would not work; that I then desired that the man should be taken back and the execution postponed; that the said condemned prisoner was returned to his cell; that I offered the Under Sheriff a certificate, which he was glad to accept. That such certificate was drawn up in my office and signed by the Governor, Chaplain, and myself, for the information of Her Majesty's Secretary of State.

I beg further to report that I am of the opinion that no blame whatever can be imputed to the Under Sheriff, who came utterly unsupported, not accompanied as of yore by his subordinates. And that the failure was entirely due to the faulty construction of the apparatus. I think when a weight was placed upon the drop, the lever withdrawing the bolts could not act.

An alternative view of divine intervention was put forward by the American judge Marcus Kavanagh. A firm believer in the death penalty, he once participated in a public debate entitled 'Does Capital Punishment Deter Criminals?' The learned judge addressed the case of John Lee's deliverance in an article published in *Mind*, September 1931: 'However, if the event was providential, may it not rather be understood as proving his guilt? Do we not place too much terror on the idea of dissolution? Is it nearly so great a misfortune as we imagine and is not all of its agony composed in its apprehension? May it not be, in short, that the crime of John Lee was so ungrateful, so cruel, so atrocious, that Providence made him suffer the death penalty not once but three times?'

Whether or not John Lee's ordeal on the scaffold was salvation or condemnation, the Governor of Exeter Prison may well have reflected on the power of divine intervention when he observed the text for the day in his diary for 23 February 1885: 'Surely it is the hand of the Lord which has done this thing.'

WITCHCRAFT

Superstitious folk saw Lee's remarkable escape from death as the work of the Devil. In South Devon, locals told of how a gypsy had walked to Exeter on the morning of the execution and kept a vigil overlooking the prison from Rougemont Hill, where she cast a spell on the gallows declaring, 'They shall not hang him!'

Another colourful story of sorcery from a correspondent signing himself LD appeared in the *Western Daily Mercury*, 7 May 1898:

Doubtless you remember the trial of John Lee for the murder of Miss Keyse, and how, strange to relate, the hangman could not hang him. There is a sort of superstition in connection with that which you may not know. Eight years ago an Exeter man lodged here, and he told me the reason John Lee was not hung was because of some supernatural power a woman (whom he knew intimately) exercised. She is termed 'a white witch'. The condemned man's friends visited this woman, beseeching her to use the power she possessed to save him from that awful death. Of course, she was to be paid handsomely for it. She doubted her ability to save him from the gallows, but promised to do her utmost.

Lee himself poured scorn on such tales: 'I believe a great deal of foolish talk went through the country about this time. Since my release I have been told how people said that on the night before the execution my mother went to the churchyard and said the Lord's Prayer three times backwards! Old Farmers also declared that I could not be executed because my family was controlled by all sorts of spirit influences. Some even went so far as to say that the Witch of the Moors would protect me. Witch, indeed! I never believed in witches' (Lee, 1908).

Remarkably, the witchcraft theory gained support from a surprising source. At the height of the campaign for Lee's release, the Home Office heard from the Chaplain to the House of Commons:

27 March 1905

The Archdeacon of Westminster telephoned this morning to say that he knew John Lee and his family well: that they were a well-known 'witch' family on Dartmoor, and there was a legend that no Lee could ever be hanged. He added that Lee had vowed to 'do for' all those who gave evidence against him if ever he should get out.

Further information was immediately sought by an official to clarify the Archdeacon's startling contention:

I wrote to Archdeacon Wilberforce to ask if he could kindly give us any further details of Lee's threats. The Archdeacon called today, and said that he only knew of the statement made by Lee at his trial, namely, that when he came out of prison he would 'do for' all those who had given evidence against him. (It should be explained that Lee had throughout complete confidence that he could not be hanged. He said no Lee could be hanged, and that 'they' had once 'tried to hang his mother' and failed.) [See Chapter 13 for an explanation of this last sentence.] All the threatened witnesses, the Archdeacon added, are now dead save one, so the risk of release is so far diminished. But he said the crime was about the worst and most cold-blooded it was possible to imagine, and did not think that, if Lee came out, anyone would give work and have anything to do with him. (HO 144/1712//A60789/62)

Archdeacon Basil Wilberforce was the son of the prominent anti-slavery campaigner William Wilberforce. The churchman was also a close friend of Lord and Lady Mount-Temple of Babbacombe Cliff. In December 1884, shortly after the murder of their neighbour Miss Keyse, Wilberforce stayed with the Mount-Temples. Both he and her ladyship were devoted supporters of the temperance cause, and to this end the purpose

Lord Mount-Temple. He and his wife were close friends of Archdeacon Wilberforce.

of his visit was to attend a three-day Blue Ribbon Mission held in Torquay. He was then struck down by illness shortly after the attempted execution of Lee, but *The Times* announced on Friday 3 July 1885 that 'Canon Wilberforce continues to make good progress towards recovery, and was able to go to Babbacombe Cliff, Torquay on Wednesday'. It is clear, therefore, that Wilberforce did not 'know the Lees well'; in fact he did not know them at all, but passed on his opinions to the Home Office based solely on gossip and superstitious nonsense gathered during his frequent visits to Babbacombe. Lord Mount-Temple died in 1888, and Wilberforce was an executor of his will. When renowned philanthropist Lady Mount-Temple passed away, Wilberforce was invited to unveil a statue to her memory on Babbacombe Downs in October 1903. Eighteen months later, Lee was understandably aggrieved when the Home Secretary gave the impression to the House of Commons that there were no plans for his immediate release because he had threatened witnesses still living; this outrageous statement was made utilising unsubstantiated comments made by a sadly out-of-touch churchman who firmly believed that witchcraft was practised on Dartmoor.

INCOMPETENCE

Executioner James Berry established a unenviable reputation for incompetence and suffered embarrassment at several executions. The former boot salesman and policeman, hailing from Bradford, Yorkshire, plied his trade as a freelance hangman receiving commissions from county sheriffs to carry out the sentence of the courts. Later in life, he came out strongly in opposition to the death penalty, but fought his conscience long enough to execute 134 men and women between 1884 and 1892.

James Berry.

Problems occurred when Berry tried to calculate the length of rope required to break the neck and bring about instantaneous death. This method known as the 'long drop' had been devised by William Marwood, whom Berry had assisted at executions while 'learning the ropes'. It was based on a system of tables which took into consideration the age, weight, build and general health of the prisoner and allowed a length of rope between six and ten feet. If the 'drop' was too short, the result was slow strangulation, with the panic-stricken official trying to accelerate the process by holding onto the condemned man's legs. In cases where too much rope was allowed, the unfortunates had their heads partly severed as the jerk of the rope sliced through their necks.

The appalling scene with John Lee produced this comment from Queen Victoria in a telegram to the Home Secretary: 'since this executioner has taken it in hand there have been several accidents' (Royal Archives, Windsor Castle). Thereafter, apprehension increased in prisons all over the country when Berry was officiating. In November 1885, the executioner arrived at Norwich Castle to carry out the hanging of wife murderer Robert Goodale and found the prison staff in a state of panic. It transpired that one of the warders had experienced a recurring dream in which he had seen Goodale beheaded instead of hanged. The warder told Berry he had experienced the dream on three consecutive nights and urged him to tell the authorities that it was inadvisable to proceed.

Berry was anxious after his recent experience with Lee, but did not believe in dreams and omens. Furthermore, he had no wish to call off the execution and lose his fee. What followed was one of the most horrific botch-ups in the annals of capital punishment, which was graphically described by Berry in his memoirs: 'When I pulled the lever the drop fell properly and the prisoner dropped out of sight. We were horrified, however, to see that the rope jerked upwards and for an instant I thought the noose had slipped from the culprit's head or that the rope had broken. But it was worse than that for the jerk had severed the head entirely from the body and both had fallen into the bottom of the pit' (Berry, 1892).

The decapitation was the only recorded instance of this happening at an execution in Britain, although two of Berry's other hapless victims, Moses Shrimpton at Worcester and John Conway at Kirkdale, Liverpool, were nearly beheaded by the drop. Mercifully, the latter case brought Berry's tortuous career to a conclusion. He resigned, although he did not accept any responsibility for the fiasco, blaming the prison doctor for interfering with his calculations and forcing him to amend the length of the 'drop'.

In his defence, it is difficult to see how even a bungling oaf like Berry could have been *unwittingly* responsible for the failure of the trap at Lee's execution. For, although he was widely regarded as the villain of the piece, his only direct involvement in the preparation of the scaffold was to carry out a simple test by pulling the lever to ensure the doors fell easily. At that time there was no requirement for the executioner to try out the equipment using a dummy, which might have highlighted the resultant problem.

THE SCAFFOLD

Close scrutiny has been brought to bear on the apparatus used for the attempted execution and several theories have evolved to explain why the trapdoors worked perfectly until John Lee stood upon them. The most amusing of these stories is the suggestion that as part of the conspiracy to save an innocent man, warders were positioned beneath the gallows and held the doors up with their hands. Slightly more plausible explanations were as follows:

RAIN

World events recorded in the *Annual Register 1885* placed the blame firmly on the vagaries of the British weather: 'John Lee, who had been convicted of the murder of Miss Keyse at Babbacombe, was brought up for execution in Exeter Gaol. The rope was adjusted, the Burial service read, and the signal given, but the drop would not act. This was repeated three times, and at the end of half an hour it was decided to postpone the execution, and subsequently Lee's sentence was commuted to penal servitude for life. The rains of the two preceding days had, it was said, caused the planks of the drop to swell, and hence the trouble.'

This simple explanation was universally accepted at the time and supported by the Chief Constable of Devon, Gerald de Courcy Hamilton, in his official report to the Under Sheriff:

Gerald de Courcy Hamilton.

9 March 1885

On the prisoner reaching the place of execution he was placed by Berry, the executioner, immediately under the cross-beam, over which was carried a rope; he was faced outwards towards the door, with both feet standing transversely on the junction of the two flaps or shutters which formed the drop. The executioner, with considerable skill and rapidity (as it appears to me), strapped the culprit's legs above the ankles, drew the cap over his face, adjusted the noose round his neck, stepped back and pulled the iron handle or trigger, to let fall the foot-boards; to my intense astonishment, however, these latter deflected only about a quarter of an inch and appeared to be tightly jammed together about the centre. The executioner and some of the prison officials standing by endeavoured, by stamping on the boards, to get them to move, but without avail. After some seconds the prisoner's face was uncovered, and he was led away to an adjoining cell or room in the prison. In the meanwhile, the executioner and the prison officials did their best to ascertain the cause of the machine not working. My own impression was that, the morning being very wet and damp, the foot-boards had become swollen, and were thus unable to free themselves when their top edges came in contact. I consequently urged the use of a plane, and pointed out the spot which I considered caused the impediment.

The prison engineer procured a plane and a tomahawk, and we eased the centre of the boards. A prison warder was made to stand on them, holding on by both hands to the rope; the trigger was pulled, and the boards fell. The prisoner was then brought out again, and the execution proceeded as in the first instance, but again the boards refused to fall. The same thing happened a third and, I think, a fourth time, between each occasion every effort being made by the officials (and I may also mention myself personally) to discover and rectify the defect, but in the natural hurry and anxiety of the situation, without effect.

After the fourth attempt to carry out the sentence, the prisoner was taken back into the prison. I remained on the spot for a short time with the executioner and some of the prison officials, still endeavouring to discover the seat of defect in the machine; after which I repaired to the office of the medical officer of the prison, where I found that officer; together with yourself, the Governor, and the chaplain of the prison, in consultation as to the course of action to be pursued under the circumstances.

A cynical correspondent signing himself 'A Friend and Neighbour of the Murdered Lady' poured scorn on this theory in a letter to the editor of *The Times*, 25 February 1885:

Sir, – It appears that John Lee, who broke the skull and cut the throat of his mistress and benefactress and then set fire to her body, is not to be hanged, because, owing to the rain on Sunday night, the drop did not work easily the next morning.

It should be announced that in future, executions will take place weather permitting.

SABOTAGE

Theories that convict labour had been used to prepare the scaffold resulting in sabotage committed by a member of the working party with advanced carpentry skills surfaced when an ex-convict told the *Referee* in May 1901 that he had met the old lag responsible a couple of years earlier in Wandsworth Prison:

> The story he told me with regard to the unsuccessful attempt to hang John Lee was this: It appears that the man I was incarcerated with was originally a carpenter, and he and several others who were undergoing sentences in the prison in which Lee was awaiting execution were directed to prepare the scaffold for this event. The drop part of it was to be made in the carpenter's shop and fitted to the rough structure in the prison yard, and it was when they were engaged in fitting the trap-doors together that the idea was conceived of inserting a flange in the sides of the flap, so that any pressure exerted from above forced the flange into a slit in the adjacent woodwork. When no weight was on them the doors fell away quite freely upon the withdrawal of the bolt. This idea was carried out. After the first attempt at precipitating the murderer into the pit below the scaffold, and when the trap-doors refused to fall inward, the man who told me the story was sent for, and with a plane was set to reduce the ends of the doors until the pit could be seen through them, thus leaving at least a quarter of an inch all round them, except where the hinges joined them to the scaffold. The hangman then withdrew the bolt and the doors fell away quite easily. The carpenter was conducted back to his cell, and two more attempts were made to hang Lee without success. It was only when the scaffold was taken down that what had been done was discovered.

Another variant of this theme was recalled by the *New Reveille*, 6 February 1975. During the First World War, Frank Ross was working as a cleaner at Chelmsford Prison. He met a warder who claimed he had escorted Lee to the scaffold. The warder told Ross that the gallows were constructed by convict labour, which included a lifer who was a master joiner. The platform was deliberately built in such a way that, when the prison chaplain stood on a warped board facing the prisoner, his weight flattened the board and jammed the trap. This theory was expanded upon in the *Herald Express*, 27 November 1984:

> Paignton pensioner Mr Vivian Bedford believes he knows why the drop refused to work – and it has nothing to do with 'divine intervention,' as the legend has it. In fact it started as just a joke.
>
> What happened, he says, is that one of the prisoners building the scaffold found a warped board and inserted it in such a place that when the chaplain, a 15 stone man, stood on the board it was pushed flat and acted as a lock on the trap doors.
>
> Mr Bedford, 72, says he proved the theory by building a quarter-scale model of the gallows with some friends.
>
> The theory, put forward 50 years ago in an article in a Midlands newspaper, answers the riddle of why the trap doors worked when a sandbag was used as the victim. Because the chaplain was not standing on the board, the drop opened.
>
> Bring Lee back – and therefore the chaplain, and it becomes 'miraculously' stuck again.
>
> Mr Bedford, of Conway Road, says: 'Fifty years ago there was an interesting article in one of the Birmingham papers. At the time I was apprenticed as a carpenter and joiner

and was interested because it said the reason they could not hang the man was because of a warped board. We built a quarter-scale model and it worked.

'The prisoners did it on purpose, probably as a joke against the warders. They had no idea it would save a man's life.'

Although it was demonstrated by Mr Bedford and his friends that it was technically possible to jam the trap with a warped board, it could not possibly have happened at the execution of John Lee. Unusually, the scaffold was not raised on a platform, but positioned at ground level with a pit below it in the prison coachhouse. The prison chaplain did not stand on a plank in front of the prisoner on the scaffold, as the Reverend Pitkin made it clear in his statement: 'I took up my position on the right of the building.'

Death-bed 'confessions' of the 'master joiner' involved became popular, as this example from barrister Ernest Bowen-Rowlands, in his book *In the Light of the Law* (1931), shows. He received the following letter from a 'well-known person' who claimed to have heard from someone the following:

An old lag in the goal confessed to him (I think when dying) that he was responsible for the failure of the drop to work in the execution of the Babbacombe murderer. It appears that in those days it was the practice to have the scaffold erected by some joiner or carpenter from among the prisoners. The man inserted a wedge which prevented the drop from working and when called in as an expert he removed the wedge and

This illustration of the attempted execution of John Lee incorrectly shows the scaffold at Exeter Prison raised on a platform.

demonstrated the smooth working of the drop, only to re-insert it before Lee was again placed on the trap. This happened three times and finally Lee was returned to his cell with doubtless a very stiff neck.

Further evidence to support this claim was given by former inmate J.R. Pile, of Bideford, North Devon, in a letter sent to the *Western Morning News*, 13 March 1945:

> Sir,
>
> About 25 years ago I read a death-bed confession of a fellow-prisoner, a carpenter, detailed either to make or do something to the trap-door of the scaffold.
>
> He confessed he told John Lee to stand on the middle board of the trap-door, as he would make that one board warp, so that when his weight was on it, it straightened sufficiently to hold the door up.
>
> As the trap-door would fall without any weight on it those concerned thought there was a divine providence behind it. There was also a sketch of the scaffold and it was headed 'The Man Who Played a Practical Joke.'
>
> P.S. According to what I read, the two men agreed that John Lee should say on the morning of his execution that he had had a dream that night that he should not be hanged.

The above story sounds extremely far-fetched, but it is interesting to note a contemporary comment in *Trewman's Exeter Flying Post*, 25 February 1885: 'Lee walked on to the drop without hesitation, placed himself in position with studied care and almost military precision.'

Executioner James Berry unveiled his own theory about the scaffold in his official report:

> 1 Bilton Place
> City Road
> Bradford
> 4 March 1885
>
> Sir,
>
> In accordance with the request contained in your letter of the 3rd instant, I beg to say that on the morning of Friday the 20th ultimo, I travelled from Bradford to Bristol, and on the morning of Saturday the 21st from Bristol to Exeter, arriving at Exeter at 11.50am when I walked direct to the county gaol, signed my name in the gaol register book at 12 o'clock exactly. I was shown to the Governor's office, and arranged with him that I would go and dine and return to the gaol at 2.00pm. I accordingly left the gaol, partook of dinner, and returned at 1.50pm. I was shown to the bedroom allotted to me, which was an officer's room in the new hospital ward. Shortly afterwards, I made an inspection of the place of execution. The execution was to take place in a coach-house in which the prison van was usually kept. Two warders accompanied me on the inspection.
>
> In the coach-house I found a beam, about four inches thick and about a foot in depth, was placed across the top of the coach-house, the ends being fixed in the walls on each

side. Through this beam an old iron beam was fastened with an iron nut on the upper side, and to this bolt a wrought-iron rod was fixed, about three-quarters of a yard long. With an hole at the lower end, to which the rope was to be attached. Two trap-doors were placed in the floor of the coach-house, which is flagged with stone, and these doors cover a pit about 2 yards by 1½ across and about 11 feet deep. On inspecting these doors I found they were only about an inch thick, but to have been constructed properly should have been three or four inches thick. The ironwork of the doors was of a frail kind, and much too weak for the purpose.

There was a lever to these doors, and it was placed near the top of them. I pulled the lever, and the doors dropped, the catches acting all right. I had the doors raised, and tried the lever a second time, when the catches acted again all right. The Governor was watching me through the window of his office, and saw me try the doors. After the examination I went to him, explained how I found the doors, and suggested to him that for future executions new trap-doors should be made about three times as thick as those then fixed. I also suggested that a spring should be fixed in the wall to hold the doors back when they fall, so that no rebounding occurred, and that the ironwork of the doors should be stronger. The Governor said he would see to these matters in future.

I spent all the Sunday in the room allotted to me, and did not go outside the gaol. I retired to bed about 9.45 that night.

The execution was fixed to take place at eight o'clock the morning of Monday 23rd ultimo.

On the Monday morning I arose at 6.30, and was conducted from the bedroom by a warder at 7.30 to the place of execution. Everything appeared to be as I had left it on the Saturday morning. I fixed the ropes in my ordinary manner, and placed everything in readiness. I did not try the trapdoors, as they appeared to be just as I had left them.

It had rained heavily during the nights of Saturday and Sunday.

About four minutes to eight o'clock I was conducted by the Governor to the condemned cell, and introduced to John Lee. I proceeded at once to pinion him, which was done in the usual manner, and then gave the signal to the Governor that I was ready. The procession was formed, headed by the Governor, the chief warder, and the chaplain, followed by Lee; I walked behind Lee, and six or eight warders came after me.

On reaching the place of execution I found that you were there with the prison surgeon. Lee was at once placed on the trapdoors, I pinioned his legs, pulled down the white cap, adjusted the rope, stepped on one side, and drew the lever, but the trapdoors did not fall. I had previously stood upon the doors and thought they would fall quite easily.

I unloosed the straps from his legs, took the rope from his neck, removed the white cap, and took Lee away into an adjoining room, until I had made an examination of the doors. I worked the lever after Lee had been taken off, drew it, and the doors fell easily. With the assistance of the warders the doors were pulled up, and the lever drawn a second time, when the doors again fell easily.

Lee was then brought from the adjoining room, placed in position, the cap and rope adjusted, but when I again pulled the lever it did not act, and in trying to force it, the lever was slightly strained, Lee was then taken off a second time, when the doors again fell easily.

It was suggested to me that the woodwork fitted too tightly in the centre of the doors, and one of the warders fetched an axe and another a plane. I again tried the lever, but it would not act. A piece of wood was then sawn off one of the doors, close to where the iron catches were, and by the aid of an iron crowbar the catches were knocked off, and the doors fell down.

You then gave orders that the execution should not be proceeded with until you had communicated with the Home Secretary, and Lee was taken back to the condemned cell. I am of the opinion that the ironwork catches of the trapdoors were not strong enough for the purpose, that the woodwork of the doors should have been about three or four times as heavy, and with ironwork to correspond, so that when a man of Lee's weight was placed upon the doors, the iron catches would have not have become locked, as I feel sure they did on this occasion, but would respond readily. So far as I am concerned, everything was performed in a careful manner, and had the iron and woodwork been sufficiently strong, the execution would have been satisfactorily accomplished.

James Berry (Executioner)

In his notebook, published long after his death, James Berry stuck to his original prognosis, but added an amazing rider which was revealed by *Thomson's Weekly News*, 19 February 1927:

A great many explanations, and a great many theories were circulated about the failure, but until this day the real truth has not been given, and it is only with reluctance that I give it now. My firm conviction is that the scaffold had been interfered with before the execution, but in what manner, I am not altogether in a position to say.

What I do know is that on the morning of the execution a warder passing a cell heard a prisoner laughing.

Now an execution has a strange effect on every man in the gaol, and sends to their knees men who have never in their lives lifted their eyes to Heaven in prayer.

The warder was so astonished that he opened the cell door and took the man to task. He was a prisoner doing a long sentence, and as a rule, was well-behaved, and the warder thought a stern rebuke would bring him back to his usual state of mind.

'What are you laughing at?' he asked sternly. 'On a morning like this too! It is a very serious matter.'

The prisoner only laughed in his face, laughed so heartily that the walls echoed with merriment. 'You will never hang John Lee this morning,' he said.

'And what makes you say that?' asked the warder. 'What nonsense are you talking?'

'Well, you wait and see,' replied the man. And again he laughed heartily.

This story I know to be true, and I know, moreover, that the scaffold was constructed by prisoners skilled in this work.

All these stories about a master craftsman lack one vital ingredient – the name of the alleged saboteur. However, during the course of our research, one finally emerged from a descendant living in Canada. According to our informant, Thomas Phillips, a joiner from Barnstaple, North Devon, was caught poaching and refused to pay a fine and was therefore sentenced to imprisonment at Exeter for three months. During his incarceration, his carpentry skills were utilised on the gallows. When he was released, his son asked him why the trapdoor had not opened at John Lee's execution. Thomas replied: 'Who taught you your trade?' and the son acknowledged, 'You did.' Thomas then added mysteriously, 'Would you say I was a good carpenter or a bad carpenter?' and the son readily agreed, 'A good carpenter.' Thomas indicated that if he had wanted a trapdoor to open, he could have made it open easily, but apparently believed implicitly in the condemned man's innocence.

With feelings running high in the run-up to an execution, it would have been highly insensitive for prisoners to have been used in the arrangement of the death of a fellow inmate. Prisoners probably assisted in the dismantling, relocation and re-erection of the scaffold in 1883, but an internal investigation into what had gone wrong at the execution included detailed statements from all the participants involved in the preparation of the scaffold. The Governor of Exeter Prison, Edwin Cowton, reported as follows:

> HM Majesty's Prison
> Exeter
> 9 March 1885

> On the morning of Saturday 21st February, the apparatus was by my order thoroughly overhauled, cleaned, and tested by the engineer officer, and a warder carpenter. On the afternoon of the same day the apparatus was again tested by the artisan warder and Berry, the executioner, the latter, after trying it twice over, reporting to me verbally that he was satisfied with it for the present use.

> On Sunday the 22nd the van-house was closed and locked throughout the day: Berry, the executioner, remaining in the prison all day.

> On Monday 23rd the van-house was cleared and prepared: at 7.15am I went with the executioner to see the rope fixed to the beam; the drop was not tried on this occasion. At 7.55 I accompanied Berry to the condemned cell and saw Lee pinioned; conducted the procession to the place of execution, the condemned man was placed under the beam, every preparation complete, and Berry pulled the lever; it would not act to release the drop; Lee was moved back at once, the drop tried and found to work; he was again placed under the beam, the lever again pulled, but it did not act; again he was removed for the preparation of another attempt; brought back prepared and placed in position, when for the third time it did not work.

> I removed Lee at once into an adjoining room, and after consultation with you, took him back to his cell.

The following statements submitted to the Governor by the artisan warder and his assistant show that they were the only two people to work on the scaffold immediately before the execution, giving no opportunity for sabotage to be carried out by convict labour:

9 March 1885

Sir,

I beg to state, for your information, that according to your instructions that myself, assisted by Assistant Warder Titford, carried the necessary preparations of the execution apparatus, on Saturday 21st February, which was afterwards tried and inspected by Mr. Berry, and found satisfactory; but I regret to say it turned out a failure at the time of the execution, February 23rd, morning, and from careful inspection find the cause of its not working is from the iron bearing bars of trap doors being too light, and lengthening with the weight of the body caused it to lock. I would add, that I carefully examined the same apparatus for the execution of Edwards, in November last [prisoner was reprieved]. I then considered it fit in every respect as it worked satisfactorily upon trial.

Charles Edwards (Artisan Warder)

9 March 1885

Sir,

By your orders, I assisted the artisan warder on Saturday, the 21st of February, to remove the van and shift bearing, etc., oil all bearings of scaffold, clean out pit and give trap three distinct trials; this was done, and found to work satisfactorily with ease, and was restored to proper order.

A.J. Titford (Assistant Warder)

HOME OFFICE INVESTIGATION

The Under Sheriff, Henry James, resigned over his part in the fiasco, despite the outcome of a Home Office investigation carried out the day after the execution by a team of officials led by Major McHardy, Surveyor of Prisons. During their visit to Exeter Prison to inspect the scaffold they discovered the reason why, when they placed a weight equivalent to that of Lee on the platform, the trapdoors would not always fall (HO 144/148//A38492):

Prison Department
Home Office
Whitehall SW1
February 25th 1885

REPORT ON THE CAUSE OF THE FAILURE OF THE MACHINERY
OF THE SCAFFOLD AT EXETER PRISON ON FEBRUARY 23RD 1885

The scaffold was fixed originally in 1879 in an old building which was afterwards demolished and then re-erected in 1882 in its present position in the van-house. It had been used on several occasions in its original position, but no execution had taken place at Exeter since its removal to the van-house.

A sketch showing the construction is enclosed, it will be seen that there are two wooden flaps or doors which form the platform, having two hinges each and those of one half of the platform stretch right across the whole width of the opening and have

Right: Transverse
view of platform.

Below:
Longitudinal view
of lever and
platform.

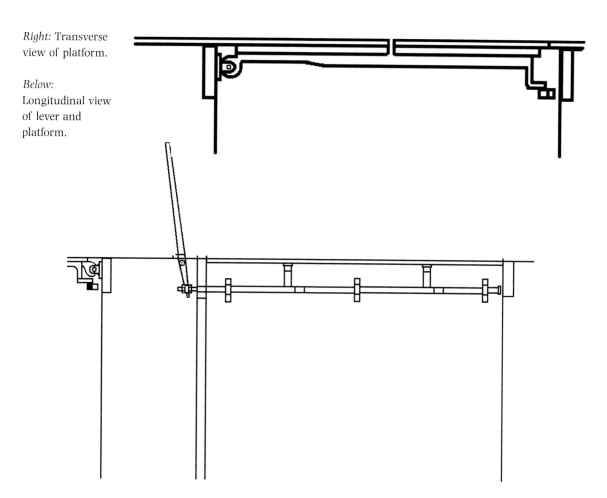

their ends supported on the draw-bolt. These two long hinges therefore practically support the floor of the scaffold. By moving the lever the support of the draw-bolt may be withdrawn from the ends of these long hinges which are then brought over cranks or bends in the bolt, and so the ends are allowed to drop down, and the flaps or doors of the platform should at once open downwards

It appears that the machine was worked on Saturday 21st by the artisan warder of Exeter Prison. It was also worked by the executioner on the same day, as was considered by the Governor and above fit for use, the executioner having made some remark about future scaffolds having the floor-boards thicker.

On Saturday it was tried several times, without, however, any weight being placed on it for execution. When the lever was then pulled it moved the draw-bolt, but the platform did not give way.

As it was thought that this was due to the wooden flaps fitting too tightly where they met in the centre, the warders tried to cut away the edges of the boarding, but this easing did not have any effect in allowing the machinery to work.

It was not until the Under Sheriff left that it was discovered there was something wrong with the iron-work.

A careful examination of the scaffold was made by Messrs Libby & Cuthbert clerks of works, who visited the prison on Tuesday morning.

They found the apparatus under cover in the van-house and apparently quite dry.

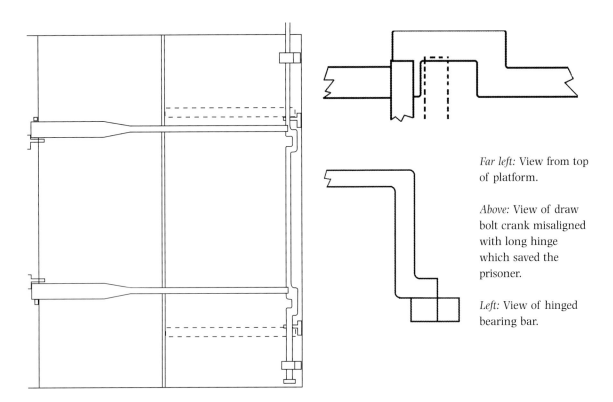

Far left: View from top of platform.

Above: View of draw bolt crank misaligned with long hinge which saved the prisoner.

Left: View of hinged bearing bar.

They examined the details of the apparatus from beneath the platform. On looking at the draw-bolt from the top where a board of the platform had been removed, signs of friction were apparent on the inner surface of one of the cranks in it.

Believing that the bearing of the end of the hinge at this point was the cause of the failure in the machinery, they tried to move the lever with a weight equivalent to 168 lbs on the platform, and the platform would not fall.

They discovered that the end one of the long hinges was resting on one eighth of an inch on the draw-bolts at the crank.

Then they tried to work the lever without any weight on the platform and found that when the lever was drawn quickly the platform fell. If drawn slowly, on one trial it remained fast, and on another it fell, but seemed to bind or grate at the end of the end of the long hinge already referred to.

They were then perfectly satisfied that the cause of the failure to act was due to the fact that one of the long hinges rested on the draw-bolt one eighth of an inch too much. It is probable that in the re-fixing of the scaffold the two sides were placed one eighth of an inch nearer than they had been before or that the long hinges had been very slightly bent in some way at the time.

Although the Home Secretary announced in the House of Commons that he had instigated an investigation into events at Exeter Prison, the official report on why the scaffold had failed was classified for a hundred years, which only served to fuel myths and endless speculation about Lee's fortuitous escape from death. The simple truth was that by placing his weight on the trap, John Lee had inadvertently saved himself. However, he had been extraordinarily lucky, for apart from the fact, highlighted by

Gerald de Courcy Hamilton, that the doors had acted when a warder balanced gingerly on them while holding onto the hangman's rope, the report of the acting engineer, A.W. Gorman, showed that when the scaffold had first been moved, it had indeed been tested with weight:

> In the absence of the engineer officer (about September 1883) I was appointed to act in his place, during which time I was instructed to go on with the new van-house and execution apparatus, which I did. The frame and trap, with their fitting, which I used were those used on a former occasion in the old hospital, being refitted to a new pit, which is about 2 feet 6 inches shorter than the old one. After having finished the apparatus I tested it with weights, and without weights; the former, by tying three half hundred weights in a piece of canvas, suspended from the beam, and placed on the trap where a person would stand, with about three feet drop, and found the apparatus to work all right without the slightest jerk or strain to the lever.

Following the bungle on the scaffold at the execution of John Lee, Queen Victoria was quick to recognise the need for a review of the procedures and immediately made a suggestion about how future gallows should be constructed in a communication to the Home Secretary: 'Surely some safe and certain means could be devised which would make it quite sure. It should be of iron not wood, and such scenes must not recur' (Royal Archives, Windsor Castle). In consequence, Lord Aberdare was appointed to head a committee to inquire into 'The Execution of Capital Sentences'. Their brief was to look into arrangements which would ensure that all 'future executions might be carried out in a more becoming manner'. In 1888, the committee published their report, making several recommendations, including the adoption of scaffold apparatus of a standard design and rope of an approved length and thickness (HO 144/212//A48697).

Fortunately, the committee did not consider the advice of the Sheriff of Devon, Octavius Bradshaw, who had been conspicuous by his absence at the execution of John Lee. It appears that he favoured the 'shove in the back' method, which would doubtless have horrified the watching pressmen even more than the debacle they had witnessed. In a letter to the Home Secretary, the Sheriff suggested that a great deal of embarrassment could have been saved by a little imaginative improvisation:

> As Sheriff for the County of Devon I write to tell you how deeply distressed I am at the disgraceful scene which took place on Monday last . . .
>
> The sentence should have been carried out in a decent way by those who accepted the responsibility, but who appear to have entirely lost their heads. I would suggest how much more satisfactory it would be if a permanent Public Executioner was appointed, and officers, whose training has fitted them to witness executions than to subject men to whom it is a real torture to be present. Had a few planks been used after the drop had first failed to act, or some similar means been adopted over the drop, we should have been saved the disgrace of all the revolting bungling that took place, and the country would have been rid of a most callous and barbarous murderer. (HO 144/148//A38492)

CHAPTER 11

If it wasn't the butler – whodunit?

It has been surmised that more than one person was concerned if not in the tragedy itself at least in its arrangement. There have been various rumours afloat on this point and even persons have been named without any warrant whatsoever.

– Torquay Directory, 26 November 1884

John Lee was condemned to death as a murderer when faced with an overwhelming tide of circumstantial evidence. The crime had all the hallmarks of an 'inside job' and Lee had talked of 'putting an end to one in the house'. The accused could not account satisfactorily for the amount of blood on his clothing and a bloodstained knife was found in a drawer near his bed. He had also threatened to 'level the place to ashes' and oil used to fuel the fire was kept in the 'butler's pantry'. As a leader in *The Times*, 5 February 1885, commented on the verdict: 'There was practically no defence . . . the only wonder is that it should have delayed the jury three-quarters of an hour.'

However, speculation about the degree of Lee's guilt surfaced soon after his arrest and continued to grow following his deliverance from the scaffold. This was bolstered by the fact that the prisoner had prepared for death devoutly, refusing to admit any guilt. Who else might have been involved in such a terrible crime? The possible twists in the real-life plot and the number of suspicious characters among the friends, neighbours and acquaintances of the victim in the case of 'Who Killed Emma Keyse?' would have graced a fictional 'whodunit' by Agatha Christie, the Torquay-born 'Queen of Crime'.

THE NOBLEMAN

One of the more outlandish theories about the death of Emma Keyse suggests that she was killed because she knew too much about the affair between showgirl Lillie Langtry and Edward, the Prince of Wales, who had visited The Glen on two occasions. The 'Jersey Lily' had relatives living in Torquay and visited the town in 1874 while she was honeymooning with the ill-used Edward Langtry. Three years later she became the royal mistress. However, if the establishment had to resort to eliminating everyone who knew of the affair, it would have resulted in mass murder, for this was surely one of the worst-kept secrets in the kingdom. Despite this, rumours about someone in high places getting Lee off persisted. The best-connected family in Babbacombe was that of Baron and Baroness Mount-Temple (William Francis Cowper and Georgina Tollemache) of

Babbacombe Cliff. The Baron was the uncle of Lord Cowper, who addressed the House of Lords following the botched execution of Lee and suggested that the government should appoint a full-time public executioner to replace part-time hangmen. Baron Mount-Temple was the stepson of Victorian Prime Minister Lord Palmerston and the nephew of another premier, Lord Melbourne. One of Baroness Mount-Temple's relatives, Mr W.A. Tollemache, was also a neighbour of Emma Keyse and became aggrieved when she renamed her house The Glen a year or so before her death: 'The change of the name in the place was the cause of some correspondence between Miss Keyse and Mr Tollemache, who had already given that title to his house [Babbacombe Glen] situated higher up the valley' (*Torquay Directory*, 25 February 1885). This quarrel has the appearance of a minor dispute, but neighbours often enter into long-running feuds over trivial matters which escalate into hatred and violence. Supposing Mr Tollemache had 'arranged' for someone to pay the disenchanted 'butler' to burn down The Glen, resulting in the unintended death of Miss Keyse? In this scenario, Tollemache had an excellent contact to save John Lee from the death penalty, for the Home Secretary was Sir William Vernon Harcourt, the nephew of Lady Mount-Temple's brother-in-law.

The Prince of Wales.

THE FISHERMAN

The petty dispute with Mr Tollemache demonstrates that Emma Keyse was not universally popular with her neighbours. The fishing community in particular had good reason to despise her, for she had instigated legal proceedings against them. This issue was raised in the obituary of solicitor Isadore Carter:

> In the Babbacombe Bay murder case, with John Lee, Mr Carter was retained by the Crown as the solicitor to prosecute. A fact which is not generally known in connection with this case was that Miss Keyse who was living in a house overlooking Babbacombe Beach, was a client of Mr Carter, and the day before the murder he had fought and won a case for her regarding certain beach rights. He returned to Torquay in the evening, and

Emma Keyse objected to fishermen 'erecting capstans in front of her house'.

was in two minds about seeing Miss Keyse that night to tell her the result, but, knowing her habit of retiring early, he decided to see her the next day. But early on that same morning, his gardener told him of the tragedy. One cannot help but comment inwardly on the probable different trend events might have taken if Mr Carter had decided to see Miss Keyse on that fatal night. (*Herald and Express*, 22 February 1936)

Apart from the obvious error in stating that Emma Keyse retired early, when it is well-established that she usually went to bed after midnight, this version of events also varies considerably with a contemporary account of the dispute published in the *Torquay Directory*, 19 November 1884:

Miss Keyse was held in great respect by the people of Babbacombe and St. Marychurch, for to the poor of these places she was a kind friend. It has been said that the fishermen had a hostile feeling against her because she objected to their erecting capstans in front of her house for the purpose of hauling up their boats. This might have been the case some time ago, but the cause of that feeling has long been removed. A test case was tried at Torquay County Court several years ago, when the decision of the judge was given against Miss Keyse. She accepted the result with a very good grace, and only on Thursday last it was stated at the St. Marychurch Local Board meeting that she had consented to a lamp being put up on her premises to guide the fishermen to the landing place during the dark and stormy winter nights.

With Miss Keyse having found a buyer for the Glen estate, it seems highly improbable that any of the local fishermen would still be harbouring grievances over the question of beach rights. However, an alternative theory evolved in 1959, when John Pike appealed to readers of the *Herald Express* for information to aid his research into the Babbacombe Murder. Two of the people who came forward mentioned the same name as a possible suspect. One of these informants, Mr Phillips of Brixham, was the great-grandson of chief boatman George Phillips, one of the principal witnesses at the trial of John Lee. According to the story that had been passed down through the Phillips family, the general feeling at the time of the murder was that Lee was certainly involved in the crime, but his hand had not committed the murder. Apparently, there had been a wild party at The Glen attended by members of the staff and others. When Miss Keyse suddenly appeared to try and disperse the happy gathering, she was struck down by a man called Stigings. The latter name turned up again in the account of a Mrs Kenneally, an elderly resident of Torquay, who had heard a story that Lee was courting the housemaid and his brother-in-law Stigings took exception to the relationship and started a fight with Lee. When Miss Keyse intervened to try and break up the brawl, Stigings unleashed his fury on the old lady and Lee then took the blame to protect his sister and the couple's children. The guilty fisherman was later found dead in his cottage on Babbacombe Beach.

A close-knit community existed on Babbacombe Beach, with many of the families interrelated. Three brothers, Richard John Stigings, Thomas Henry Stigings and William Gasking Stigings, were nephews of William Gasking, landlord of the Cary Arms, and, if Mrs Kenneally's version is to be followed to its natural conclusion, then one of them was married to Amelia Lee, whose brother John was 'courting' their half-sister Elizabeth Harris. Confused? You needn't be, because Amelia Lee was single and remained in service after leaving The Glen.

Two of the Stigings brothers were involved in the legal proceedings against John Lee. William made a model of The Glen which was produced in court, while Thomas was a witness recalled in John Lee's autobiography: 'Jane [Neck] and I at once called a man named Stiggins [*sic*], who was living in one of Miss Keyse's cottages on the beach. He was a fisherman.' According to Lee, Thomas Stigings was the first person summoned to The Glen. Yet surprisingly, this witness was not called upon to testify at the inquest or

William Gasking Stigings.

magistrate's hearing, but appeared at the trial, largely contradicting the evidence of others by insisting that the axe produced to fight the fire by Lee had been handed to him, not George Pearce. Shortly after the murder his family moved to a new address in Babbacombe, where he and his wife Charlotte gave Jane Neck a home following the death of her elder sister, Eliza, which was reported in the *Torquay Times*, 10 December 1886: 'Eliza Neck, one of the servants of the late Miss Keyse, at Babbacombe, and an important witness at the trial of John Lee, died suddenly at the Glen late on Sunday night. Since the time of the well-known tragedy, Eliza Neck and her sister Jane Neck, have been living in the house, being maintained by gratuities received from curious strangers who visit the now celebrated spot.'

Following the death of their employer the two sisters had simply continued to reside in the burnt-out cottage, which had been emptied of all its contents at an auction held on site and attended by hundreds of curiosity seekers in April 1885. Jane spent her last years lodging with the Stigings and their seven children until her demise, which is recorded in the *Torquay Directory* of 15 April 1891: 'Jane Neck, one of the two elderly servants of the late Miss Keyse, died on the 5th instant, at the age of 77. . . . The late Jane Neck was one of the principal witnesses at the inquest and trial of John Lee, the alleged murderer, when she stated that she had been in the service of Miss Keyse since 1836.'

Although there were no suspicious circumstances, the third brother, master mariner Richard John Stigings, died at the age of fifty in June 1886. According to his death certificate, he was a diabetic whose condition caused him to suffer kidney failure. The cause of death was determined by Dr Herbert Chilcote, who himself died later that year of bowel disease at the age of forty-six. In recognition of the doctor's services to the poor and sick, a monument was erected to his memory in St Marychurch.

THE BUILDER

Another reference to the possible incestuous involvement of John Lee and Elizabeth Harris emerged during the week of the hundredth anniversary of the botched execution, when a local man approached the *Exeter Weekly News*, 22 February 1985:

> An Exeter man believes he has an answer to the mystery of 'the man they couldn't hang'. . . .
>
>   Over the years, theories as to how Lee escaped death have abounded, ranging from practical explanations like swollen wood, to intervention by supernatural forces. But Mr. Ken Goss, of Friars Walk, Exeter, has a much simpler explanation, which he firmly believes to be the true reason Lee cheated the gallows. Lee protested his innocence, says Mr. Goss, because he did not murder Miss Keyse, his elderly employer. And he did not hang because of a conspiracy concocted by the real murderer to save his neck. . . . Mr Goss, 62, told the *Exeter Weekly News*: 'I was told in 1937 by my grandfather, Bill Holloway with whom my mother and I lived in Torquay. He swore me to secrecy and said I should not repeat what he had told me until 100 years after the attempted hanging.'
>
>   Even now, Mr. Goss will not allow us to publish the name of the man he believes was the killer. 'He still has descendants living in Torquay today, and I do not want to bring trouble on them,' he said.

Mr. Goss revealed that the man was a wealthy and well-respected Torquay builder, who was friendly with Miss Keyse. According to Mr. Holloway's version of events, Lee was climbing the back stairs to his quarters at Miss Keyse's home, when he met the murderer coming down. Lee had got a young lady 'into trouble', something which was severely frowned on at the time, and the murderer blackmailed him into taking the rap, probably agreeing to pay him a sum of money for going along with the plot.

The builder managed to convince Lee that he would never hang, which explains why he appeared so calm as he walked to the gallows. 'He nearly gave the game away by looking up at the rope,' said Mr. Goss. 'Somehow, the carpenter rigged the gallows and I think the hangman must have been in on it too, because he supplied the rope. The story going round the fishing families of Wellswood and Babbacombe at the time was that the noose was treated with a substance fishermen use to stop ropes stretching.' . . .

Mr. Goss is still trying to trace a document which he says gives details of the plot. It was shown to him by an uncle in 1945, but he has not seen it since.

'I think one of my cousins must have it,' said Mr. Goss. 'I hope they haven't disposed of it, because it substantiates my grandfather's theory.'

And he added: 'I swear the story is true. I'd be prepared to swear on the Bible.'

The only 'wealthy and respected builder' living in the immediate vicinity of The Glen was Frederick Matthews. His finest achievement in Babbacombe was the completion of All Saints Church in 1874. A week before the Babbacombe Murder, the St Marychurch Local Board, on which Frederick Matthews occupied a seat, announced a plan to build a

The Downs overlooking Babbacombe Beach. Frederick Matthews was arrested for picking flowers from the gardens.

pier on Babbacombe Beach. Matthews was successful in obtaining the contract and the pier was completed in 1890. Lord Mount-Temple and W.A. Tollemache were leading lights in the project, and their kinsman architect L.F. Vernon Harcourt gave his services free of charge. The structure was dedicated to the memory of Levison Vernon Harcourt. For reasons not satisfactorily explained, the press reported that the opening event was boycotted by the very people it was built to serve – the local fishermen.

Frederick Matthews then fell from grace in humiliating fashion. In March 1894, he was arrested for picking flowers from the public gardens on Babbacombe Downs. The Local Board met and discussed the fate of a former member and decided that they could not intervene in the matter. The chairman observed: '. . . the picking of flowers had been going on for a long time. He had been informed that Mr Matthews was in the habit of doing it' (*Torquay Times*, 14 March 1894).

This incident caused a split in the builder's family. Frederick Matthews's brother Thomas left the company, where he had been foreman, to set up his own building business with borrowed capital, but went bankrupt three months later with debts totalling over £600.

Ten years earlier, Frederick Matthews had been a member of the inquest jury which had found John Lee guilty of 'wilful murder', and now he was charged with a trifling but embarrassing offence which had ruined his reputation. One wonders about the state of mind of the elderly businessman who felt the need to steal flowers when he lived in a fine residence, complete with its own garden, in the road leading to Babbacombe Beach.

THE SMUGGLER

If Frederick Matthews was the builder in the story told by Ken Goss, what possible motive could he have for committing murder? One possibility is that he was involved in smuggling activities, which were rife in the area. Only two days after the Babbacombe Murder, two French seamen were brought up before the magistrates at Torquay Police Court, having been apprehended concealing bottles of brandy: 'Some difficulty was experienced in eliciting from the defendants any facts relating to the charge, and eventually to settle the value and quality of the decoction itself, a bottle was uncorked, and to the amusement of those in Court, was passed round for the gentlemen on the Bench to determine its quality. Fines of five shillings were paid' (*Torquay Times*, 21 November 1884).

This story illustrates the fact that smuggling was not then considered to be in any way disreputable but a rather heroic pastime. Further tales were recalled in 1922 by William Henry Grant (1836–1924), the last chairman of St Marychurch Urban District Council before the area was incorporated into Torquay Borough Council in 1900. His account mentioned some interesting names associated with the Babbacombe Murder: 'Smuggling was intensive at times and was carried on chiefly by the Babbacombe fishermen. The fishery was then a very important industry, and there were several large owners of fishing gear, boats, seines, nets, etc. There were the Messrs. Thomas, Harris, Matthews, Gasking and others' (Pateman, 1991).

The Thomas family were fishermen and ran a business catering for tourists at Oddicombe Beach and Anstey's Cove – situated either side of Babbacombe Beach; boat owners Richard Harris and William Gasking were witnesses at John Lee's trial; and businessman Frederick Matthews was a juror at the inquest into the death of Emma Keyse. John Lee was short of money, knew all the local mariners and was ideally placed at The Glen to act as a lookout. Mr Grant recalled that the darkest night of the month was selected and a watcher on shore would guide the cargo vessel with a system of signals given with a lamp. Once landed in Babbacombe at appropriately named spots such as Smugglers Cove or Brandy Cove, the heavy kegs would be collected: 'They would be carried to many destinations, anyone who could be trusted might order a couple and they would have to employ a carrier at their own risk. . . . The Babbacombe Coastguard station was then one of the principal on the coast. The chief officer was a captain or lieutenant and a warrant officer, a chief

William Gasking.

boatman with about twenty navy men as ordinary guardsmen, besides two revenue cutters patrolling the channel and bays, so those engaged in the matter had a very formidable opposition to contend with.'

At the inquest, while questioning a witness, John Lee involuntarily stated that he had gone to bed still wearing his collar and necktie, which suggests that he had not removed these uncomfortable items of clothing as he intended to get up for some purpose later that night. Therefore, did Matthews meet Lee at The Glen late at night and disturb Miss Keyse, who descended the stairs and died for her trouble? Perhaps Lee then covered up for the builder's crime by using his signal lamp to set fire to the place. At the inquest, witness Charles Sutton testified that he had been told by Lee that Miss Keyse had been burnt through a benzoline lamp being overturned. Once arrested, perhaps Lee loyally refused to 'split' on his fellow conspirators even at the cost of his own life. Furthermore, William Grant said that the adventurers had little to fear from informers, as people were afraid of reprisals against themselves and their families.

According to William Grant, Jonathan Thomas was a favourite model for artists and it was the old salt's likeness that appeared on adverts of the period for Lifebuoy soap. A Paignton resident, W.B. Spry, recalled his boyhood memories of the arch-smuggler for readers of the *Herald Express*, 15 August 1959: 'I used to listen to that grand old man of Oddicombe, Mr Thomas, describe dramatically all the circumstances of the tragedy, the trial of John Lee, and the abortive execution. At the end of his description, with the intimacy of personal acquaintance with every character in the case, he never failed to add, with absolute certainty in his voice, "He never did it! No more than I – he never did it!"'

THE 'WOOD CHOPPER'

During the campaign for Lee's release from prison, Stephen Bryan of Leigh received information from Londoner Emma Balkwill, who had been told by a Mrs Caunter of Torquay that the Babbacombe Murder had been committed by a 'wood chopper'. Bryan evidently wrote to Mrs Caunter, but to the puzzlement of his informant received no reply (Bryan Letters, Exeter Prison Museum):

> 682 Kings Road
> Fulham
> 17 August 1907

> I received your letter this morning, I cannot think why Mrs. Caunter don't answer your letter as she was anxious for me to make it known to someone in London to get Justice done to John Lee. But there was one thing she mentioned, it was that the old wood chopper's family lived near her at Torquay and she was afraid they would do her an injury if she told what she knew. I believe she told me that she was cook at Miss Keyse, she must not go back from what she told me and my daughter or what I have told you. I can swear to, I would go down and see her if I could afford it. I hope she will own up to what she said as it will be very unpleasant for me. Would you advise me to write to her on the subject, if so, please send me her address back, which is on the postcard, if you say not to, I will not do so.

> I am sir, yours truly
> Emma Balkwill

> PS. I may tell you that I have been at Chelsea Railway station as attendant Ladies Rooms for fourteen and a half years.

Bryan eventually succeed in getting Mrs Caunter's cooperation, but following Lee's release received a strange request from Emma Balkwill, which he curtly dismissed:

> Leigh, 23 January 1908

> Dear Madam,
>   I beg to acknowledge receipt of your postcard, which you posted on the 18th ult. I note you request me to return to you, a photo of Mrs. Caunter's house, situated at Torquay, also a postcard which she sent to you. I regret to inform you Dear Mrs. Balkwill, that I am unable to do so, for the following reasons, namely, after I received certain letters from you and the above named which referred to John Lee's case, I promptly sent the same to the Chief Detective Inspector, Criminal Investigations Depart. New Scotland Yard, London, and as you forwarded me the above for the purpose of assisting poor John

Smuggler 'Jonathan Thomas' dangles a 'noose' with a cryptic message.

Lee, it seems strange to me that you want them back now he has been released. I also am aware that you have wrote to him since he has arrived home. Further I desire to acquaint you I have sent John Lee, Mrs. Caunter's address and no doubt she will be found. She will then have an opportunity of saying what she knows about The Babbacombe Crime, and if in case you desire to obtain the aforesaid photo & postcard, you must apply to the above named official at Scotland Yard. At the same time I am afraid that they would refuse such an application, you are at liberty to make what you think of this letter.

I beg to remain yours faithfully,
Stephen Bryan

The correspondence from Mrs Caunter, the documents sent to Scotland Yard and, crucially, the name of the suspect have not been located, and it is therefore only possible to surmise. It may be recalled that, following his spell in prison for theft, John Lee was invited by Miss Keyse to return to The Glen and 'work in the garden with my gardener for a while'. Much of The Glen estate was woodland, and the 1881 Census reveals that nineteen-year-old Simon Bartlett was the 'gardener'. However, his name was never mentioned during the murder inquiry. If the two young men had been working alongside each other, then Bartlett would have gained a useful insight into Lee's attitude towards Miss Keyse which would have been of interest to the jury. Perhaps there is another explanation for his non-appearance in court. The prosecuting solicitor Isadore Carter stated at the magistrate's hearing that the prisoner 'did work in the house and also acted as gardener'. Therefore, had Bartlett been dismissed to rehabilitate a petty criminal? If so, he might have planned a terrible revenge. Having lived at The Glen, he would have been fully aware of the household routine and known the layout of the rooms – vital knowledge if he wanted to gain access to the premises, kill his former employer and then 'plant' evidence on the unsuspecting occupant of his old bed in the pantry.

THE SILVER DEALER

Without naming and shaming the suspect, John Pike revealed another theory on the seventy-eighth anniversary of the murder to the readers of the *Herald Express*, 15 November 1962:

> It seems that on the night of the murder three or four men, including Lee, were entertaining women at The Glen when Miss Keyse interrupted them. Apparently one of the men at the party was a 'dealer' in silver and in a position to pay the hangman.
>
> Mr. Pike said he did not think that Lee was totally innocent of the crime, but he thought that someone else could have struck the blow and paid Lee to 'carry the can' assuring him that he would not hang. This could have been the dealer. . . . According to Mr. Pike, there is little doubt that Lee was at the house, but it was highly possible that he did not commit the crime.

The late Mr Pike's research notes, preserved at Torquay Reference Library, show that the name of the silver dealer was self-proclaimed 'bad boy made good' George Tregaskis, an acknowledged connoisseur of the antiques trade who was equally renowned for his violent temper. The information about his involvement in the case came from the son of a local character called 'Old Oliver'. At the age of sixteen, Mr Oliver senior went down to the scene of the crime and saw Tregaskis, who was asked to account for his movements by the police. The dealer had visited Miss Keyse several times before her untimely end, and 'Old Oliver' used to say that Tregaskis was interested in obtaining Miss Keyse's 'plate'.

Tregaskis revelled in a 'tough guy' image, which he carried from his schooldays. As an *enfant terrible* he once turned on a teacher, causing him to flee for his life. In his youth, he became a useful amateur boxer and also gave tuition in the noble art to members of the gentry, including a son of Isaac Singer, the American sewing machine magnate, who spent his last years in Torbay at Paignton. Later in life, Tregaskis became an hotelier. Following his retirement at the advanced age of seventy-eight, he spoke frankly about his connection with the murder in an article published in the *Torquay Directory*, 11 September 1935:

> Mr. George Tregaskis, who has sold his hotel at Torquay, told me a very interesting story the other night. As most of our readers are aware, he was for a long time in the antique business and was very well known to all collectors, including Miss Keyse, who was the victim of the Babbacombe murder, 50 years ago. John Lee was convicted of the offence, and, as everybody knows, was never hanged, although the executioner tried three times.
>
> Miss Keyse had some valuable *objets d'art*, and occasionally asked Mr. Tregaskis to go up and look them over. He would have done a deal with her on one occasion, but she said she did not wish to part, and the expert got the idea that she was simply approaching him with the view to sucking his brains and finding out what was the value of certain articles without actually consulting him in a professional capacity.
>
> A week before the date of the tragedy Miss Keyse wrote him saying she would be prepared to sell some candlesticks and other stuff. Would he call? He decided to see her once more in the hope of picking up something valuable.

The hotel owned by George Tregaskis.

The evening arrived when he thought of going to Babbacombe, but just outside he met a friend, and instead went to the theatre. A few hours afterwards he was told that Miss Keyse had been murdered. Mr. Tregaskis said he did not remember ever before knowing fear, but when he heard the news of the tragedy his hair stood on end. He felt that he had narrowly escaped being suspected of a very serious offence.

The point he makes is this. Had he gone up that night and secured some valuable pieces he would have brought them away, and probably sent on a chit in the course of a day or two. Then it would have become known that he had visited the house, for the goods would have been found in his possession. The real murderer might, of course, have been traced, but at the time he thought that grave suspicion would have fallen upon him.

Mr. Tregaskis can also look upon the affair from another angle. 'I have always thought,' he said, 'that had I visited Miss Keyse that night she might not have been murdered because probably the negotiations would have gone on for a long while, and it might have been late before I left the house.'

Mr Tregaskis' life story . . . shows that he was a person who got into many scrapes in his young days. On one occasion, before he was married, he was accompanying a lady home from a social function at night. In those days public houses closed at 11pm, and for half-an-hour the square in front of the Market Inn partook of the nature of a fair, and men were often about looking for trouble. As he passed one group on this occasion a man made a rude remark which was overheard by his lady friend. She took his arm and urged him not to mete out punishment to the offender. Mr. Tregaskis was itching to teach the man a lesson, but the lady had her way, and he went home, promising on the way that he would not go back and chastise the 'rough.' Up to a point he kept his word, but when he put his key in the door and opened it he came over all of a tremble. His hand shook, and he said he felt that nothing could prevent him going back to the square and seeking out the rude one. When he got there he found a knot of 'roughs' and asked them who had been offensive to him and his lady earlier on. A big fellow stepped forward, and before he knew what was happening Mr. Tregaskis had hit him with his left and one with his right and finally bowled him over with another left. The man lay still, and one of his pals said: 'You should not hit a man like that.' Mr. Tregaskis immediately offered to fight him as well, but there was no 'take-up,' so he went back home and went to bed.

An hour or so later there was a knock on the door, and his landlady came to tell him that the police wanted him.

He dressed and went below, and the officers of the law told him that they were afraid he had done his man in. He must accompany them to the Police Station. They were very decent about the whole matter, and seemed to believe he had received considerable provocation, but at the same time they thought it likely that the man might not recover as he was still unconscious. Tregaskis was not actually confined to the cells, but was detained in the office, talking to the night staff.

Fortunately, the man recovered, and no charge was made.

'You see', he said, 'I was pretty well known, and although a fighter, I was never a bully, but if anyone insulted me and went about looking for trouble they usually got it.'

The fact that Tregaskis was willing to talk about these events suggests that he had nothing to hide, but on the other hand, it is known that men of a boastful nature often feel compelled to claim the 'credit' for committing a crime. Why should Tregaskis, described later in his obituary published in the *Torquay Times*, 12 August 1938, as 'a notable personality' in Torquay's 'business, social and sporting life', choose as his chief claim to fame being a peripheral involvement with a murder which had occurred over fifty years earlier? Had he seen something among Emma Keyse's valuables that he coveted, then perhaps elicited help in obtaining it from John Lee, or Elizabeth Harris if they were romantically attached? One expensive item of jewellery did go missing on the night of her death and was never accounted for: 'On Wednesday it was rumoured that a valuable ring the property of the late Miss Keyse was missing. It is well known to her relatives and servants that she was in the habit of wearing this ring, and of taking it from her finger and placing it on the dressing-table in her bedroom on retiring to rest. The other rings which the deceased wore were found on her body, but the diamond ring in question was missing' (*Torquay Times*, 21 November 1884).

THE LOVER

Without the support of the father of her child and shunned by her family for giving evidence against her half-brother, Elizabeth Harris was forced to seek refuge in the work-house where she gave birth to a daughter, Beatrice, on 24 May 1885. In letters to his family, written from the death cell, Lee left no doubt that his half-sister held the key to what had really happened on the night of the murder. Suspicion naturally fell on the unknown lover of the pregnant cook, which was compounded in a long statement made to the vicar of Abbotskerswell by the condemned man a few days before his intended execution. The statement of the prisoner was reported in the press, but its substance was dismissed when submitted to the Home Secretary. In it, Lee said that on the night of the murder he was woken by strange noises coming from outside the pantry. On looking out into the hall, he saw his half-sister, Elizabeth Harris, creeping down the stairs, accompanied by a masked man. He later saw a bloodied knife in Elizabeth's bedroom, but did not say anything to the authorities as he felt it was a cowardly act to make such serious allegations implicating a woman.

Elizabeth Harris.

This 'confession', missing for ninety years, was discovered at Exeter Prison by a BBC team filming the documentary *The Man They Could Not Hang*, broadcast in 1975. It was found hidden between the pages of the prison governor's diary for 1885. Sadly, since the diary was passed to HM Prison Service Museum, the statement has seemingly been lost again. Lee did not actually name the person he thought was the 'masked man' until a few days after the aborted execution – and thankfully that document survives. Following incessant questioning, the information was finally extracted by the prison chaplain, who immediately forwarded this communication to the Home Office:

Exeter Prison
27 February 1885

For the information of the Home Secretary, I send you the following particular.

After pressing John Lee, for the 50th time almost, to tell the name of the man, whom he states as being at the Glen with his half sister, on the night of the murder of Miss Keyse, he yesterday said he would not swear to him, but he believed him to be Cornelius Harrington, a Babbacombe fisherman. His half-sister, he said, can give the man's name.

John Pitkin

(HO 144/148//A38492)

Following this rather less than positive identification from Lee, the Chief Constable of Devon, Gerald de Courcy Hamilton, was instructed to investigate the claims, which suggested that the motive of the 'masked man' was the theft of a cash box. The plea was dismissed out of hand in a damning report delivered to the Secretary of State:

Chief Constable's Office
Exeter
20 March 1885

Sir

In further reply to your letter of the 13th instant respecting the written statements of the convict John Lee . . . I have the honour to inform you that I have personally made careful enquiries in order to ascertain if there is any truth in them and I can arrive at no other conclusion than that they are absolute fabrications, for the following reasons:

1st Elizabeth Harris declares most positively that the allegations made by the convict respecting her and the supposed man are 'lies' and having subjected her to cross examination I am unable to see any reason to doubt the truth of the evidence she gave at the trial, and which she declared, she is ready at any time if called to reiterate on her oath.

2nd Cornelius Harrington is one of a respectable crew of fishermen resident in Babbacombe, who was never known at any time ever to have been on Miss Keyse's premises and who I am informed was in his quarters on the night of the murder, and against whom there does not seem to be the slightest ground for suspicion.

3rdly The extreme circumstantiality of the convict's statement defeats its own object and establishes its falsity, and is moreover contradicted on numerous important points by incontrovertible evidence of facts, as for instance, such a cash box and writing desks as described were never known by any of the old servants in the house to have existed, no property of any sort had been stolen, and the only cash box the deceased lady was in the habit of using was a small wooden one, which I found in its accustomed place intact, when I searched the rooms and wardrobe. . . .

I would beg to call attention to the fact that the story now put forth by John Lee was only committed to appear by him on the Wednesday previous to the day fixed for his execution although he was represented by Counsel at the Coroner's Inquest, the Magisterial investigation and the trial at Assizes and it bears strong evidence of having been built up by the prisoner upon the foundation of the suggestions thrown out by his Counsel at the Assizes that there might have been the possibility of the half-sister, Elizabeth Harris, having admitted a man who might have perpetrated the murder. (HO 144/148//A38492/51)

There is one surprising omission from this report: the chief constable, reportedly an 'intimate friend' of the victim Emma Keyse, evidently did not establish who the father of the child was and does not state whether he actually asked Elizabeth if she was willing to divulge the man's identity. This would have been the only sure way of eliminating anyone from the scenario described by Lee. She was of course quite entitled to withhold this information, but the secretive nature of her affair and the fact that her daughter was born in the workhouse indicate that her lover was either married or from a higher station in life. If she had been courted by a single working man, social pressure embodying Victorian family values would probably have led him to 'do the right thing' and enter into a 'rush marriage' to legitimise the birth. Another possibility is that Elizabeth had a fleeting romance with Cornelius Harrington, about whom little is known, or someone else she barely knew during the Babbacombe Regatta. This social event with an annual fair was the highlight of the summer season. It was held in late August, the time of her child's conception, and would have allowed her to escape the rigours of life in service and given her a rare opportunity for a sexual encounter. The secret of Beatrice Harris's parentage might have been easily solved if Elizabeth had given a clue to the identity of her lover when naming her child – as her own mother had done thirty years earlier in similar circumstances. At the time of the 1851 Census, nineteen-year-old Mary Harris was working in the picturesque Dartmoor village of Widecombe, as a general servant for farmer Nicholas Esterbrook, his wife and two sons of working age. Four years later she left the farm under a cloud when her pregnancy came to light and subsequently christened her daughter Elizabeth Hamlyn *Esterbrook* Harris – indicating that she had been taken advantage of by a member of her employer's family.

CHAPTER 12

Whispers from the law chambers

I am one of those who was never fully satisfied of his guilt.

– Walter Molesworth St Aubyn, 1885

Defence barrister Walter Molesworth St Aubyn expressed his concern at the validity of the case against his client John Lee, and it transpired that he was not the only member of the legal profession to have reason to doubt the verdict of the court. For, while the suspects outlined in the previous chapter may be considered to be merely the object of the authors' musings, local gossip or a figment of Lee's imagination, equally fantastic stories emerged from seemingly unimpeachable sources – respected figures of the legal establishment in Torquay.

One of these accounts was revealed in an article published in the *Herald Express*, 15 November 1962:

> The Torquay Borough Librarian (Mr. J. Pike) has been trying to solve the mystery of what happened to Lee after he left this country.
>
> In 1959 the Herald Express published an article about Mr. Pike's research, which was taken up by newspapers in other parts of the country. As a result Mr. Pike received information from people all over Britain. All of it appeared to be speculation. But a local man came forward with information, not about his whereabouts after his release, but about the abortive hanging. The name of Mr. Pike's informant cannot be revealed, but this man was fully convinced that the hangman was 'got at.'

John Pike was naturally reticent to name names at the time the article was published, as his informant had died just a few months previously. Many years later, he generously shared his knowledge of the case with fellow researchers and revealed that the man who had told him this sensational story was leading Torquay solicitor Percival Almy (1872–1962). 'Pa' Almy, as he was popularly known, was head of the legal firm Almy & Thomas. A man of many distinctions, he served in local courts for over sixty years and was a president of the Devon and Exeter Law Society. He was selfless with his time and boundless energy. His list of long-serving involvements in a variety of organisations was staggering and include the following positions: President of Rotary International of Great Britain and Ireland, a life-member of the governing council of the National Society for the Prevention of Cruelty to Children (NSPCC). At local level he was a founder member of Torquay Chamber of Trade, served as president of Torquay Round Table, president of Torquay Rotary Club, chairman of Torquay's United Nations Society, and for fifty-five years was an indefatigable secretary of the South Devon branch of the NSPCC. Almy had made his mark by 1892, the year that Torquay received a royal charter of incorporation, granting increased powers of self-government. Aged twenty-one, Almy was elected a town councillor and utilised his legal expertise in the capacity of deputy town clerk. That same year he also obtained an interview with Oscar Wilde for a theatre magazine, a meeting that possibly inspired him to publish a book of his own verse – a writing talent he was to develop further as he later became a notable author on local history.

The word of 'Pa' Almy has to be respected. Although he was a schoolboy at the time of the Babbacombe Murder, he became a contemporary of all the legal figures who had been involved in the case. He had obviously learned something about the affair which he would not elaborate upon but which had totally convinced him of the truth of his startling revelation to John Pike: 'You can take it from me Berry was got at.'

Following John Lee's unlikely escape from the gallows, the possibility of part-time, freelance hangmen being open to bribery and corruption was raised by the *Globe*, 24 February 1885: 'If a criminal's death is to depend upon the proper working of a trap and lever, and if such proper working is to depend entirely on the amount of personal care the hangman may choose to bestow thereon, it becomes evident that the hangman has it in his power to override the sentences of judges. Our executioners are private and unofficial persons; and it is always possible that any of these may some day find himself exposed to very serious temptation, if it once gets abroad that he is so entirely master of the situation.'

Percival Almy.

James Berry's personal motives for becoming an executioner were questioned by the Sheriff of Devon, Octavius Bradshaw, in a thinly veiled letter of criticism to the Home Secretary after the debacle at Exeter Prison: 'I would further suggest that the choice of permanent executioner should be made from Prison Warders who have their occupation and wages direct from the Government, and not Boot Makers, etc., who are only too eager for the office of Hangman to gain notoriety and promote their private business and who hold receptions after executions giving every loathsome detail to their audience . . .' (HO 144/148//A38492).

The much-maligned Berry became the first executioner to publish his memoirs and later became an evangelist, embarking on lucrative tours and giving a lecture entitled

'From Public Executioner to Preacher of the Gospel'. While in office he had absolutely no scruples about seeking any money-making opportunities. Once, he tried to obtain the dress of an executed woman in order to sell it to Madame Tussaud's. For years he swindled buyers by charging them one shilling for a piece of the noose allegedly used on Lee, despite the fact that he had previously sold the rope intact to a Nottingham publican, Dan Dominic. Could these acquisitive instincts have made him receptive to a bribe? The possibility is certainly supported by the experience of the world-famous escapologist Harry Houdini. The American showman toured England and was approached by Berry while appearing at Bradford in November 1901. What transpired was revealed by author Harold Kellock in his biography *Houdini: His Life-Story* (New York, 1928): 'James Berry, a former public hangman had taken to the less gruesome occupation of running a public-house, and, on the side advertised himself as a phrenologist and character reader, able to give "excruciatingly 40 minutes continuous entertainment". He offered to make wagers of several thousand dollars that he could tie Houdini and hold him, and agreed to split his winnings if the Handcuff King would pretend he could not escape. "Guess he didn't know how I was brought up," was Houdini's comment in his diary.'

This anecdote clearly illustrates that former policeman Berry was a corrupt individual capable of offering bribes; therefore, it is not hard to believe that he would have been willing to accept a great deal more money to save Lee than the official £10 fee which was on offer to execute an innocent man.

The defence counsel at Lee's trial suggested that Elizabeth Harris's lover could have been responsible for the murder, and the belief persisted that Lee covered up for that person. There has been speculation that the father of the cook's child was a member of the nobility and that collusion among Freemasons in high places influenced officials to 'fix' the execution. Alternatively, it is believed that Harris was involved with a highly respected local businessman who bribed the executioner. The validity of these conspiracy theories appears to hinge on Lee's conviction that he would not die on the gallows. Whatever the truth of Percival Almy's claim, it appears that Lee's survival was the subject of a gambling coup, for this extraordinary comment appeared in the *Torquay Directory*, 3 March 1885, after the failed execution:

> One theory which *pretends* to account for the miscarriage of justice is that the two folding boards, which formed the drop, bulged upwards in the centre, probably owing to the rain. . . . There is another which is given as a matter of gossip. Very, many Englishmen make all kinds of incidents and events the subjects of bets. Fortunes have been won and lost in making spiders run across a hot plate. . . . Accordingly, when Lee was arrested, bets were laid that he would not be hanged. The remarkable escape by Lee from death by accident or *otherwise* has been quite a windfall to those who laid against his being executed. (Authors' italics)

Although Almy gave no indication of who might have approached Berry, John Pike linked this story to an allegation, dealt with in the previous chapter, that local 'silver dealer' George Tregaskis had been implicated and questioned by the police about his whereabouts on the night of the murder. Six months after the reminiscences of Tregaskis appeared in the local press, further astounding claims appeared when the death of Isadore Carter (1849–1936) was announced in the *Herald Express*, 22 February 1936:

His death at the age of 86, brings before the public eye once again one of the foremost legal minds of the Westcountry, and recalls the cases of Charlotte Winsor and John Lee . . . in both of which unprecedented incidents occurred making legal history. . . .

In 1865 the famous Charlotte Winsor trial took place at the Devon Spring Assizes when Mr. Carter was 16. His father was retained by the Crown to prosecute. Prior to the hearing, his father was taken seriously ill, and the son took responsibility of handling the case. . . . Charlotte Winsor was indicted for murder with a woman called Mary Jane Harris [the mother of a baby whose lifeless body had been found wrapped in newspaper in a Torquay lane]. . . .

Isadore Carter.

It was the practice of women who had a child to dispose of to take it to Winsor, a witch-like woman, who was cunning enough to make the mother a participator in the murder, so she would not 'split'. . . . It is believed that one of her methods of dispatching babies was to hold an arm and a leg, and make the mother hold the other arm and leg. They would then hold the baby over a tub of water . . . gradually lowering it until it was immersed, when it would be left until it drowned. . . .

[When the jury failed to reach a verdict] . . . Mr. Carter induced Harris to turn Queen's evidence, and when the next trial came round . . . the jury had little difficulty in returning a verdict of 'Guilty' against Winsor. . . .

[Following an unsuccessful appeal against the verdict] . . . the Home Secretary, however, then intervened because sentence of death had been lying over Winsor's head for such a long time that it was deemed a matter of common humanity that it should be transmuted to penal servitude for life. Winsor died serving her sentence, and her effigy is, or used to be, in the Chamber of Horrors at Madame Tussaud's.

Mr. Field Fisher [Carter's law partner] somewhat reluctantly confessed to a remarkable contention held by Mr Carter, but unsubstantiated by the old solicitor, who would never commit himself on the point. It was Mr. Carter's belief that John Lee was a son of the woman Harris, who was first indicted with Winsor in that first sensational case twenty years before . . . Whether there is any truth in this it is impossible to say, and what reason Mr. Carter had for holding that opinion will never be known . . . but if there was anything in it, it gives food for thought to those interested in hereditary crime.

The startling contention that mother and son both stood trial for murder and avoided execution had previously surfaced in a message to the Home Office from the venerable Archdeacon Wilberforce in 1905 (see Chapter 10). The story is groundless, although there is some credence in the folklore saying 'They'll never hang a Lee'. Mary Lee (née

Harris) was married to John Lee senior and lived at Abbotskerswell, whereas Mary *Jane* Harris was single and lodged in Torquay, where her child was fathered by a farmer named Nickells. Mary Lee gave birth to John in August 1864, two months before Mary Jane Harris's son Thomas Edwin Gibson Harris was born on 6 October 1864. Baby Thomas was smothered by Charlotte Winsor in December 1864, when John Lee was four months old. Mary Lee was some ten years older than Mary Jane Harris and it is clear that they were not one and the same person, although there is a family connection. When Mary Jane was questioned by the police about the fate of her son, she claimed that Thomas was alive and well and being cared for by her aunt Betsy Stevens – the mother of Mary Lee. Betsy was living with her second husband, William Stevens, at Pepperdon Farm, Kingsteignton, near Newton Abbot. The couple were raising Mary Lee's illegitimate daughter Elizabeth Harris, but were completely unaware that Mary Jane Harris had recently given birth to a child. It appears that Mary Lee and Mary Jane Harris were cousins, which in later years evidently created some confusion in the mind of Isadore Carter.

With Carter barely cold in his grave, even more incredible revelations emerged with an assertion from an unnamed informant of John Lee's innocence in a sensational article published in the *Herald and Express*, 18 March 1936:

The Man They Could Not Hang

For over half a century the world has thought that John Lee committed the Babbacombe murder, although he declared to the Court: 'I am innocent'. Tonight, for the first time, the Herald & Express is able to reveal John Lee's own story of what happened on that terrible night. He had served over twenty years in prison, and as his crime was expiated in the eyes of the law, he stood nothing to gain by lying.

With the death of the late Mr. Isadore James Carter, the well-known solicitor, of Torquay, who passed away at the advanced age of 87, there disappeared the last personal link with the notorious Babbacombe murder. Mr. Carter was the prosecuting solicitor, and it was largely due to his own investigations on the spot that John Lee was arrested and accused of the murder. It was largely to Mr. Carter that his conviction was due.

But were Mr. Carter's deductions correct? Did John Lee actually commit the murder?

> *The Herald & Express is able tonight to reveal entirely new facts about the affair which go to prove that John Lee did not strike the blow which killed Miss Keyse, but that he knew who did so.*
>
> *Despite this, he stood on trial for the crime, was convicted for it, walked three times to the scaffold, suffered imprisonment for twenty-two years and finally went to his grave without making any public statement on the matter.*

We reveal this story – which will prove that truth is stranger than fiction – on the authority of a man whose name is respected by every citizen of Torquay, but who for obvious reasons, cannot be identified. Nor, for equally obvious reasons, can any other

The Glen, with a colonnade leading to the Music Room on the right.

names be mentioned, for, although none of the principal characters now survive, there may be descendants to whom pain might be passed.

Was John Lee Guilty?

About the year 1890 there stood at the side of an open grave, in a South Devon town, a well-known local resident and his two sons. The man who had been buried was a public man of the town who had been well-known, highly respected and very popular throughout South Devon. The young men were, also in their turn, to become public men in the area. As they were moving away from the grave and the mourners were dispersing their father turned to them and said:

> *'We have buried this afternoon the secret of the Babbacombe murder.'*

At the time they did not realise the significance of their father's remark. It was nearly twenty years before they did, but long before that they were aware that their father knew a good many secrets of the dead man.

By an amazing coincidence John Lee himself gave them the explanation when he was released from prison.

Lee knew nothing of that funeral when the two men stood at the open grave. He did not know that the brothers, to whom he went on his release, knew of the existence of the man who had been buried. All he knew was that he felt he had been suffering under a grave injustice for twenty-two years, he wanted to obtain redress, and he had decided to talk the matter over with the two men – to have their advice as to what to do to get satisfaction.

The story he told them explained their father's remark about the secret of the Babbacombe murder, and their surprise as the facts were unfolded can be better imagined than described.

He started by declaring that he was not the Babbacombe murderer but that he knew who was, and that he had shielded him for over twenty years, only to discover, on his release from prison, that the murderer was dead.

> *The name of the murderer he gave. It was the name of the man at whose graveside the men on the opposite side of the table had stood.*

Lee went on to explain what happened. The man in question was, he said, well-known to everybody for his public activities. He was much respected. Everybody knew him. What everybody did not know was that he was 'carrying on' with a young woman who was known to Lee, and who had access to the servant's quarters at the Glen. Thus it was that, with the assistance of Lee, the man in question had arranged a supper party for himself and the woman, and for Lee and another girl, in the kitchen of the Glen on the night of November 15, 1884.

Everything went well. The household was in bed and the party 'below stairs' was proving a great success. Apparently they must have made more noise than they bargained for, because some time after midnight, without any warning, the door was thrown open and there stood Miss Keyse in her dressing gown. It was a dramatic moment as described by Lee. He declared that Miss Keyse was livid with rage. She ordered them out of the house and told Lee to fetch the police.

> *High words followed. If the police came on the scene the public career of the man who had arranged the party was at an end. Lee did not know what to do. His own future was anything but bright. Miss Keyse, in her rage, smacked the face of the man. There was a scuffle and a struggle. The man picked up a chopper and the next thing Lee knew was that Miss Keyse was lying dead on the floor.*

Naturally everybody was very panic-stricken, but, according to his own account, Lee kept his head. His idea was that they should make it appear that there had been an attempt to burgle the house and that they should set the place on fire. He argued that, with a thatched roof and the house in such an isolated position, fire would wipe out all traces of what had happened before the flames could be extinguished. Lee had very carefully prepared the story that was about to be told, and as he was the only individual who was to tell any story he did not imagine there would be very much difficulty about it.

So the stage was set. The body was removed to the dining-room, where it was found, the midnight visitors went away, Lee soaked the place with paraffin and in due course set it alight and retired to his bedroom. He put his hand through the dining-room window after he was aroused by the cries of the maid who had smelled the fire, and, in doing so, cut his arm.

Lee explained how he went to give the alarm at the Cary Arms, and afterwards to tell the police about the discovery of Miss Keyse's body. He carefully told the story he had prepared and, having told it, never budged from a detail. Even when it was shown that the window was broken from the outside and not the inside he did not try to explain it. He protested from beginning to end that he did not kill Miss Keyse and even now, after he had completed his sentence, he was here again declaring his innocence though confessing the part he played in the proceedings. He did not explain who cut Miss Keyse's throat.

It was the sole survivor of all the people referred to in this article who told these facts to a Herald & Express reporter and he gave some further particulars.

> The man concerned, and who was declared by Lee to be the murderer of Miss Keyse, was known, says our informant, to have been critically ill for a long time after the murder, though nobody at that time – or ever – associated him with the crime. As a matter of fact, he never really recovered, and gradually became demented. He died in a mentally unbalanced condition.

Few people had the slightest idea that he even knew Lee, or Miss Keyse, or the Glen. But there were a few who knew something, and when in his madness he shouted things which the doctors put down to his state of mind, there were one or two people – our informant's father was one – who knew what he was referring to, and what had driven him insane.

> It was also, said our informant, afterwards discovered that the money for the defence of Lee was provided by the man in question.

Over twenty years ago the writer of this article had occasion to interview James Berry, the executioner, and asked him whether Lee made any statement to him. This is what Berry replied:

> 'When I walked into the cell to pinion him I said: "Well, Lee do you want to say anything?" Lee shook his head. Then he tapped his breast over his heart and went on: 'What I know about this business will remain there. I am innocent."'

Obviously, even after this lapse of time, names cannot be mentioned, but there is no question whatever that the statements referred to in this article were made by Lee and the other persons mentioned and if Lee spoke the truth – and other events seem to prove that there was more than 'something' in what he said – it looks as though after all this time the world has come to what really happened in the Glen on the night in November over fifty years ago.

The writer of the article who, 'over twenty years ago', 'had occasion to interview James Berry' was undoubtedly the newspaper's respected leading journalist, Reg Cowill, but the man who claimed the credit for obtaining this remarkable 'scoop' was junior reporter George Matthews, who, some forty years later, had risen to become editor of the *Herald Express* when the BBC interviewed him for the 1975 television documentary *The Man They Could Not Hang*. Unfortunately, the newsman was not very forthcoming beyond confirming that there was a 'definite' connection between the article and Carter's death.

With the timing of Matthews's story, it is natural to assume that Carter was either the father, or one of the two sons, who had attended the funeral of the deranged murderer of Emma Keyse, then salved his conscience by arranging for the truth to come out after his death. Like their father, Frederick, Isadore and his elder brother, Francis, were both solicitors. However, Francis worked in Bristol for sixteen years before joining Isadore from 1894 to 1901. This partnership began after the funeral of the alleged killer and was dissolved before Lee left prison.

Therefore, it appears extremely unlikely that Isadore Carter was directly responsible for the story. True, he had two sons of his own, but he was in no position to take them to a funeral 'about the year 1890', for circumstances prescribed that he would have so little contact with them that their names were not even mentioned in his will, which was made three years after the scandal of a divorce that was announced in the *Dartmouth and Brixham Chronicle*, 30 January 1885, just before the commencement of the trial of John Lee:

LOCAL DIVORCE CASE

The petition of Mrs. Annie Miles Carter, for divorce, by reason of her husband's (Mr. Isadore James Carter, solicitor, Torquay), adultery, and desertion, was heard before Sir James Hannen, on Monday, the 19th ins. Dr. Pritchard appeared for the petitioner. The respondent was not represented. – In the course of her evidence, Mrs. Carter stated, she was married in 1872, at Exmouth, and, resided with her husband at Torquay and Newton Abbot, and there were three children of the marriage. About three years ago, the respondent became very intimate with a Miss Constance Onslow, of Plymouth, and this occasioned frequent quarrels between the husband and wife. Finally the respondent left his home, and went to Shaldon, where he resided with Miss Onslow, his sister, Miss Carter keeping house for them. Proofs of adultery having been given, by two servants at different times in the service of the respondent, the president pronounced a decrement with costs, the petitioner to have custody of the children of the marriage.

Carter's wife and children were not the only members of his family to distance themselves from his unseemly conduct. The philandering solicitor's indignant sister wrote the following letter to the editor of the *Dartmouth and Brixham Chronicle*, 6 February 1885:

Sir,

Having seen in the Dartmouth and Brixham Chronicle, for January 30th, an account of Mr. Isadore Carter's divorce from his wife, Mrs. Annie Miles Carter, in which my name is mentioned with regard to circumstances in the case in a most untruthful matter. I write to deny entirely what the above mentioned paper states with regard to me. I was certainly living with my brother at Shaldon, when Miss Onslow came to us on a visit; but as soon as ever my suspicions were aroused with regard to improper conduct, I left the house never to return to it. I think it but right that I should protect myself by defending myself against such a rash statement as has just appeared in the Dartmouth and Brixham Chronicle with regard to me, viz., that I kept house for my brother and Miss Onslow, knowing the relationship existing between them, for this is what the statement necessarily implies.

I am sir, faithfully yours,
Bessie Carter

The only probable connection that Carter's death had with the 1936 *Herald and Express* article was, as Matthews stated at the time, that the prosecuting solicitor was thought to be the last surviving link with the murder case. The source of the story probably chose this moment to speak out as it could no longer embarrass a professional colleague, for in his conversation with the BBC, Matthews gave one slight clue when he refused to name his informant in order to protect surviving members of the family, particularly a son who he affirmed was at that time well-known locally. In all probability, this offspring was the South Devon Deputy Coroner, John Hutchings, as the evidence points strongly to the fact that his father, Ernest Hutchings, most certainly 'a man whose name is respected by every citizen of Torquay', gave the story to George Matthews.

In 1905, Mary Lee had engaged the services of solicitor Herbert Rowse Armstrong to campaign for her son's release. Shortly afterwards, Armstrong moved to the Welsh border town Hay-on-Wye, where he was successful until he found himself on the wrong side of the law when he poisoned his Teignmouth-born wife, Pearson Friend, a crime for which he was executed at Gloucester Gaol in 1922. Before setting up on his own, Armstrong had practised as the Newton Abbot representative of the Teignmouth-based firm Hutchings & Hutchings. Upon his release, John Lee engaged them to represent him. Ernest

Ernest Hutchings.

Hutchings and his older brother John also had a branch in Torquay where Ernest became the country's youngest town councillor when gaining election in 1901. He later formed an advantageous partnership in the town, practising as Kitson Hutchings Easterbrook & Co. The change evidently occurred in 1908, for in October of that year a solicitor's letter written on Lee's behalf was received by the Home Secretary asking that their client be allowed to address religious societies. The heading of the stationery had recently been altered from Hutchings & Hutchings, with the latter name crossed out and 'Kennaway' – the name of their promoted associate – crudely inserted above.

Ernest Hutchings became a leading citizen of his adopted town advocating the provision of many leisure and sporting facilities, which helped to develop Torquay as a modern holiday resort. Declining offers to become Mayor of Torquay or parliamentary candidate for the Liberal Party, he served as a county councillor and for thirty-four years was the Coroner for South Devon, succeeding Sydney Hacker, who had presided over the controversial inquest into the death of Emma Keyse.

George Matthews did not indicate whether he actually knew the name of the alleged 'demented' killer, but an important clue to his identity appears in this extract from John Lee's petition to the Home Secretary submitted on 1 November 1887: 'I wish to bring before your notice that the Solicitor that my parents employed to look after my case, was between the coroners inquest and the trial taken with a fit of insanity and all that I had told him about the case and all that he himself had prepared was of no use and just as the trial commenced his brother took the case into hand but he had nothing ready for my Counsel' (HO 144/148//A38492/71).

Lee's mentally unstable solicitor Reginald Gwynne Templer was admitted to a sanatorium founded by Thomas Holloway. It was officially opened in June 1885 by an old acquaintance of Emma Keyse, the Prince of Wales. Born in Plymouth, the son of a naval officer, Thomas Holloway was a self-made millionaire who ploughed over £200,000 into building the sanatorium at St Annes Heath, Virginia Water, Surrey, to benefit members of the middle class who were suffering from 'curable' mental disorders. The opulent building was designed by architect William Crossland in the Flemish style. The red-brick exterior was trimmed with Portland stone, which John Lee would later spend many years quarrying while in prison. The walls of the magnificent recreation hall were adorned with portraits of famous Britons, including Queen Victoria, Prince Albert, Shakespeare, Wellington, Raleigh, Nelson, Cromwell, Disraeli, Gladstone, Francis Bacon and Isaac Newton. *The Builder*, 7 January 1882, described Holloway's sanatorium as a 'sumptuously decorated palace', a far cry from the popular conception of Victorian lunatic asylums provided for the poor. The magnificent surroundings seemed ideally suited to patients suffering from delusions of grandeur. *The Times*, 16 June 1885, reported on the accommodation provided at Holloway's: 'Indeed it is not too much to say that the place is more than comfortable – it is luxurious.'

Holloway also owned a country house nearby at Sunning Hill – Tittinghurst Park – which would later, in turn, become the home of Beatles John Lennon and Ringo Starr. Much of his personal fortune had been made by playing the stock market, following humble beginnings producing patent medicines. This worldwide business venture began with an ointment possessing a 'healing genius' made out of beeswax, resin, lanolin and olive oil that were mixed in a saucepan in his mother's kitchen. Holloway later

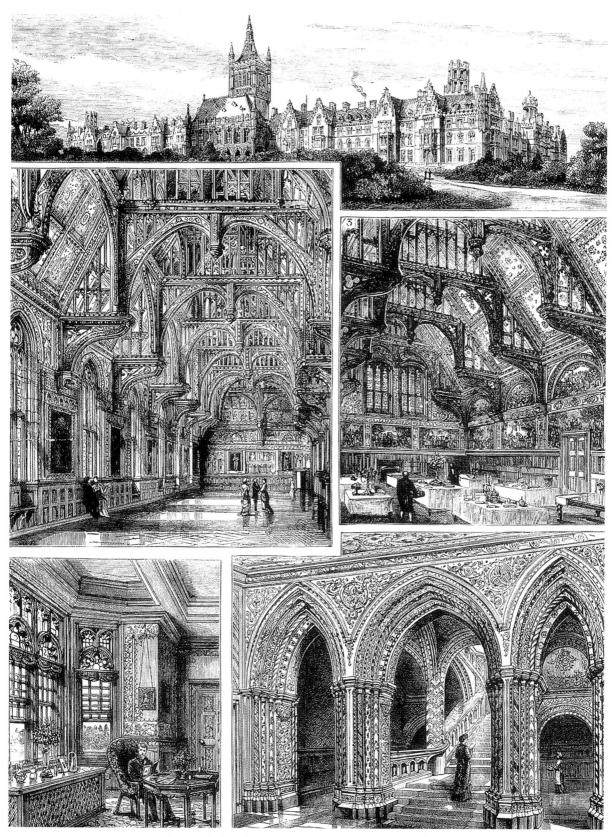

Holloway's Sanatorium: 'a sumptuously decorated palace'.

manufactured 'quack' pills, containing a rhubarb root base, which were nothing more a mild laxative, yet he convinced the public through expensive advertising campaigns that they would cure virtually any serious medical condition, including skin diseases and cancer. It was also claimed that they would cure general paralysis and venereal disease. Holloway's Pills could not, however, cure the ailing Reginald Gwynne Templer, who had syphilis. He died of 'general paralysis of the insane' on 18 December 1886 and was buried five days later in 'a South Devon graveyard' at Teignmouth Cemetery: 'The death took place on Saturday in London, at the age of 28, of Mr. R.G. Templer, solicitor, of Teignmouth. The deceased practised in the district for some time, appearing on behalf of John Lee, the Babbacombe murderer, both at the inquest, and at the subsequent magisterial investigation. Soon after Lee's committal, however, Mr. Templer's health gave way, and, in consequence, his brother, Mr. C. Templer, acted in his stead in the matter of instructing the defending counsel at the trial at Exeter' (*Torquay Times*, 24 December 1886).

Reginald Gwynne Templer.

The funeral report published in the *Teignmouth Gazette* did not include a full list of mourners, but it would be surprising if Ernest Hutchings's father, Thomas, the first chairman of Teignmouth Urban District Council did not attend with his sons. The deceased's father, Reginald William Templer, and Thomas Hutchings were close professional acquaintances as they were both heads of law firms in Teignmouth.

Reginald Gwynne Templer, the eldest of six children born to Reginald William Templer and his wife, Emily Gwynne, practised law in Newton Abbot and resided at Teignmouth. The family claimed that their ancestors had settled in Devon after landing at Brixham with William of Orange in 1588. A Heritage Trail, the Templer Way, now commemorates the Haytor Granite Railway and the Stover Canal, which were constructed by the family in 1820 to transport goods from Dartmoor to Teign-mouth docks. They also provided a church at Teigngrace, a small village on the Stover estate near Newton Abbot, where Reginald Gwynne Templer's grandfather was rector for many years. Following the death of her first husband, Thomas, Elizabeth Keyse married George Whitehead and the couple settled at Teigngrace, where in 1823 her seven-year-old daughter was baptised Emma Ann Whitehead Keyse by Reginald Gwynne Templer's uncle, the Reverend John Templer. This strong connection with the deceased prompted Reginald Gwynne Templer immediately to offer his services to the police on the day of the murder, despite the fact that his greatest successes had apparently been gained whilst defending clients:

6 Bridge Terrace
Newton Abbot
15 November 1884

Dear Mr Barbor,

   I am much shocked at reading the case tonight of the fearful tragedy at Babbacombe. Miss Keyse was highly known to me, & known to friends of mine. It is a case which I should take the keenest interest in supporting the police in their investigations and in assisting to bring the murderer to justice. I have no claim whatever upon you personally to ask for this favour but if, in considering the employment of an advocate for the preliminary investigation, you may deem me qualified to assist you I will devote my best energies to the case & shall be equally obliged to you for this exhibition of your confidence in me as a young advocate who has shown already some aptitude for and attention to business. I defended the Newton murder case, re: Leveridge & the attempted murder at Shaldon re: Ricketts – both successfully.

Yours truly,
R. Gwynne Templer

(Epton Collection, Galleries of Justice)

   When Templer wrote this letter, he was probably unaware that John Lee had been taken into custody. Perhaps, if the young solicitor was the guilty party, he hoped his offer would be accepted by the police so that he would be in a position to monitor the investigation and be in a position to cover up his involvement if necessary. Whatever the reason, it seems amazing that after failing to be invited to appear for the prosecution, Templer then turned up in court representing the accused. This may simply have been a case of youthful ambition triumphing over sentiment, or even part of a police ruse to use Templer in order to try and extract a confession from the prisoner; otherwise, knowing the victim so well, why would he have chosen to defend Lee if he did not implicitly believe in his innocence? In the final analysis, what better reason would he have than to try and protect the man who had attempted to cover up a murder he himself had committed when Emma Keyse discovered him visiting his lover Elizabeth Harris at The Glen? The *Herald and Express* article states that Lee's legal fees were paid for by the man in question. Lee himself admitted in his autobiography that these amounted to £60, equivalent, in his case, to over five years' earnings. Charles Nicholson MP discovered that a public appeal had raised only £12 for the defence; therefore, it is natural to assume that Templer waived his own fee and took care of all other expenses.

   Although readers of the *Herald and Express* were assured that 'there is no question whatever that the statements referred to in this article were made by Lee and the other persons mentioned', the story contains a major flaw, in common with the tales of the 'fisherman' and the 'silver dealer', that there was a late-night 'supper party' at The Glen. If such a party had taken place in any of the other unoccupied buildings on the estate, then it might have been feasible, but Emma Keyse was in the habit of retiring very late, and it is hard to imagine anyone waiting for her to retire until the early hours of the morning on a dark, windy, winter's evening in such a remote spot in order to enter the house. If people had been admitted to the kitchen by John Lee and Elizabeth Harris, then it would have been impossible to hold a whispered conversation without Emma Keyse or her elderly servants overhearing. The only possible explanation can be that the term 'supper party' was simply a euphemism for a sexual liaison between the two couples, Templer sleeping with Elizabeth and, presumably, John with his girlfriend Katie Farmer.

The latter was a notable absentee from the roster of witnesses paraded before the courts. The lovers' letters were read out in court at every stage of the proceedings, implying that the suspect had been harbouring evil thoughts as he was 'unsettled' and planning to 'do something which may not be to your liking'. These comments, written over a month before the murder, were given a sinister appearance by the prosecuting counsel, who misled the trial jury when he stated in his opening address that they had been written 'four days' before the death of Miss Keyse. If she had been called, Katie's evidence might have given a clear insight into how the couple had resolved their future plans. In addition, it was alleged that they had conversed shortly after the murder in this report from the *East and South Devon Advertiser*, 22 November 1884: 'On Saturday morning prisoner, being sent to acquaint Colonel McLean, a friend of the deceased, with what had occurred, called upon a girl named Kate Farmer, with whom he keeps company, and passed the remark to her, "You'll see us all marched to the police-station."'

A simpler explanation for Lee's involvement is that he was simply well rewarded for letting Templer in and out of the house. On the night in question Miss Keyse could have followed Templer down the stairs where an argument ensued and Lee witnessed the murder before covering up for his half-sister's lover. It appears that Templer may have known 'the cook' for some time, for the 1881 Census reveals that before finding a position at The Glen, Elizabeth was employed in the household of bank manager Edward Chant of Teignmouth.

If the various stories absolving John Lee of blame are to be dismissed as total fabrication, there remains one outstanding puzzle. If he was the sole perpetrator of the crime, who had had the good fortune to escape from the gallows, before gaining the opportunity to rebuild his life with the general public perceiving him as a hero, then it seems inconceivable that, having served more than half his life in prison, he would waste precious time trying to prove the existence of a 'confession' supposedly made by his half-sister, Elizabeth Harris. Yet a month after his release, in letters obtained by John Pike, he was corresponding with a Mr Newland of London, a well-wisher who had seen an erroneous syndicated article claiming that 'the cook' had made a statement clearing him on her death-bed:

Abbotskerswell
21 January 1908

Dear Sir,

Your letter to hand, many thanks for it and your kind words of sympathy. I am pleased to know that you are reading Lloyd's and that you read about the case at the time of the trial, you will be able to judge better than those who have only read my side of the case, I say that I am innocent, but other people are quite justified in keeping their own opinions. Almighty God is my judge, I am going to trust him always. He has brought me safe so far and he will to the end, yet bless his Holy name.

I am going to London, trying to find out about the confession of the cook, I do hope I can trace it back. Dear sir, 23 years ago no one thought to see me again, but man proposes but God disposes. I thank you again for your kind letter and I pray God to bless you always.

I wish to remain your obedient servant
John Lee

After receiving an invitation by reply from Mr Newland, Lee agreed to meet him personally and made it clear that nothing was too much trouble in his search for information:

Abbotskerswell
24 January 1908

Dear Sir,

I shall be in London tomorrow 25th January. I shall be at Paddington Station about 2pm. I do not know if your place is far from that Station. Please do not put yourself out of the way. I am only an ordinary man and can make myself at home . . . or can you advise on what hotel I can stop at because I have a lot of people writing to me about this confession. If I can find your place I will come and see you and perhaps you can tell me which place to stop at. I will have a talk with you when I see you.

I wish to remain your most obedient servant
John Lee

The visit to London proved fruitless and Lee wrote of his frustration to Stephen Bryan on 7 February 1908: 'I have been to London trying to find out about the confession of my step-sister, the cook who lived with me at the house of Miss Keyse. I have had a lot of letters [from] people who have read about it. Hundreds have read it in London, but we cannot find out the year to search up the newspapers.'

In a further letter to Stephen Bryan, written on 15 May 1908, Lee appeared to have made an important breakthrough in his quest: 'I have had some very extraordinary letters from London. Some ladies there write and say that my step-sister, the cook at Miss Keyse, died some years ago and confessed to a Salvation Army officer that she committed the crime.'

By 13 July, as letters arrived from sympathisers around the world, Lee was in a position to let Bryan know the identity of the person who had allegedly been at the death of Elizabeth Harris.

I put an advertisement in the 'People' newspaper, also did a young woman who lives in Kent offering a reward for the 'Warcry' containing the confession of the Babbacombe

Murder by the cook upon her deathbed to Major Pearson, a Salvation Army officer about 15 or 16 years ago. Plenty of people write and inform me that it was in the newspapers, but they forget what paper it was. One man in Belfast, Ireland wrote and told me that his sister had got a paper containing the confession, but he could not get at it for a while. I also have a letter from Queensland, Australia. A young woman told me that she read all the confession in the Sunday Sydney Herald. So I wrote and asked her if she could get it for me. (Bryan Letters, Exeter Prison Museum)

The Home Office could find no evidence to substantiate these claims and unbeknown to Lee, the fate of the cook had been explained in an article published in the *Torquay Directory*, 30 June 1886:

A Resident of Torquay who is spending a short time in London writes:– 'There is a curious report current here respecting the late murder case at Babbacombe. Lee, so it is said, is out of prison, his half-sister having confessed on her death-bed that she committed the crime. Lee having received a sum of money has gone abroad.' This is evidently the revival of a report to a similar effect which prevailed in the neighbourhood last November and reproduced here again in April. In the last-named month we received a letter of enquiry from the manager of one of the leading London dailies respecting it, and could find no foundation for the story. Elizabeth Harris, the half-sister referred to, went abroad soon after the affair, and the last that was heard of her was that she had settled comfortably in one of the Australian colonies.

This report of the cook's destination was passed by the authors to Alan Elliott, an Australian with ancestral links to the Lees of Abbotskerswell. He has been building up the family tree on a website and quickly located records to establish that Elizabeth Hamlyn Esterbrook Harris had sailed to Queensland. Having had to abandon her baby to the tender mercies of the poor law guardians, she started a new family after marrying labourer Robert Dukes on 9 May 1892. They lived at Maryborough, the Fraser Coast immigration port for free settlers, before moving inland to Brooweena. The couple had two daughters, Sarah Jane and Elizabeth Esther, who were born on 26 May 1893 and 3 January 1895 respectively. A son, Robert William, born on 26 July 1896, was fated to become a casualty of the Somme, dying from his wounds on 13 November 1916. On the first day of that month the family had been celebrating the wedding of his sister Elizabeth Esther to Emil Staib. The Dukes' eldest child, Sarah Jane, married Tom Jakeman on 5 February 1925 and shortly after their first wedding anniversary, Elizabeth Dukes passed away aged seventy on 26 February 1926 – forty years after supposedly making her well-documented 'death-bed confession'.

The role of the Torquay solicitors, who went to their graves believing they were each harbouring a dark secret, is hard to fathom. If they had obtained inside information about the case, such respected upholders of the law might have been expected to lay it before the proper authorities. Was Ernest Hutchings's story about Reginald Gwynne Templer linked to the bribery of the hangman proposed by Percival Almy? It is conceivable that they discussed the case, for following the death of Ernest Hutchings, this tribute was paid on behalf of all Torquay solicitors by Percival Almy who recalled that 'he had been associated with Mr. Hutchings since the early days when he was usually on one side in a case and Mr. Hutchings on the other. But they never let their professional animosities enter their private lives and were the best of friends' (*Herald Express*, 25 March 1957).

Ernest Hutchings had been conspicuous by his presence at the funeral of Isadore Carter, for he and Caryl Field Fisher were the only solicitors to attend and send wreaths. At the time of the murder, Carter was living with his mistress at Shaldon, near Teignmouth. Did he become aware during the legal proceedings that his opposite number, Reginald Gwynne Templer, had been implicated in the murder? Or did he spot a clue earlier at The Glen? He claimed that he assisted the police at the scene of the crime and was closely involved in the decision to arrest John Lee. If this is true, it may explain why he had apparently been dreading Lee's release, for when Henry Percival James was taken into partnership by Caryl Field Fisher in 1952, he sat at Carter's old desk and found a pistol hidden in a secret compartment which he learned 'Isadore Carter had kept to hand, because John Lee had sworn to kill him, when he came out of prison' (Epton Collection, Galleries of Justice).

CHAPTER 13

John Lee – a victim of circumstance?

You say you are innocent; I wish I could believe it.

– Mr Justice Manisty

Had the execution of John Lee been brought to a natural conclusion, then justice would have been seen to be done. The case would then have quickly faded from the public memory with no question raised about the condemned man's innocence or guilt. The bungle on the scaffold, however, stimulated debate about the whole handling of the case. Links of a flimsy nature made up the chain of circumstantial 'evidence' against John Lee, which was supported by powerful corroboration in the way of 'threats' against his employer, who had provided a substantial 'motive' for such a dreadful attack on her person by reducing his wages by sixpence a week. Therefore, it was surmised that Lee had brought a hatchet into the house to exact a cold-blooded revenge on a helpless old lady, whom he himself had acknowledged as being his 'best friend'.

CIRCUMSTANTIAL EVIDENCE

The direction of the police investigation was summed up a week after the crime in the *Spectator*, 22 November 1884:

> The police think they have caught the murderer, and the facts certainly limit in a curious degree the range of speculation. The murder was clearly committed from within, all the doors and windows being fast, and none of the women present in the house are so much as suspected of having any hand in it. . . . As the murdered lady was first stunned, and then nearly had her head cut off by some sharp weapon, the crime would seem to be beyond their physical capability. . . . The police therefore, are reduced to two theories, either that the murder was committed by John Lee, a young footman who had been convicted of theft, but who had been sheltered by Miss Keyse, partly out of kindness, she having known him as a lad, and being desirous that he should have a second chance to redeem himself, and partly out of attachment to one of her servants whose kinsman he was; or by a burglar or other stranger who had concealed himself in the house. This latter supposition should not be dismissed too readily, for it is not inconsistent with the evidence as to the absence of any forcible entry, and has occurred repeatedly in the history of crime. It tallies too, with a few of the known facts, more especially these – that Miss Keyse had evidently been disturbed after ascending to her room late at night by

Where the body was found in the dining room

Pantry and hall where the murder occurred

Butler's pantry fold-up bed behind door

(left)
Miss Keyse's
bedroom

(right)
Where the murder
took place,
outside the pantry

Scene of the crime.

some noise below, had crept down in her nightdress to see if there was cause for alarm, and had been struck senseless, probably at the foot of the stairs, by a furious blow with a weapon not yet identified. Any one familiar with her habits would have selected a better opportunity. The police, however, reject this explanation, alleging that any such occurrence must have been heard by the footman, John Lee, who slept in a room off the staircase passage, and believing that they have found evidence that he had carefully arranged the firing of the house. No trace of any escape of the stranger is discovered, and they consequently fix their attention on John Lee, against whom the circumstantial evidence looks black. . . .

This in essence was the case against John Lee. A total of thirty-two witnesses gave evidence during the inquest, magistrate's hearing and trial, although not one of them had actually heard or seen anything of the terrible deed. Reinforcing the volume of circumstantial evidence was the amount of press bias against the prisoner. Following his arrest, every aspect of his career, character and former conviction were distorted, with derogatory comments about his physical appearance thrown in for good measure as demonstrated in this appalling example published in the *Torquay Directory*, 26 November 1884:

The career of Lee . . . has not been of the best. When old enough for the purpose, Miss Keyse took him as a page. A naval gentlemen, of Paignton, has informed us that a few years ago a lady sent him two boys with the object of getting them on board HMS Implacable, at Devonport, for service for the navy. One of these was Lee. . . . [who] after the first novelty had passed over, did not like his new life, and sought to bring about a change. After two years he was invalided. . . . The gentleman referred to says he did not like Lee's looks from the first, and wrote to the lady saying he did not expect much from her protégé. After this Lee, was occupied in various pursuits, and was at length engaged by Col. Brownlow, from whose residence he stole some plate, and underwent a term of imprisonment. When he came out of gaol he had no place to which he could go. All applications for situations were barred by the fact of his recent conviction. Miss Keyse, under these circumstances, took him back, and gave him board and lodgings and a few shillings a week, whilst he sought for employment. Miss Keyse herself did all in her power to get him a situation. She pleaded personally with tradesmen in Torquay to take him on. To these she urged that it was very cruel not to give the boy a chance to retrieve his character. The poor lady declared that Lee had faithfully promised never to err again – that he would shut up shop, do errands, clean boots, in fact, do anything to earn an honest living, and she was so satisfied of his earnestness that she offered to become guarantee for his honesty. All these efforts failing she endeavoured to get him to emigrate. Lee, however, seems to have been adverse to this, for he had formed sundry friendships at St. Marychurch which he was loath to break off, and which he would be obliged to do if he left England. . . . Lee's personal appearance is by no means prepossessing. He is tall, well-built, and has a powerful frame; he seems to be very muscular, and evidently possesses great strength. His lower lip protrudes and droops, he has thick lips and half-open mouth; his nose is straight with an upward tendency. His head recedes behind almost to a point, and his black hair dishevelled and with no attempt at a parting; either in the middle or the sides, descends over his low forehead to the eyebrows. There is a peculiarity about the eyes: they lack lustre and expression, and are such as may be met with in our lunatic asylums. Altogether his appearance does not indicate any ordinary degree of intelligence. But personal appearances and accidental circumstances have nothing to do with the case in hand; they are simply surroundings which may or may not have had their influence in the crime which the coroner is now investigating. There is this to be said: The prisoner may be assured of having a fair and impartial examination, and whatever the result of the verdict of the jury may be, that will be further analysed by the Grand Jury at Exeter.

The extent to which British newspapers could report such prejudicial information regarding suspects would continue for almost a century, until curbed by Parliament with the introduction of the Contempt of Court Act 1981.

LEGAL REPRESENTATION

MR TEMPLAR SOLICITOR FOR THE DEFENCE

The prosecution was helped by the lack of meaningful legal representation for the defendant. Lee was not represented at the opening of the inquest and clumsily attempted to question witnesses himself. When solicitor Reginald Templer was engaged, he fell ill before the trial and his brother stepped in to instruct the circuit barrister. Lee's indifferent demeanour at the preliminary proceedings did not endear him to the public and an appeal to pay Lee's legal costs raised a paltry amount. Contemporary newspaper criticism of the arrangements for the defence was scathing. The *East and South Devon Advertiser*, 21 February 1885, commented:

From the first there has scarcely been but the opinion entertained by the public, viz., that John Lee was the brutal murderer. So strong was this opinion even before the prisoner's committal that there were not a few of the public who would have ignored the English mode of administering justice, and would have inflicted lynch law upon him – in other words would have taken his life much after the same way poor Miss Keyse came to her tragic end. . . . Most of the public prejudged the man; they were impregnable to any theory that might be advanced in his defence. Even one of the jurymen at the inquest figured among the number, for if he could have his way he would hang the prisoner without affording him a trial at the Assizes, and not withstanding at the time the prisoner, acting under the advice of his solicitor, had reserved his defence. Between the time of his committal and his trial, even in the absence of the nature of his defence, public opinion even further ripened into a belief that he was the murderer, and the most wild and incorrect reports, all more or less prejudicial to the prisoner's position, were circulated. In saying this much we do not in any way wish to exonerate the man. We heard the evidence that was given at the inquest, before the magistrates, and at the final trial at the Assizes, and we cannot but believe ourselves, it was his cruel hand which committed the dreadful act. Still, whilst we believe this, we are bound in common justice to say that there is some room for doubt. And we do not hesitate to assert that doubt might have been greatly been strengthened in our minds, as well as in that of others, if the prisoner at the outset could have commanded money, in like manner as the prosecution did in netting around him a strong evidence of guilt. Very rightly the prosecution spared no expense, not a stone was left unturned in fact, to produce even the most trifling bit of evidence against him. The prisoner on the other hand, had no such facilities. Shut up in the cells at Torquay he was debarred even an interview with his father, and though he was afterwards defended by a solicitor, that gentleman falling ill, and remaining so up to the time of the trial, he was unable to render the counsel (Mr. St. Aubyn) who represented the prisoner at the Assizes but comparatively little assistance. The loss sustained in this respect must have been all the more severely felt, when two eminent counsel were engaged for the prosecution. Not only was the evidence against the prisoner very strong, but it was systematically linked together, in the absence of any material cross examination to snap or weaken any of the links, that the jury had no other alternative but to return the verdict which they did. Had Mr. St. Aubyn been more fully instructed it is possible many more facts might have been elicited in cross-examination on the prisoner's behalf.

This view was not formed with the benefit of hindsight; Lee's predicament was highlighted before the start of the trial by the *Dartmouth and Brixham Chronicle*, 16 January 1885:

With the approach of the assizes at Exeter, to commence on the 29th inst., public interest is being revived in the Babbacombe murder case. As counsel for the prosecution, Mr. A. Collins, Q.C., and Mr. Vigor have been retained by the Treasury. There is little probability of the services of a barrister being secured privately in the interests of the accused, John Lee, the appeal which has been made for the subscriptions for the defence having met with a meagre response. As a counsel is certain in the end to be allotted by the judge to the prisoner, it would be only fair to all concerned that the arrangement should be made speedily. Otherwise prisoner and his counsel will alike be placed at a serious disadvantage.

While campaigning for Lee's release, barrister and Member of Parliament Sir Charles Nicholson raised concerns about the safety of the verdict in a letter to the Home Office dated 16 March 1906:

Is he guilty? The evidence was purely circumstantial. The judge in his summing up said that it was consistent either with guilt or innocence. Lee denied any complicity in the crime from the first. His quiet firm denial after the verdict made a remarkable impression

'There was blood on his arm. But it was admitted . . . he cut his arm badly
in breaking a window to let out the smoke.'

on the judge. He denied it to the Prison Chaplain up to the moment of starting to the
scaffold, in the full certainty that he stood on the brink of a certain grave. He denied it at
the close of the terrible ordeal through which he went on that occasion. . . .

The circumstantial evidence brought against him seemed very considerable, but every
single point of it was capable of explanation consistent with his innocence.

There was blood on his arm. But it was admitted that on the discovery of the fire he
cut his arm badly in breaking a window to let out the smoke. The prosecution suggested
that he did this, inflicting a serious wound on himself, to account for the blood!

Paraffin had been used to start the fire and paraffin marks were found on his clothing.
But he was in the daily habit of cleaning and trimming all the lamps in the place!

A knife and a chopper, kept on the premises, to which he had access, were produced as
the weapons used in the murder. Yet the knife was a very blunt one while the wound in
the throat was of unusual depth. Prosecution could get their own medical evidence to go
no further than it was possible by extraordinary strength to inflict such a wound with
such an instrument. Lee was not of extraordinary strength. There was never any
substantial reason to suppose the chopper, which Lee himself fetched from an outhouse
to help in cutting down burning woodwork, had any connection with the murder at all,
except it was there to be produced.

The faulty nature of the circumstantial evidence would probably have led to an
acquittal but for the fact there was evidence of his having threatened to kill the old lady
and set the house on fire. This evidence was given by the young servant girl though,
strangely as it must appear, she did not say a word about it at her first appearance before
the Coroner. (HO 144/1717//A60789/64)

FORENSIC EVIDENCE

Many aspects of the investigation would have benefited from forensic science, which was then in its infancy. In the 1880s there was not even a method of detecting crime by fingerprinting. Edward Henry, the Commissioner of the Metropolitan Police, set up the first fingerprinting bureau at Scotland Yard in 1901. It was not until 1935 that the Metropolitan Police set up the Forensic Science Laboratory in London. Many of the points raised by Charles Nicholson had been reinforced by the prosecution's use of evidence submitted by two local doctors and Home Office expert Thomas Stevenson:

BLOOD

The victim had suffered a dreadful loss of blood and the accused had cuts on his arms, but the constant references to 'blood stains' were often the object of pure speculation by the medical experts, who could only identify blood as 'mammalian' – that is, as either that of a 'human being or an animal'. There was also no way of distinguishing one blood group from another or determining the age of bloodstains unless they were considered 'fresh', that is, up to six weeks old. Thomas Stevenson conducted a microscopic examination on the knife produced as the murder weapon, but for all he knew, the trace of blood found could have come from a rabbit being prepared for the cooking pot. One critic wondered whether it was blood at all: 'Possibly it was the remnant of a spot of gravy, for the "trace" was found between the handle and the blade, where remnants of dirt of all kinds might be expected in an old knife. Yet it came up as "evidence" against John Lee' (*Sunday Chronicle*, 12 February 1905).

PARAFFIN

Much was made of the smell of oil on Lee's clothes, but there was a plausible explanation detailed in the *Sunday Chronicle*, 12 February 1905:

> Then again it was a strong point in the indictment that Lee's clothes smelled of paraffin. As stated before, paraffin had been poured on the body of the murdered lady and on other places where it was attempted to set fire to the premises. Its presence on the clothing of the accused was put forward as significant evidence of guilt. Yet, if there had been no murder his clothes would have smelled just the same, for it was part of his daily duty to trim and clean the lamps! And, further, he had helped carry the paraffin-soaked body of his murdered mistress to the outhouse where it was placed after the discovery of the crime.

It is certainly hard to see how anyone who had been at The Glen that morning could have emerged without their clothes likewise affected by the paraffin-drenched premises.

HAIR

As for the 'human hairs' found on Lee's socks, Home Office analyst Thomas Stevenson identified two strands with a 'reddish tint' that were similar to those of the victim, while others were 'greyish or whitish', but even if the owners of the hairs could have been positively identified, it would hardly constitute evidence of Lee's guilt as he had been moving around the house for hours after the murder without putting his boots on. The insignificance of this evidence was highlighted by the *Sunday Chronicle*, 12 February 1905: 'Yet the most remarkable piece of evidence appears to have been that afforded when Lee's stockings were subjected to a microscopic test. A number of hairs were found to be attached to the wool. It is to be supposed that such things might be found on anyone's stockings. But in this case, two of the hairs were claimed to be the same colour as those of Miss Keyse. The others were of different colours, probably those of the other inmates of the house where he had lived for some months. But none the less those two were relied upon to prove that he had murdered the old lady . . .'.

WEAPONS

The police were observed by a reporter searching Babbacombe Beach for weapons on the morning of the murder, so how confident were they that the hatchet and knife produced had actually been used in the attack on the victim?

> When Lee and some neighbours were trying to cope with the conflagration one of them asked for a weapon to cut down some burning timber. Lee ran to fetch a hatchet which was kept in an outhouse for chopping sticks. That hatchet was produced at the trial as the weapon with which Miss Keyse's head had been battered. The doctor who was first on the scene [Chilcote] thought the wounds could not have been inflicted with it, but another [Steele] was found to swear they might have been, and that was sufficient. (*Sunday Chronicle*, 12 February 1905)

As for the minute trace of blood found on the head of the hatchet, it may in all probability have run off the bleeding arm of the man who carried it in – John Lee.

During the magistrate's hearing, Lee's solicitor, Reginald Templer, protested that Jane Neck had identified knives four times and each time made a different statement. The confusion arose because a pantry knife used for trimming candles and one used for gardening were produced, as is explained in this extract from the *Torquay Directory*, 3 December 1884: 'These two knives are very much alike; they have each white bone handles, and the blades are worn down to half their original length; there is just this difference between them, the former is blunt and the latter is sharp, being kept in that condition by Miss Keyse, who had a sharpening stone inside the front door.'

SERGEANT NOTT

P.S. Nott produces the axe.

A modern-day barrister from Devon, Barry Phillips, has made a special study of the Babbacombe Murder, and although considering the weight of evidence against Lee to be 'damning', developed this point in an article published in *Counsel*, November/December 1996:

> St Aubyn also failed to notice a vital point relating to one of the prosecution exhibits. A knife stained with blood was produced in court which had been found in the pantry in a table drawer near to where Lee slept. At one point during the committal proceedings Jane Neck, another of the servants in the house, had stated that this knife was not the one that was normally kept in the pantry. She thought it was another knife usually kept on the table in the hall. If this was correct, there appeared to be a strong case for arguing that evidence had been planted on Lee and that he had been set up. If Jane Neck's testimony at the committal hearing had been studied more closely, one of the principal prosecution exhibits produced in court to incriminate Lee might well have formed a central part of his defence.

The possibility of manufactured evidence is amplified by the discovery of a more likely murder weapon reported by the *East and Devon Advertiser*, 28 March 1885:

> We may mention that since the trial a table knife, measuring about ten inches in length, the blade of which was stained with blood, and enclosed in a sheath roughly made of a piece of wood, and with a leather covering has been found in an inclosure some distance from the house, but not far away from the highway. It had a very sharp edge and towards the top was a notch, and supposing this was the instrument with which the murder was committed – and those who have examined the knife are disposed to think it is – it would fully account for the notch found in the vertebrae of the deceased lady's neck. We are not aware, however, that the knife was ever seen to be in possession of the prisoner Lee, so that it is quite open to possibility the knife might have been placed where it was found by some other person. We should hope the matter will be fully inquired into, especially should it afford a particle of evidence in favour of the innocence of the prisoner.

John Lee should have been long dead when this information was released and even with the discovery of this vital clue, the case was not reopened. Of course, the weapon may have been wielded by the accused, then disposed of on his way to Compton House; however, the appearance of the blood-stained smaller implement wrapped in paper found in the drawer in the pantry further reinforces Barry Phillips's point about planted evidence. If Lee was the guilty party, who would have put it there other than the police?

THE POLICE INVESTIGATION

Many other aspects of the police investigation left much to be desired, and it was certainly not as thorough as it first appeared. The day after the victim was found, Jane Neck discovered that a previously full can of lamp oil kept in a cupboard beyond Lee's bed was empty, which linked Lee to both the murder and the arson. A 'blood stain' on the can was only noticed while being examined by a member of the inquest jury. Incredibly, P.S. Nott was allowed to produce further evidence 'discovered' one week after the crime. He had returned to look for a missing ring owned by the deceased and found a match in her bedroom 'similar' to those found in Lee's trouser pocket. On the instruction of the chief constable, Nott also took up the carpet in the hall and found 'two blood marks as though a knife or something of that kind had been wiped on it'.

The fact that the scene of the crime was not sealed off and the female servants continued to live at The Glen gave an obvious opportunity for someone to further incriminate John Lee. The increased aroma of paraffin on Lee's clothes also raises the possibility of altered evidence. When Lee's trousers were produced in court Dr Chilcote stated: 'I notice *now* a smell of oil about them. Did not do so when the PC called upon me at my surgery.' Dr Steele agreed with Chilcote on this point but offered a somewhat feeble excuse: 'In consequence of the general smell of smoke and fire about the house on Saturday last, I did not notice the smell of Petroleum Oil, but did on Monday. Can smell Petroleum about the trousers *now*, most distinctly.'

There was a gasp of disbelief in the courtroom when Molesworth St Aubyn declined the opportunity to cross-examine P.S. Nott, but the defence counsel also did little to question the validity of other crucial evidence presented by the prosecution. It was the Crown's contention that Lee had broken windows with his fists merely to inflict cuts which would account for the victim's blood on his clothes. When Lee summoned help from the Cary Arms, he apparently left finger-prints of blood on the gate, but landlord William Gasking testi-fied that in relation to the cuts on Lee's arms, there was no blood 'about him' when he and the manservant later moved the body. He was not asked at what point he had spotted the blood-stains on the alleged murderer's shirt and trousers. The police were adamant that the windows had not been broken from inside the house, yet P.S. Nott testified that broken glass was found three feet away outside the window. Chief Officer of Coast-guard Thomas Bennett con-firmed that a strong wind had been blowing dead against The

Fingerprints of blood were found on the gate of the Cary Arms.

Glen – which could explain why much of the glass landed in the dining-room when the inside shutters were opened. Jane Neck testified, 'The glass was broken when I went out on the lawn and shouted, "Fire".' This reinforces the point that if Lee smashed six windows from the outside after the general alarm was raised, how is it possible that none of the constant stream of arrivals saw him doing this, or that no one, inside or outside the house, heard the sound of breaking glass?

Much was made of the fact that Lee had acted suspiciously when he hesitated to answer Gasking's call to lift the corpse. However, this behaviour seems entirely consistent with the natural revulsion of a youth viewing a mutilated body. Surely, a

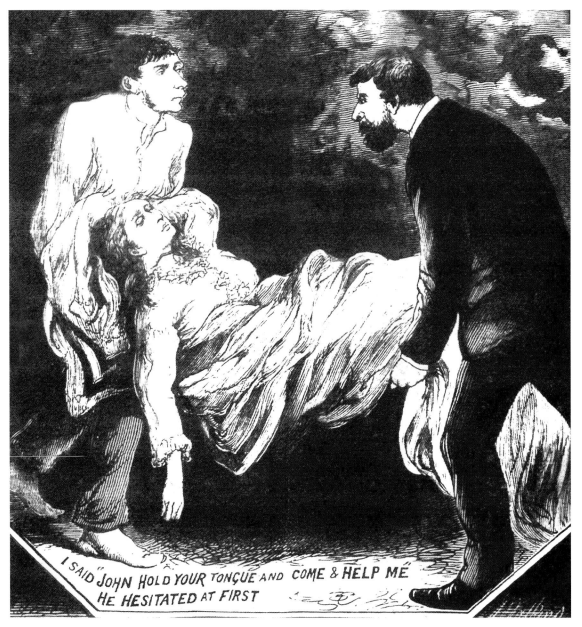

'Surely, a heartless murderer . . . would not have felt any reluctance about approaching the victim of his own handiwork?'

heartless murderer, who had already dragged the body from the hall to the dining-room, would not have felt any reluctance about approaching the victim of his own handiwork? Lee was also criticised for informing people that 'Miss Keyse was burnt to death', when it was obvious that she had been murdered, yet three other witnesses did not immediately realise that the horrendous neck burn hid a wound. Eliza Neck, who discovered the body, called out to the servants, 'Miss Keyse is lying on the dining-room floor'; Richard Harris admitted at the trial, 'I did not notice at first that the lady's throat was cut; I thought it was a burn'; William Gasking, recounted in an interview with the *East and South Devon Advertiser*, 22 November 1884: 'Richard Harris, who had just arrived, and I took her out to the outhouse. She was quite dead. I noticed there was something wrong with Miss Keyse's throat, but I was too intent upon putting the fire out to make particular observation.' Therefore, it would have been far more suspicious if Lee had revealed in his conversations that he did know the real cause of death.

Sydney Hacker, Coroner.

Barry Phillips noted that Lee's counsel should have done far more to highlight the deficiencies of the police investigation, whose conclusions were allowed to pass virtually unopposed:

> The failure of St Aubyn to test adequately the prosecution case did not go unnoticed. A local newspaper, the *Torquay Directory*, was quick to point out that he failed to ask a single question of Sergeant Nott, who had carried out a search of The Glen and whose evidence in chief had taken two-and-a-half hours to complete. At the very least, an effective cross-examination might have deterred the trial judge, Justice Manisty, from commending Sergeant Nott openly for his efforts before sending out the jury to consider its verdict.

THE CORONER'S HANDLING OF THE CASE

There can be little doubt that a verdict of 'wilful murder' at the inquest greatly damaged Lee's chances of a fair trial at the assizes. No statement was made on behalf of the defence, yet the verdict was reached by a jury of local people from a close-knit community who knew the deceased well and had knowledge of the circumstances in which she had re-employed the accused. It is likely that some gentlemen of the jury had been approached by Miss Keyse in an effort to secure a position for her convicted man-servant. Many members of the jury attended the funeral of the victim and one of their number, the Reverend Wrey, Vicar of St Marychurch, whom Emma Keyse had prompted to speak words of wisdom to John Lee upon his release from prison, was hardly unbiased when he spoke passionately in a special sermon about the cruel irony of the fate that had befallen a valued member of his congregation: 'Why did God let that poor, good old lady be murdered?'

Barry Phillips also believes that the Coroner's handling of the inquest prejudiced the outcome of Lee's trial. In a further extract from the article in *Counsel*, November/December 1996, he states:

> A close study of Lee's case suggests, however, that it may not have been the strength of the evidence given against him at his trial that really sent him to the gallows. The coroner who conducted the inquest into the death before Lee's trial went very much farther than simply investigating cause of death. He invited the inquest jurors to return a verdict of wilful murder against Lee if they considered it justified by the evidence. This they duly did without hearing any effective cross-examination of witnesses, or an account of the fateful night from Lee, who was not legally represented during the early part of the inquest.
>
> The damage the verdict did to Lee's prospects of receiving a fair trial later at the Assize Court was incalculable. The verdict, along with Lee's criminal record, was widely recorded by a press which was far less restrained than it is today by the laws relating to contempt of court. Little more than two months after the inquest, the Assize jurors, many of whom would have been privy to local accounts of the murder, were to be asked to consider objectively the evidence against Lee. Every one of them might well have known that Lee had a criminal record and that an earlier jury had already found him guilty of the crime for which he stood accused.
>
> A few who followed Lee into the true crime encyclopaedias suffered similar injustices at coroner's inquests. It is frequently forgotten that Lord Lucan was named by a coroner's jury as responsible for the murder of his children's nanny without ever having faced a criminal trial.

The high-profile case surrounding the disappearance of Lord Lucan in 1974 served as an important reminder regarding coroner's inquests and the damage that they might inflict on an individual's right to a fair trial. Three years on, the Criminal Law Act 1977 came into effect and the coroner's jury was no longer able to name an individual as responsible for the death of a person.

MOTIVE

A baffling aspect of the Babbacombe Murder was the apparent absence of motive. If John Lee did indeed plan to kill Emma Keyse with murder aforethought, then a parallel can be drawn with his previous conviction for theft when his solicitor affirmed, 'It was evident that if a man had intended to be detected he could not have acted more foolishly than the prisoner had.'

INSANITY

Before taking John Lee back at The Glen, Emma Keyse had described him as 'simple-minded' in a letter to the Reverend Pitkin; therefore, was he stupid enough to make frequent 'threats' against his employer that he fully intended to carry out?

A discontented John Lee in conversation with the postman: 'was he stupid enough to make frequent "threats" against his employer that he fully intended to carry out?'

Was Lee a simpleton or insane? His parents implied the latter in the petition organised to try and save their son from the death penalty. According to the *East and South Devon Advertiser*, 23 February 1885, the foreman of the jury at Lee's trial believed that the verdict would have been very different if a plea of insanity had been entered: 'He stated that he felt most confident that the prisoner was not of a sound mind, and in that opinion, he said, he was joined by several other jurymen.'

More details of Lee's strange behaviour were revealed by Dan Vile, the editor of the *East and South Devon Advertiser*, 28 February 1885:

> We were present at each examination of the prisoner . . . and we watched his demeanour very closely, and not only did that indicate signs of insanity, supposing he was the murderer, but it was further confirmed by his extraordinary conduct on the scaffold. We venture to affirm there is not a man in the United Kingdom, presuming him to be in his right senses, and still capable of perpetrating such a tragic act as the prisoner stands

accused of, who while believing in the punishment of sin hereafter – and we have every reason from the prisoner's letters, penned just before he went to the scaffold, he believed in an after state – could have faced and gone through those terrible, those cruciating pangs of death, and with the like fortitude, and with a lie of the deepest dye on his lips as the only feature to meet his God. Now what did the prisoner tell his mother on Saturday last when he was under the impression that would be the last time he would see her on earth? . . . we had a detailed account of that interview from the old lady amid a shower of tears, and with an assurance that she believed her son was innocent, and if not innocent, his mind was so utterly deranged as to be unaccountable for his actions and what he said. . . . The prisoner had been previously made acquainted of the intended visit, and when he was informed of her arrival he rushed out of the condemned cell to the usual place assigned for interviews with great alacrity, to use the words of his mother with that cheerfulness 'as though he was going to a theatre.'. . .

We considered last week there were very strong indications that he was not sane, and we feel assured there has been much stronger facts since, to prove that this is so. When fourteen or fifteen years, he was eccentric, and frequently when at home would rush frightened from his bed-room into that of his parents and it would take a very long time to pacify him; when, afterwards in service at the Dart Yacht Club Hotel, he deemed it more expeditious to batter up plate than to clean it and was discharged; and supposing he is guilty, he preferred to commit one of the most diabolical murders ever enacted rather than either submit to have his wages reduced 6d. a week, or seek employment elsewhere; when the jury at his trial were considering their verdict of life or death he was below feasting over a hearty meal, and afterwards came into the dock to receive sentence of death with his mouth full of food, and to depart afterwards from the court with a smile; when in the condemned cell to write the letters of a saint when steeped in the deepest dye of iniquity and guilt; to write letters to his parents and sister couched in the most loving and tender terms, and at the same time to be guilty of threatening to throw the table on which they were penned to the warder in charge; to cry like a child at his mistress rebuking him, and to face the gallows three times, encounter the agonies of death without the slightest apparent discomfiture. Certainly if the ingredient of insanity are not associated with all these acts we do not know what insanity can be.

Lee, in fact, never exhibited signs of violence during his long incarceration. The incident referred to in the newspaper article was a joke by Lee which occurred when the two warders guarding him fell asleep one night in the condemned cell: 'In the morning I said to them: "You're a nice pair to be looking after a man. If I were dangerous, I could have broken a leg off that table and knocked out your brains!" . . . Violence? One of them used to stick his knife in the door and hang up his coat! I wonder how many times I could have crept out of bed and got at that knife' (Lee, 1908).

As dealt with previously, in Chapter 7, the issue of Lee's mental state was officially addressed in September 1906. Not surprisingly, he had displayed symptoms of depression when it became clear that there was no immediate hope for his release. It is a testament to Lee's strength of character that two eminent psychiatric examiners concluded that despite the prisoner spending over twenty years in custody, there was absolutely no 'sign or indication of mental derangement'.

FINANCIAL GAIN

Bearing in mind his conviction for stealing from his previous master, it was suggested that Lee might have been disturbed by Miss Keyse in the act of theft which had been going on for some time: 'It appears, however, that several articles have been missed from the house; these articles have been traced to St Marychurch, and are said to have been sold by the prisoner Lee' (*Torquay Directory*, 26 November 1884).

A policeman was observed carrying articles including a guitar and a musical box into St Marychurch Town Hall during the inquest, but none were produced in court to try and implicate Lee in theft. These items could have been presents from Emma Keyse to John Lee. The prosecution suggested a cut in his already low wage was Lee's motive, but although this reduction had occurred only two weeks before her death, one of the Neck sisters testified that Miss Keyse had promised to make it up to Lee with gifts. If so, it is possible that he had no use for these and simply sold them to subsidise his meagre income.

If Lee was capable of murderous thoughts over losing sixpence a week, it follows that the possibility of a bequest could drive him to carry out his threats. There was speculation in the press that Lee stood to gain from Emma Keyse's will, but an article in the *Dartmouth Chronicle*, 20 February 1885, refuted this: 'Reports have been in circulation in Torquay and neighbourhood, during the last few days to the effect that the late Miss Keyse had left by her will, in addition to a substantial sum for the two elderly servants, Eliza and Jane Neck, £200 to Elizabeth Harris, the cook, and £50 to John Lee, her murderer. These reports are incorrect. The two old servants have been bequeathed £1,000, but nothing has been left to either Elizabeth Harris or John Lee.'

In fact, the Neck sisters (and long-serving gardener William Discombe, who had pre-deceased his employer) were supposed to receive only an equal share of the *interest* accumulated from an investment of £1,000. There was a greater shock in store for Miss Keyse's relatives when they learned the net value of Emma Keyse's estate from their legal representative, Isadore Carter (the amount totalled slightly less than the pittance later left by John Lee's mother). The details were published in the *Torquay Directory*, 8 April 1885:

> The will of the late Miss Emma Whitehead Keyse, of the 'Glen' Babbacombe, who was murdered by John Lee, the butler, has been proved in the Exeter Court of Probate. The will is in the handwriting of the deceased, and is on two sides of a sheet of foolscap. It was made on the 16th December, 1875, the deceased was murdered on the 15th November 1884. The will is proved by Amelia Hamilton Edwards, wife of the Rev. J. Edwards, of Croft Rectory, Leominster, Hereford, the sister of the deceased; power being reserved to grant probate to George Maxwell, a nephew; the other executor, Arthur Oakes Wilkinson, renounced. The testatrix directed that in case the 'Glen,' at Babbacombe, which was given her by her mother, was not sold previous to her death, it should be disposed of by her executors to the best possible advantage. She provided that of the proceeds £1,000 should be invested and the income should be applied for the benefit of her servants, William Discombe, and Eliza and Jane Neck. To her sister, Charlotte Baldry, Miss Keyse bequeathed a legacy of £1,000, and to her other sisters,

Mary McLean and Harriet Maxwell, she gave her plate and various articles of vertu. She further provided small legacies to her nephews and nieces and other relations, and left the residue of her estate to Mrs. Edwards. On the affairs being wound up, it was found that the gross value of the estate was £1,079. 6s. 6d. Against this there were debts to the extent of £984, and after meeting these and the funeral expenses there was only a balance left of £31. 18s. 6d. to meet the legacies before mentioned. There was, however, some leasehold estate, but no real property. Mr. William Burd, of Okehampton, is the solicitor for the executrix.

MR WHITEHEAD

With the stigma of a murder attached to the place, the sale of Emma Keyse's leasehold property, valued at £13,000, fell through following her death. When it came up for auction in August 1889, it failed to attract an opening bid of £2,000, and a buyer was not found until June 1890. In the meantime, the executors had a pathetic balance of £31 18s 6d to meet cash bequests totalling £2,060. It therefore seems that while Miss Keyse was outwardly trying to preserve her social status, her wealth had evaporated and she had been forced to make economies and reduce Lee's wages out of sheer financial necessity. In his evidence at the inquest, George Whitehead testified that his sister-in-law had been planning to change her will recently, but the one proved was made in 1875. The Coroner, so determined to hear every tangible scrap of evidence, stated that Mr Whitehead would appear again after having an opportunity to look into Emma Keyse's affairs. In the event, the witness was spared the embarrassment of being recalled at the inquest, and did not appear at the magistrate's hearing or assize trial. Courts therefore never learned whether the victim's personal circumstances and future plans might have been a factor in the events leading up to her death.

ARSON

If John Lee had planned a murderous attack on Emma Keyse, it makes no sense to believe that he was concealing a hatchet on the off chance that his intended victim might come back down the stairs. As Lee himself pointed out: 'If I had wished to murder her I could have done so whilst she was sitting alone in the dining room writing after the servants had gone to bed. Or I could have done it upstairs' (Lee, 1908).

It is reasonable to suppose, however, that the victim may have smelt smoke and discovered her servant carrying out his threat to burn the house down, thus forcing him to eliminate the witness to his crime. A vindictive act of arson does not necessarily mean that he wished to kill any of the occupants, but it would have brought an abrupt end to the owner's plan to sell the property. Having set fire to the house, Lee could then have sounded the alarm to save his mistress – an act which would have portrayed him as a hero instead of a worthless felon in the eyes of those who thought him unworthy of employment.

THE ROLE OF ELIZABETH HARRIS

If Elizabeth Harris was an innocent bystander who simply came to believe that her half-brother was the murderer and that she might also have perished in the house fire started by him, then it is perfectly understandable why she offered her damning testimony to the prosecution, despite the fact that in doing so it alienated her from her own mother. However, Barry Phillips argues that the defence counsel missed an opportunity to try and discover whether she was implicated in the crime:

> At Lee's trial St Aubyn pointed out in his closing speech that Elizabeth Harris, Lee's half sister and one of the servants at The Glen, was pregnant at the time of the murder. He claimed it was quite possible that there was more than one man in the house at the time of the murder. The other, he suggested, could have been Harris's lover, for whom no account had been made.
>
> St Aubyn failed, however, to draw on an important event to support this point. Remarkably, in Harris's earlier testimony during the committal proceedings, she had stated that on the night of the murder she had not descended the stairs of The Glen for some thirty minutes after she had become aware that the house was on fire. She gave evidence that the early part of her activities after she had been roused by smoke was occupied by her attempts to put out a fire near to her bedroom.
>
> Why Elizabeth Harris chose to remain upstairs by her bedroom and not check to see that her mistress was safe – as did the other servants – was never explored by St Aubyn. One explanation is that Harris knew that someone had killed her mistress and that less suspicion would be directed at her if she was the last person in the house to attend downstairs where the foul deed had taken place. (*Counsel*, November/December 1996)

It is certainly puzzling to understand why St Aubyn suggested that Elizabeth Harris's lover was present on the night of the murder, yet made no attempt in cross-examination to find out who he was. In his summing up, the defence barrister said that he could not ask the cook who the father of her child was. Did this imply that he thought it would be an ungentlemanly thing to do, or was he under instructions from his client not to ask the question of his half-sister? In the latter respect, the thought occurs that John Lee was initially arrested on suspicion of murder simply because he was 'the only man in the house'. The same conclusion might therefore be reached when naming the father of Elizabeth Harris's child. Psychiatrists have identified and documented a condition called Genetic Sexual Attraction, which they have found to occur when blood brothers and sisters meet after experiencing entirely independent upbringings. In these cases, siblings often share physical and emotional characteristics which, if they were complete

Elizabeth Harris roused the Neck sisters then suspiciously 'she was the last person in the house to attend downstairs where the foul deed had taken place'.

strangers, would make them naturally attracted to each other. As they do not have the shared childhoods, or experience of one another growing up, that would work to produce a normal, healthy relationship, Genetic Sexual Attraction acts like a magnet, producing an incredibly strong bond which draws them together into an adult sexual relationship. This often results in dire consequences, in terms of facing the possibility of criminal charges and producing strained relationships with other family members.

Elizabeth Harris had obviously been in a position to facilitate her half-brother's return from prison to The Glen. While working together there they would have become close for the first time. It emerged in evidence that she listened to his troubles and carried out

'Elizabeth Harris had . . . been in a position to facilitate her half-brother's return . . . to The Glen.'

domestic chores for him, such as washing and ironing his clothes. They were young people living with three elderly women in an isolated house. Although John was allowed to wander out in the evenings, Elizabeth, as a single female, did not enjoy the same freedom and must have led a somewhat lonely existence with little time off for socialising.

Elizabeth Harris had gone to bed early, feeling unwell, no doubt from the effects of her pregnancy. She testified that her employer had not been told: 'I asked Jane [Neck] not to say anything about my illness to Miss Keyse as she might think more of it than was necessary.' However, it would have become obvious that something was amiss when the cook did not attend evening prayers. Did Miss Keyse call into Elizabeth's room to see if she was feeling better and learn the truth before descending the stairs to confront the father? In order to keep the relationship secret the lovers killed Miss Keyse and then set fire to the house. This would explain Elizabeth Harris's involvement in the crime, as so many aspects of the case suggest she was. This scenario would also explain why John Lee wrote to his sister Amelia 'you must forgive Lizzie' and that he should have 'told the truth earlier' and was prepared to take the punishment 'which I deserve for not opening my mouth'. He was ashamed of facing the consequences of the illicit relationship and was willing to pay the price to protect his lover and their unborn child. It could also explain why Lee tried to break off his engagement to Kate Farmer. Elizabeth Harris's cruel attitude toward her half-brother may have been to protect her secret lover, but it could also have been caused by self-protection, a revulsion of their taboo relationship and a feeling of terror at having been left carrying their – possibly deformed – baby.

Unfortunately, Harris was not allowed to complete this interesting outburst at the inquest: 'The prisoner had talked to her about murder and said two should never be involved in murder because one . . .'. At this point, she was interrupted by the Coroner who asked why she hadn't said all this before and she replied, 'I had tried to screen him.'

Upon gaining his freedom, John Lee spent an enormous amount of time and energy attempting to 'clear his name' by tracking down the source of the 'cook's confession'. Why did he bother if he had committed the crime in isolation? As Charles Nicholson noted, the cook's plight was even ignored by her own mother, Mary Lee, who herself had suffered the shame of having a child out of wedlock, yet apparently had no sympathy for her daughter or interest in the welfare of her first grandchild: 'It is a fact that shortly after his trial and attempted execution she became the mother of an illegitimate child, by some lover whose identity never transpired, but who is believed to have been in the habit of visiting her at the house, and who may have been there on the night of the murder. She was Lee's half-sister. Very soon after the case she disappeared, was said to have left the country, and to this day has not been heard of even by her mother who is also Lee's mother' (HO 144/1717//A60789/64).

Mary Lee clearly did not believe her daughter's version of events and chose to stand by her son as testified in this article in the *Torquay Times*, 15 September 1922: 'It is a somewhat extraordinary fact – and one that is utterly inexplicable to those who are intimately acquainted with the circumstances attending the awful crime – that even to this day there are persons in Torquay, St. Marychurch, and Babbacombe, and also farther away, who stoutly adhere to their opinion in favour of Lee; and it is also well known that his poor old lonely mother, in her little cottage at Abbotskerswell, held firmly to her belief in his innocence to the very last day of her life.'

MOTIVELESS

An article entitled 'The Motives of Murder' appeared in the *Spectator*, 22 November 1884, commenting on the public obsession with the need to provide a motive. The author reasoned that a member of the criminal classes did not require any motive to carry out the senseless killing of Emma Keyse:

> John Lee is as yet untried, and he may, of course, be the victim of a series of accidental coincidences, or may have committed the murder, without premeditation, because discovered by his mistress in an act of theft; but, if the accusation is brought home either to him or to a burglar, the occurrence will be a fresh illustration of the imbecility of the general judgement about the motive of murder. The public, which could not commit such crimes, does not understand those who could, and habitually lays too much stress upon the absence or presence of sufficient motive. Most men and women want more motive for murder than is ever present, or likely to be present in their minds; but the murderers want but little. An immense majority of men would not commit a murder for any gain whatever; but a large proportion of murderers are tempted by some gain which seems to onlookers very small. In a great number of the recorded cases the murderer had no adequate motive at all, and was moved by either small greed, or petty fear – as of evidence against him – or revenge for apparent trifling injury, such, for instance, as comparatively trivial prosecution. . . . Murder after murder has been committed merely to avoid work, or to seize some coveted object, or, as is alleged in this case, out of angry fancy over which a malignant nature had brooded, till, let us hope, it had partially affected the reason. No murder, if it is a true murder at all, can have an adequate motive; and the distance between one impelling cause and another is exaggerated in the general judgement. . . .

Motive or not, it is hard to accept that the whole truth of what occurred at The Glen on that fateful night in 1884 ever came out in court. Many questions still remain un-answered. The household staff of The Glen were in turmoil because Miss Keyse had dis-posed of her property in such a way as to have serious ramifications for all of her four servants. If Miss Keyse had been invited to spend a quiet retirement at the home of one of her many wealthy relatives, it may even have spelt the end of a long association with the Neck sisters. The cook was 'in the family way' with no prospect of marriage and her truculent half-brother had refused to take his employer's advice that emigration offered the only escape from his criminal past. It is difficult to believe John Lee's assertion that he was totally innocent of any wrong-doing. Most damning of all, he contradicted his story that he had slept through the events by making a statement to the prison authorities about seeing Elizabeth Harris's 'masked' lover in the house. That said, some doubt remains about the degree of his participation. Did he act purely on his own, or did he become embroiled in events which resulted in a cover-up involving his half-sister? Whatever the answer, it is clear that he felt absolutely no gratitude or loyalty to Emma Keyse, the woman who had believed in him and taken an unnecessary risk with her reputation and ultimately her life, which resulted in her death certificate recording 'wilful murder by John Lee'.

Perhaps the nature of the relationship that existed between Emma Keyse and John Lee is best summed up by a quote from Oscar Wilde. He and his wife, Constance, a relative of Lady Mount-Temple, stayed at Babbacombe Cliff in November 1892. Wilde visited the scene of the infamous crime when swimming and boating with his two sons on Babbacombe Beach. Ironically, in view of the public build-up of sympathy for John Lee that had formerly been reserved for his alleged victim, the master of the epigram was working on a new play, *A Woman of No Importance*. During his three-month sojourn at Babbacombe, Oscar granted an interview to solicitor and budding author Percival Almy, which appeared in the magazine *The Theatre*. The article recorded the great man's opinion of criminals, a philosophy which, alas, had not been shared by the late Emma Keyse: 'Never attempt to reform a man, men never repent.'

Sources

OFFICIAL DOCUMENTS, THE NATIONAL ARCHIVES

ADMIRALTY RECORDS

ADM 188/135: Record of service of seaman John Henry George Lee
(service number 110179), 1.10.1879 to 6.1.1882

ASSIZE RECORDS

ASSI 21/71: Devon Assizes: Crown Minute Book
ASSI 25/56/18: Devon Assizes: Indictment
ASSI 21/21 (part 1): Devon Assizes: Depositions
ASSI 26/21//64326 Torquay Court Records

HOME OFFICE RECORDS

HO 144/148//A38492: Criminal Cases: Lee, John
HO 144/1712//A60789: Prisons and Prisoners: Commuted death sentence where
prisoner was required to serve more than 20 years
HO 144/212//A48697: The Execution of Capital Sentences 1888

PRISON COMMISSION RECORDS

PCOM 8/87: Registered Papers: Lee, John, Exeter 29 January 1885

THE ROYAL ARCHIVES, WINDSOR CASTLE

Queen Victoria's Journal, August 1846
Queen Victoria's telegram to Sir William Harcourt, 23 February 1885

GALLERIES OF JUSTICE, NOTTINGHAM

Epton Collection: John 'Babbacombe' Lee papers – case notes of solicitor Isadore Carter

EXETER PRISON MUSEUM

Bryan Letters: Stephen Bryan's correspondence with John Lee, Fred Farmer, Mrs
Caunter, Mrs Bond
Norton File: miscellaneous papers on the case of John Lee

ON-LINE DATABASES

www.ancestry.com
www.census.pro.gov.uk
www.ellisisland.org
www.1837.online.com

BRITISH NEWSPAPERS & JOURNALS

The Builder, Cheltenham Examiner, Counsel, Daily Mail, Daily Mirror, Dartmouth and Brixham Chronicle, Devon County Standard, East and South Devon Advertiser, Express and Echo, The Globe, Gloucester Journal, The Graphic, Herald and Express (later issues *Herald Express*), *Illustrated London News, Illustrated Police News, Lancashire Evening Telegraph, The Listener, Lloyd's Weekly News, Mid-Devon and Newton Times, Newcastle Evening Chronicle, New Reveille, News of the World, Paignton Observer, Radio Times, Referee, The Spectator, The Star, Sunday Chronicle, Tavistock Times* (later issues *Tavistock Times and Gazette*), *Teignmouth Gazette, The Theatre, Thomson's Weekly News, The Times, Torquay Directory and South Devon Journal, Torquay Times and South Devon Advertiser, Totnes Times and Gazette, Trewman's Exeter Flying Post, Western Daily Mercury, Western Morning News*

OVERSEAS NEWSPAPERS AND JOURNALS

Australia: *Bacchus Marsh Express, Everyones, South Australian Advertiser*
Canada: *Toronto Globe*
USA: *Milwaukee Sentinel, Mind, New York Herald, Washington Post*

Select Bibliography

REFERENCE WORKS, GUIDES AND DIRECTORIES

The Annual Register 1885

A Chronological Record of Events Relating to Torquay and Neighbourhood, published by authors R. Dymond and J.T. White, *c.* 1881

Great Western Railway Guide to Devonshire, *c.* 1875

Guinness Book of Records, Guinness Publishing Ltd, 1970

Kelly's Directory of Devonshire (various editions 1883–1939)

Who's Who of British Members of Parliament, ed. M. Stanton and S. Lees, Harvester Press, 1976.

BOOKS

Berry, James. *My Experiences as an Executioner*, London, Percy Lund & Co., 1892

Bowen-Rowlands, Ernest. *In the Light of the Law*, London, Grant Richards, 1931

Elliott, John. *Palaces, Patronage and Pills. Thomas Holloway: His Sanatorium, College and Picture Gallery*, Egham, Surrey, Royal Holloway, University of London, 1996

Ellis, Arthur. *An Historical Survey of Torquay*, published by author, 1928

——. *Royal Occasions in Torquay*, published by author. 1935

Holgate, Mike. *The Secret of the Babbacombe Murder*, Newton Abbot, Peninsula Press, 1995

Honeycombe, Gordon. *More Murders of the Black Museum*, London, Hutchinson, 1993

James, Ann. *Murders and Mysteries in Devon*, Exeter, Obelisk Publications, 1996

Kellock, Harold. *Houdini: His Life-Story*, New York, Harcourt, Brace & Co., 1928

Keyse, Frank. *The Babbacombe Murder*, published by author, 1988

Lee, John. *The Man They Could Not Hang*, London, C. Arthur Pearson, 1908

Pateman, Leslie Lownds (ed.). *Pictorial History of Babbacombe and St Marychurch, vol. 2*, Babbacombe and St Marychurch Traders' Association, 1991

Pike, Andrew, and Cooper, Ross. *Australian Film, 1900–1977*, Melbourne, Oxford University Press in association with the Australian Film Institute, 1980

Pitkin, Reverend John. *The Prison Cell in Its Light and Shadows*, London and Edinburgh, Sampson, Low, Marston & Co., 1918

Walbrook, H.M. *Murders and Murder Trials, 1812–1912*, London, Constable & Co., 1932

Waugh, Ian David, *Who Killed Emma Keyse?*, published by author, 2000

Index

Page numbers in *italics* refer to illustrations